THE POPULATION EXPLOSION

AND CHRISTIAN RESPONSIBILITY

The Population Explosion

and Christian Responsibility

RICHARD M. FAGLEY

New York OXFORD UNIVERSITY PRESS 1960

To Mary

ৡ► For many years one of my responsibilities has been to provide church leaders in the ecumenical movement with background data and analysis on various international problems which might help them to arrive at informed policy decisions. Indeed, the seed of the present survey grew out of such memoranda. In a sense, it is a memorandum on a larger scale and addressed more widely to our clergy and laity, as well as to interested people outside the churches. I make no pretentious claims concerning this review on aspects of the contemporary population problem. I have relied principally on the more readily available and familiar resources, without attempting an exhaustive survey of foreign works. The practical urgency of the issues here presented, rather than the ideal of comprehensive scholarship with the delays that that entails, is the dominant concern. In fact, I have reluctantly eliminated a good many references helpful to the special student in the hope of securing a wider audience. The need to confront the implications of the population explosion is now, not a decade from now.

This is a book about the dilemmas posed by the new pressures of population and the need for a more widely held and vigorously supported Christian doctrine of responsible parenthood. It is not a book about 'overpopulation.' That is a highly ambiguous term, for it ignores the possible improvement of underdeveloped resources. Moreover, it implies that a certain percentage of human beings are 'surplus.' That is a conclusion which Christians cannot accept. Rather, rates of population growth may be dangerous in relation to rates of development, and need to be restrained by responsible parenthood. That is the subject dealt with here.

In a real sense, this is an unfinished work. It does not close with a rousing conclusion like a musical finale. One reason is that the

Protestant consensus on responsible parenthood is in process of becoming, and does not lend itself as yet to *fortissimo* treatment. The other reason is that I prefer to let the facts, which seem to me thoroughly convincing, speak for themselves rather than stress my own percussion. My concern is less to preach my own convictions than to offer the reader the various data by which he can convince himself, for no one else can do it as well.

Every author is indebted to the work and help of others, and I am more indebted than most. Indeed, if I were to list my debts, I would hardly know where to begin; those to whom I am most indebted already know my gratitude. I must mention, however, my special obligation to my colleagues in the Commission of the Churches on International Affairs, both for their encouragement and for their willingness to shoulder an extra load that this report might be prepared. It need hardly be added that I take personal responsibility for the views here expressed, and that these views in no way commit either the C.C.I.A. or its parent bodies, the World Council of Churches and the International Missionary Council.

I must also express appreciation for the competent help rendered by the staff of the Oxford University Press.

Richard M. Fagley

Chappaqua, New York
September 1959

Acknowledgments

The author wishes to thank the following publishers for permission to reprint selection from their publications:

Charles Scribner's Sons for passages from *The History of Religions*, vol. 2, by George Foot Moore; and *The Ante-Nicene Fathers*, the American reprint of the Edinburgh edition; The University of Minnesota Press for a passage from *The Population Ahead*, edited by Roy G. Francis, copyright 1958 by the University of Minnesota; George Allen and Unwin, Ltd., for a passage from *Population and Planned Parenthood in India*, by S. Chandrasekhar; Association Press, Inc., for references from *What Christianity Says About Sex, Love, and Marriage* by Roland H. Bainton; The Paulist Press for quotations from The Encyclical Letter of Pope Pius XI, *On Christian Marriage*; and The Division of Education of the National Council of the Churches of Christ in the United States of America for permission to use the Revised Standard Version of the Bible for Biblical references. In addition, the author wishes to thank the following periodicals for permission to quote: *The Month* for passages from an article, 'Christian Theology and the Population Problem,' by John L. Russell, S.J., in the April 1958 issue; *Impact of Science on Society*, published by UNESCO, for passages from an article, 'The Control of Human Fertility,' by Sir Solly Zuckerman.

Contents

THE POPULATION EXPLOSION

AND CHRISTIAN RESPONSIBILITY

Population and Parenthood

᠅ 'Everywhere the victim is man.' The Executive Committee of the World Council of Churches said this in a statement concerning the conflicts of our time and their injury to human freedom, justice, and peace. It provides a suitable text for the subject of our inquiry. For these same values of man's earthly existence are also menaced from an unexpected quarter: an accelerated proliferation of human life itself. By a combination of historical circumstances, which we will examine, the gift, the miracle of procreation, whereby man and wife share in God's creative work, has seemed to become a factor of social disequilibrium, intensifying the factors which victimize man in large sections of this planet. Of course, it is not the miracle of birth which causes the present dilemma, but the fact that through want of knowledge and training on the part of parents, this miracle is in the aggregate invited too frequently in relation to the available material conditions which support human life.

The problem of population and parenthood is in the first instance a problem of time. It is a temporal problem in the sense that the issues of today differ from those of previous centuries and may well differ from those in centuries to come. It is a temporal problem in the sense that it stems not from the fact of human increase, but from the *rate* of that increase in relation to the tempo of economic and social development, and the absorptive capacities of varying civilizations. It is the speed with which the human sum is growing in various parts of the world that poses the sharp questions which this generation must face. In this sense, despite the fact that more permanent issues are posed for the Christian conscience, the analysis here presented is very much a tract for the times.

It is also a tract for the times in that it is motivated by the strong conviction that God is speaking to the churches and to the nations in the dire accents of the population explosion, calling us all to redress the neglects of the past and to use the knowledge and insight vouchsafed to us in more responsible ways. The grim dilemmas we now face would not have occurred, at least in such harsh and urgent form, if we had given better heed to the principles of stewardship inculcated in His Holy Word, and applied them more conscientiously both to material resources and human procreation. But the Lord has various ways of teaching us our duty. If we refuse to learn in one way, we are taught by sterner means of our own making. This is the conviction which underlies the analysis here presented.

Although the concerns of the general reader have been kept in mind, in purpose this book is a call to Christian action, addressed in the first place to churchmen who share the Evangelical heritage. It is a call to the parson and interested parishioner to take an active part in the task of building a more worthy and dynamic Protestant position on the complex of problems represented by the terms population and parenthood. As I shall try to explain in a moment, such a position is a debt we owe both to the family and to the world, but most of all to the Author of our faith. The chapters which follow attempt to summarize various data — demographic, economic, technical, theological — to help the reader arrive at an informed conviction. The presentation tries to be objective: points negative to the argument and not merely those which support are included. But the reader should not be misled by the effort to make a balanced and honest presentation of the evidence into thinking that the underlying purpose is impartial or academic. Underneath is the belief that the total picture, with its complexities and shades of gray, is convincing evidence that responsible parenthood is a Christian doctrine whose time has come, and which calls for church and personal support.

Population and parenthood are two aspects of the same phenomenon. Population is the social aspect, and parenthood the personal and family aspect. It should be stated that parenthood is used in this treatment in a narrow, primordial sense, virtually equivalent to procreation. The fuller dimensions of parenthood which have evolved in human history, the care and nurture of children, the safeguarding of their material welfare, the training for responsible adulthood, the companionship of family life — all this unfortunately must lie outside the direct scope of the present volume. Yet it is because of this broader meaning that parenthood has acquired, which in fact introduces principles of limitation in regard to procreation, that it is used in preference to the traditional term.[1] Responsible parenthood, in the context of the population explosion, more often than not means restricted or limited procreation in view of the total responsibilities of parenthood. It is more than a euphemism for family planning or limitation, not to mention 'birth control.'[2] It implies a basically affirmative attitude toward procreation.

The current rapid increase in humanity, or the current phase of a longer-range increase — the 'explosion' described in the next chapter — can be dated roughly from 1930, when a widespread decline in death rates began to occur, a decline which has accelerated in spectacular fashion since World War II. At the time it was not noticed very much except perhaps by a few students of population trends, the demographers. European opinion at the time was much engrossed by predictions of race or ethnic 'suicide,' derived from projections of falling birth rates — the combined effect of World War I, the depression, and wider use of contraceptives.[3] So the signs of the times were read by few. It was hard to 'shift gears' from concern over 'race suicide' to anxiety about runaway expansion.

Besides, the signs were no bigger than a man's hand. There had been throughout history rises and falls in fertility and mortality.[4] Perhaps this was a passing phase of a cycle. It was not until the end of World War II, when the antibiotics and new insecticides produced during the war became available for public health programs, that the signs became unmistakable. The prophecies of the demographers took on a more strident tone. Then came the Chinese census of 1953 which revealed a much more dynamic population situation in that sub-continent than had been expected. By this time the evidence was so plain that even churchmen like myself began at last to stress the matter.

A special reason for concern was that the center of the massive new increase in population, as we shall see, was found in the continents of Asia, Africa, and Latin America, for which brave new efforts at developmental assistance were sought in the West. The poorer countries of the world, already caught in three revolutionary ferments — the struggle for independence and nationalism, the revolt against outmoded social patterns, and the revolution of 'rising expectations' — were now seen to be involved in a fourth, intensifying and complicating the others — the demographic revolution. Thus Hugh Keenleyside, then director of U.N. technical assistance and one of the more outspoken public servants on the dangers of the new population pressures, pointed out that 'there is no foreseeable possibility of national production coming anywhere near to matching' the 3 per cent rate of population increase in Ceylon. As for India's First Five Year Plan, he added: 'By running as fast as they could for five years the people of India had succeeded only in remaining just about where they were.'

It can be argued that higher standards of material comfort, as pursued in the West and under Communism, or even the pursuit of more than the bare necessities of material existence, do not constitute a necessary human ideal. Certainly a lessened preoccupation with creature comforts in the richest countries could produce a higher quality of life. Is it necessary for the economically less developed countries to do much more than manage to stay where they are? The point is that the revolution of 'rising expectations,' however it may have been stimulated by contact with the West, has become thoroughly indigenous. If the Eastern countries' dreams of a more prosperous life are more modest than their

Western counterparts, they are held just as fervently. And it is these dreams which are placed in jeopardy by the demographic revolution. A Special Study under the Rockefeller Brothers Fund indicated that in 1956 the per capita gross national product in the industrialized free societies was ten times that in the less industrialized free societies; by 1976 it was likely to become *fifteen* times as great.[5] The gap between the two worlds is widening, partly because of more rapid economic development in the West, and partly because of more rapid growth of population in the poorer countries. Thus, a rapid expansion of population in these countries tends to defeat their efforts to raise living standards through economic development.

Despite the high stakes posed for world development, it cannot be said that the population-parenthood problem began to receive major public attention until a year or so ago. There was a considerable increase of books and articles, but most of them were read by limited circles. The grim dilemmas of the atomic age occupied the forefront of the stage, and the explosive human situation remained in the wings. There was hardly a whisper of the population problem in the halls of the United Nations or the legislative assemblies of the Western nations, save in private conversations.[6] Of the hundreds upon hundreds of multilateral and bilateral assistance projects, I know of only four that have been related in some way to family planning.[7] Indeed, the official disregard of the population question has probably been a major factor in public apathy and ignorance.

The difference between studied silence in public and private expressions of apprehension on the part of government officials reveals part of the reason why the population explosion has been the most neglected great social issue of our time. The prevalent idea among Western and intergovernmental officials is that Roman Catholics form the only significant group which cares about the question of 'birth control,' and that they care enough to penalize any person or program which directly or indirectly promotes the use of contraceptives. This is the explicit or implicit reason I have been given in a number of private explanations by government and U.N. officials. Why enter upon a controversial subject and jeopardize the constructive work they were trying to do? The memory of the retreat by the U.S. Occupation in Japan, when the question of contraceptive assistance for the Japanese people was raised, and of the early retreat of the World Health Organization, before the representations of several governments, when it was proposed to include work in this branch of health — these have made a strong impression.[8]

Rather than dig into such major examples of political action by Catholic organizations and governments, since this is not of particular relevance to my argument, I take instead a mild little example in Northern Rhodesia. The semiofficial journal for Africans, *Nshila*, published in its 3 February 1959 issue a story on the evil of prostitution which contained this sentence: 'The idea of limiting the family — known as "birth control" among Europeans — is only now starting to interest African people.' Within a week the editor received a letter from the Jesuit Manager of Schools of the Chikuni Mission, regretting the 'veiled advocacy of "birth control," ' and asking cancellation of subscriptions for the Mission schools 'unless you can assure me that they [future issues] will not again offend in this domain.' Actually, in this case, the threat did not work; the Chief Education Officer replied that he could give no such assurance. In earlier years and other places, however, the result was undoubtedly different.

Now, I do not question the right of Roman Catholic individuals, organizations, and governments to use their political and economic influence in behalf of policies they believe to be right, provided the essential rights of others are not infringed. Whether such influence has been used wisely or in accord with official Catholic policy lies outside this analysis. The point that is important here is that Protestant individuals, organizations, and governments share in responsibility for the prevalent official neglect of the population-parenthood complex of issues by their failure to assert an equally conscientious if different position. If there had been such a counterpoise of conviction, governments and international organizations would unquestionably have faced up to these urgent issues a long time ago. Administrators of aid programs would have acquired the courage to move forward in ways they privately know to be right. A more adequate Christian witness in this area is a key to a more realistic approach by governments. Conversely, *our* neglect and inaction have been a major factor in governmental neglect and inaction. *This* is the point we need to ponder in penitence.

An equally strong case for penitence can be made when we consider the other aspect of the population-parenthood question: the family East and West and its need for religious counsel in rapidly changing societies. I am much less qualified to speak in this area, though I recognize that it is more fundamental in the Christian perspective than the public witness. The Anglicans and some of the Lutheran and Reformed churches have done commendable work in regard to marriage and family guidance. The majority of our churches and councils, however, are just beginning to measure up to their responsibilities in this field. A common assumption seems to be that, because husband and wife must finally make in Christian conscience their own decisions regarding responsible parenthood, the church is thereby freed from obligation to provide spiritual and ethical guidance. This is hardly worthy of the Good Shepherd whom we seek to serve.

There are understandable reasons why the 'birth control' movement grew up in the 19th century largely without benefit of clergy. The motives of those who led this movement, beginning in the 1820's with the self-taught Englishman, Francis Place, were quite heterogeneous. Free-thinkers, social reformers, and socialists shared a secular, indeed anticlerical, attitude. A perusal of some of the literature reveals the name of only one 19th-century clerical defender, the Reverend Moncure Conway, pastor of the South Place Chapel in London, who spoke against the 1879 proceedings against Charles Bradlaugh and Annie Besant for circulating contraceptive literature, and whose liberal Nonconformist congregation submitted a memorial in their support. There can be little doubt that most of our Victorian churches took an attitude that differed little from that of the Roman Church.

Indeed, as we shall see in due course, it was not until the depression of 1929 that Protestant denominations began to speak out cautiously in favor of family limitation. The French Jesuit, Stanislas de Lestapis, writes of the 'birth control' movement being 'systematically implanted in Anglo-Saxon and Scandinavian countries, where it has ended by gaining the favor of the Reformed confessions, obtaining thanks to them the official sanction of the public powers.' There is a measure of truth in this, in that Protestants have become increasingly active in support of the availability of contraceptives. Yet I think Father de Lestapis gives us too much credit. The importance of secular influences should not be minimized. Indeed, the growing use of contraceptives for the spacing of children among all sectors of the population is no doubt a major underlying factor.[9] The specific Protestant contribution must be thought of mainly in the future tense, not the past.

Even the first signs of an awakening Protestant consensus may have helped somewhat to break down the walls of public indifference and neglect in recent months in regard to the population problem. In any case, the walls are crumbling rapidly, as the consequences of the demographic revolution become inescapable. During the past several months, there has been a marked change in the amount of attention given to the population problem, particularly in the American press. The metropolitan papers now carry almost daily some item relating to this complex of issues. Day by day the fears and inhibitions of the past pass away.

More important, there are the first small signs of public attention at the governmental level. In December 1957 the U.N. General Assembly approved unanimously a resolution calling for greater recognition of the relationship of demographic and developmental problems, a resolution introduced by José Encinas of Peru, with the support of the Italian, Mexican, and Pakistani delegations. While not much has been done to follow up this initiative, the 1958 General Assembly heard in the general debate more references to mounting population pressures than the preceding sessions; and the new appraisal of future U.N. economic and social programs gives significant attention to this area. Under-Secretary Philippe de Seynes said, in opening the session of the U.N. Social Commission on 27 April 1959:

> In a number of countries the excess of births over deaths now exceeds 3 per cent of the population, a rate of increase which is without precedent in human history . . . The need to overtake such rates of population growth with a greater expansion of production, at a time when there are so many obstacles in the way of rapid economic and social development of the underdeveloped countries, represents a challenge to social techniques such as no country in the world has had to face until now.

While the U.N. still avoids speaking frankly of the need for population policies and family limitation, a breech in the dike has occurred in the United States. The Draper Committee, made up of former senior civil servants appointed by the President to recommend on foreign aid, urged in a report on 23 July 1959 that American aid programs supply 'birth control' advice to friendly nations that request it. According to the United Press summary of the recommendation, the committee urged assistance, on request, in the formulation of plans designed to deal with rapid population growth; in increased aid relating to maternal and child welfare in recognition of the immediate problems; and in strong support of research 'leading to the availability of relevant information in the formulation of practical programs . . .' Translated into everyday language, this apparently means help on family planning campaigns, greater welfare programs, and research on improved contraceptives. The silence of the Congress on the reception of the report was said to be 'stony,' but the report signifies the beginning of the end of the long night during which the maligned ostrich was imitated.

Another sign of approaching dawn is the recent report prepared for the Senate Committee on Foreign Relations by the Stanford Research Institute. The report points out *inter alia* that 'while some $30 billion are spent each year on the worldwide attack on mortality, only a few million dollars are allocated to programs which affect birth rates.' New approaches to the problem of

population pressures are said to be 'urgently required.' One pro-
posal is the provision of research funds for larger-scale testing of
devices needed by peoples who want to check their population
growth.

Evangelical Christians, through past inaction, share in responsibility for the long night. In a positive sense, we have an urgent
obligation to speed the dawn of a more worthy approach. The
chapters which follow are offered as possible tools for this task. I
add a few notes on these various tools.

The only short way to describe the population explosion is by
means of statistics, which some find difficult and tending to ob-
scure the flesh-and-blood people behind the statistics. The key
figures are the birth rates and death rates expressed in numbers
per thousand, the difference indicating the rate of increase, usually
expressed in percentages. Thus the new state of Guinea, according
to the U.N. 1958 *Demographic Yearbook*, has the highest birth
rate, 60 per thousand, but also the highest death rate, 40, the
difference of 20 indicating a 2.0 per cent rate of increase. The rate
of increase is the key element in future forecasts. So the Chinese
economist, Ma Ying-chu, noting a rise in the rate of increase from
2.2 to 3.0 per cent, which means a doubling every 23 years, predicted in June 1957 a Chinese population of 2.6 billion in 50
years. The main value of the forecasts lies in illustrating the thrust
of the present and prospective tempo of growth; there are too many
variables to regard the longer-range forecasts as predictions in any
strict sense. As the chapter tries to make plain, the population explosion is a present reality, not merely a forecast.

Chapter III finds the main ingredient in this explosion to be the
advance of 'international disease control.' As Dr. R. L. Hood, chief
of the International Quarantine Section of W.H.O., has stated
in *World Health*:

> It is not fantasy to say that, given the kind of cooperation, medical
> knowledge, and resources which W.H.O. represents, the majority of
> the old pestilences could disappear in our generation and with them
> most quarantine restrictions on international travel.

Some of the stakes involved in the paradoxical consequences of this beneficent prospect also are suggested.

Three alternative or complementary ways of coping with the mounting population pressures in the underdeveloped world are next considered: the rather dim prospect of moving a substantial number through migration, the various possibilities for increasing food supplies, and the question of curbing the rate of increase through population policy and family planning. The potentialities for new nutritional resources are not discounted, despite the difficulties. The main issue is the problem of *time*. It is not easy to feed a hungry baby on future expectations of a larger larder.[10] The conclusion is that, at least in the densely populated countries, no strategy can win which fails to include a real program to control and reduce fertility.

To assess the possibilities here requires a review of the technical situation in regard to contraceptives. I have tried to summarize medical advice on this point. The immediate prospects for the poorer countries do not seem too bright. As Dr. S. N. Mwathi, a Presbyterian elder as well as an M.D., wrote in *Rock*, a Christian monthly in Kenya: 'all the methods at present in use are either too expensive or too complicated.' Also the educational problems are formidable. Maurice Pate, executive director of UNICEF, put his finger on a key point:

> The greater the value attached to life, the more educated people become, the more they become aware that a life from the moment of conception should at least have a chance to strive for health and happiness, the better the chances that the population problem will be solved.

The correctness of this point, however, only indicates the dimensions of the educational task. To quote Dr. Mwathi again:

> We have spent a good deal of time telling people how to improve their farming and agriculture. But we haven't spent enough time in telling them how to improve the health of the children whom God gives to them, by proper methods of family spacing.

Because of the crucial importance of religious attitudes and doctrines for any extension of family spacing, the balance of the book is devoted to a survey in this area. After a preliminary chapter on the non-Christian religions, which presents the view that cultural rather that doctrinal obstacles form the main hurdle,[11] we turn to the Bible, with a sub-chapter on post-canonical Judaism. More attention is paid to specific texts than might otherwise be justified, because of the historical use made of such texts. Also, a relatively full account is given on the early fathers of the church, because of the mind-set contributed to subsequent doctrine in both the Eastern and Western churches; for the Eastern Orthodox, indeed, the main body of doctrine is to be found here. The three following chapters attempt to delineate the differing positions of the three main branches of Christianity. The final chapter summarizes developments in the ecumenical movement and gives some personal views and conclusions.

Raymond Pearl of Johns Hopkins, who took in *The Natural History of Population* a biological approach to the population problem, said, in reference to the 'enormous' growth of population from the altered balance of nature, that no species had yet been able to adapt itself 'swiftly and skillfully enough to survive this combination of circumstances.' He found the only chance to lie in the fact that man 'has shown himself in the past to possess somewhat greater innate powers of adaptability than any other organism ever known.' Man's resources are not nearly that limited. God made man in His own image, and also offers him resources far deeper than innate human powers, when man has the penitence to turn to them.

The Population Explosion

꿍 Population explosion is a useful term to describe the present and prospective increase in the human inhabitants of this smallish planet called Earth. It is more than a scare word uttered by propagandists for this or that social panacea. It is more than an hypothesis by students of population trends, the demographers following in the footsteps of Malthus. It describes in the first instance a present reality. We are living in the midst of an accelerating growth of world population that can truly be called explosive. The hard facts of census data, rather than demographic theory, provide the inescapable core of this concept.

At the time that Jesus walked among men, the world's population may have totaled 300 million persons, concentrated principally in the Mediterranean basin, India, and China. The Secretariat of the United Nations Population Division, after reviewing various estimates, suggests 'that the world's population was likely to have been between 200 and 300 million at the beginning of the Christian era.' During the present generation from 1930 to 1960, the *increase* in the world's population will be approximately 900 million, or three times the total of the New Testament period. This increase of 30 years, moreover, may be twice as large as the global total at the time of the Reformation. This is the population explosion.

The annual net increase is now 1.6 per cent, which means some 44 million more persons each year, 120,000 each day, 5,000 each hour, more than 80 per minute. The 1957 *Demographic Yearbook* indicates that these figures are already on the conservative side. The increase from mid-1955 to mid-1956 was 47 million persons, or close to 130,000 per day. The current figure, incidentally, is much closer to the high forecast for growth to 1980 than to the medium forecast made by the United Nations Secretariat in 1954. The medium figures meant an average annual increase of 39 million a year; the high, 51 million.[1]

The growth of the world's population continues to accelerate through a combination of factors. Even if the rate of growth were constant, the net increase would expand as the base is enlarged, comparable to the growth of savings at compound interest. The rate of growth, however, for reasons to be examined later, is not constant but continues to rise in the larger part of the world. On top of this, as data and methods for collecting information improve, it is usually found that previous estimates of population were too conservative and require upward revision. Thus, the population explosion is proving more dynamic in character than was realized even a few years ago.

The biggest recent factor in the upward revision of population estimates was the Chinese census of 1953. The effort to enumerate this major segment of mankind showed that previous estimates fell short of the actuality by 100 million or more. Furthermore, it showed that the composition of the Chinese population, with 45 per cent 18 years of age or younger, was such as to augur explosive future growth. Improved statistics in other areas and more careful analysis have added to the picture of a zooming world population.

Thus, the ink is hardly dry on a projection of population growth into the future before it is outmoded by new evidence of dynamic growth.[2] The forecasts by the United Nations demographers as to world population in 1980 have been successively increased, as follows:

	World Total, 1980
1951 estimates	2,976 to 3,636 million
1954 estimates	3,295 to 3,990 million
1958 estimates	3,850 to 4,280 million

This latest total, moreover, is already in need of some upward revision. A more recent and detailed Secretariat study of population
growth in South-East Asia shows that mortality in this region was
overestimated in the 1958 world forecast, so that several million
more need to be reckoned into the total.[3]

While the details of forecasting future growth of population
may be rather technical for the layman, there is nothing particularly mysterious about the business. It is the projection into
the future of present population growth, under varying assumptions
as to factors affecting the rate of increase. One assumption in the
United Nations forecasts is continued advance in medical knowledge at a steady rate, an assumption which seems on the conservative side in that medical science seems to be advancing at an
accelerating rate. The estimates vary according to low, medium,
and high assumptions regarding birth rates: an immediate reduction, a reduction by 1975, or no reduction.

These population forecasts show the shadows that present trends
cast on the future. They are a warning as to what may be, not a
prediction of what will be. Neither the horseman of famine nor
the horseman of atomic holocaust enters into this picture, except
as malnutrition and war have affected the rates of growth which
are being projected. That new factors will alter the outline the
demographers would be the first to admit. Their projections merely
extend the curve of the graph.

What is important to note is that the curve projected is an
extension of one expressing the actual numerical growth of mankind. What is doubly impressive is that the similar forecasts of
some decades ago have been met, indeed surpassed, by the facts of
life. Consequently, the conscientious calculations of those expert
in the study of population have a major claim to attention. As
data accumulate and improve in quality, their case is continually
strengthened. Indeed, the evidence argues that the demographers
have been understating rather than exaggerating the population
explosion of the 20th century.

What the students of population are saying can be gauged by
the estimates of the United Nations Population Branch. These

might be called 'middle of the road' estimates, higher than some and lower than others. In their latest world-wide projection, *The Future Growth of World Population* (1958),[4] the United Nations demographers indicate that mankind as a whole (now approaching 2,900 million in number) confronts the prospect of reaching the three billion mark about 1963, and of zooming to more than six billion before the end of the century, some 40 years away — indeed, of approaching the seven billion mark by the year 2000 if birth rates do not fall off after 1975. As indicated before, these calculations do not attempt to judge whether food supplies can be developed rapidly enough to sustain such a phenomenal increase in people. They merely show the kind of pressures being generated. As the authors say in their preface:

> With the present rate of increase, it can be calculated that in 600 years the number of human beings on earth will be such that there will be only one square metre for each to live on. It goes without saying that this can never take place, something will happen to prevent it.

As a mathematical exercise, the portrait of the hypothetical population explosion can indeed be carried a step further. John L. Russell, S.J., in a theoretical article in the April 1958 issue of *The Month* of London, speculated that, assuming a population that doubles itself every hundred years — a rate of increase considerably below the present rate — the present world population would have resulted from an Adam and Eve created about 1000 B.C. He carries this into the future:

> One thousand years hence, at the same rate, there would be two million million people . . . In 2,500 years from now, the population would be so densely packed that there would be one man on every square yard of the earth's surface, including the sea. In 5,000 years the weight of human beings would be equal to the total weight of the earth, and in 14,000 years to the estimated total weight of the universe.

Needless to say, such exercises are of value only to demonstrate that the present rate of increase cannot last, and that the population problem cannot be solved unless the rate of increase itself is greatly modified. The important consideration at the moment is the significance of the short-range projections showing the prospect that the mass of humanity will double during the next generation or so. This is not a speculative exercise. This is the logical implication of the known facts. This is the continuation of a population explosion already well under way.

To grasp the scope of this challenge it may help to see it in historical perspective. Our knowledge of population levels in the distant past is almost as dim as projections into the distant future. Yet students of the subject, by piecing together the fragmentary clues, have acquired useful if rough notions of past populations. Archaeological evidence, an occasional census record, extrapolations from later estimates, and the like, go into the detective sector of demography. Also, some idea of the size of population can be gleaned from knowledge of its economic base.

It can be concluded, for example, that primitive peoples were relatively sparse in numbers, because it takes a considerable territory to support a few people by hunting and gathering. A handful would need many square miles to survive. There would be a constant danger of overpopulation. This illustrates, incidentally, the tricky character of that term. Overpopulation can be defined only in relation to the available resources, and, at a higher stage of civilization, in relation to the values of a society. The meaning of available, moreover, depends upon the skill of a given society for utilizing the resources to which it has access. It may well be that a larger percentage of primitive men, at certain stages, suffered from overpopulation than is the case with contemporary man in the midst of a population explosion.

The domestication of animals and cultivation of crops permitted a very considerable increase. Then came irrigation, the division of labor, the greater degree of order which made possible the relatively densely populated centers of civilization as in Egypt, Mesopotamia, India, and China. The rise and fall of empires were reflected in considerable fluctuations in the levels of population. Yet even at their peak, the ancient empires were small by modern standards. Scholars estimate the total population of the Roman

Empire at the beginning of the Christian era in the neighborhood
of 60 to 80 million.

While peoples waxed and waned, the small net increase in the
global total over the centuries is the striking conclusion of the
various studies. Plague, war, famine, or decay and disorder would
take their toll, and then the upswing of the cycle would return.
The consensus is that after some 50 centuries of historical development the world's population in 1650 came to 500 to 550
million. Somewhat divergent estimates by A. M. Carr-Saunders
and Walter Willcox [5] put the population of Asia at nearly three-
fifths of the total, that of Europe and Africa at around 20 per cent
each, and that of the Americas at roughly 2 per cent. It might be
noted in passing that despite modern talk about 'the rising tide of
color,' the tide was relatively higher three centuries ago. In 1650
the area of European settlement accounted for only 22–24 per
cent of the total population, according to the two estimates.

By 1750, the sum of mankind came to roughly 700 million
people, Carr-Saunders putting the figure somewhat higher and
Willcox slightly less. In retrospect, one can see the first evidence
of our present population explosion. After centuries of a rather
cyclical pattern in the over-all, an upward spiral was under way.
Willcox puts the net increase of the century at 224 million (from
470 to 694), Carr-Saunders puts it at 183 million (from 545 to
728). Whether the expansion amounted to 48 per cent or only
34 per cent, here were signs of things to come. The man most able
to read the signs was the Reverend Thomas R. Malthus, whose
Essay on the Principle of Population appeared in 1798.

At some point between 1820 and 1830, according to the estimates of the two modern demographers, mankind reached the
billion mark for the first time in the long ages of human evolution
and economic and social development. By the end of the hundred
year period, 1850, the world total stood at from 1,091 million
(Willcox) to 1,171 million (Carr-Saunders). Whereas the preceding century had seen a population growth of perhaps 200 million, the century ending in 1850 had witnessed an increase of
400–450 million. The composition of this increase is also instruc-

tive. The Asian sector remained at 60 per cent or slightly more, the African segment fell to 8 or 9 per cent, the Americas now accounted for 5 per cent, while Europe had risen to roughly 24 per cent of the total. The acceleration was most evident in the lands of the Industrial Revolution. Europe and Northern America in two centuries had virtually tripled in population, while the less developed societies in the rest of the world were doubling.

In the 1850–1950 period, which saw humanity pass the two billion mark with ease around 1930, the more developed societies continued to grow at a faster rate than the less developed world. The rate of increase, however, was decelerating, slowed down by lower birth rates as well as by the effects of two world wars. Europe and Northern America increased about one and a half times, while the less developed world was again doubling.

A closer look at this century reveals a key to an understanding of the present phase of the population explosion. For the past hundred years has been a period of transition. If we examine the figures for 1920 to 1950, the increase for the more developed world stands at 23 per cent. For the less developed world as a whole during the recent decades the increase has been 45 per cent. And for Latin America the growth amounted to 79 per cent. The slowing down of population growth in the industrialized societies has been succeeded by a new and far greater population explosion in the underprivileged societies of Asia, Africa, and Latin America.

This new mushrooming of population pressures, which began in Latin America, has spread to most of Asia, and is now developing in Africa, is the heart of today's demographic problem. If trends now discernible are projected into the future, as United Nations demographers have done in *The Future Growth of World Population*, the stark dimensions of the problem can be seen. In the period from 1950 to the end of this century, the figures in the United Nations study indicate that the more developed countries confront a prospective population increase of 74 per cent. *The peoples of the less developed world confront a prospective increase of 180 per cent!* In United Nations parlance, incidentally, the less developed world is defined as Asia except for the U.S.S.R. and Japan; Africa except for the Union of South Africa; the Americas except for the U.S.A. and Canada; and Greece and Yugoslavia. In this vast world, where two-thirds of mankind already live, is the center of the new population explosion.

For those endowed with a mathematical imagination, the fact that the underdeveloped world as a whole now confronts a rate of population growth of more than 2 per cent each year will bring home the tragedy and challenge of the new population explosion. For those not so endowed, it may be helpful to remember the family caught in this maelstrom of rapid social change. To the ferment of a new nationalism, the discontent of social revolt, and the 'revolution of rising expectations' in regard to economic development have been added the pressures of a demographic revolution. The family caught in this fourfold revolution lives on the margins of subsistence. Its annual income ranges from $50 to $200 per person. Its diet is lacking in protective foods—indeed often in calories. Its land is likely eroded or in need of fertilizers. The seeds it plants are low in yield. Its tools are primitive. It is burdened by debts that continue from father to son. As President Eisenhower said in addressing the Colombo Plan Conference:

> In vast stretches of the earth, men awoke today in hunger. They will spend the day in unceasing toil. And as the sun goes down they will still know hunger. They will see suffering in the eyes of their children.

These are the people caught in the present phase of the population explosion — the second stage of the rocket. But unlike the peoples of the West among whom for the most part the Industrial Revolution grew hand in hand with the expansion of population, these people by and large are experiencing a rapid growth of population *before* the achievement of large-scale economic and social development. And the pace of population growth is more rapid. The largest increase known in Europe during three centuries of expansion was an increase of 54 per cent in the years 1850–1900, large-scale migration to the New World helping to make the net rate of increase more moderate. Compare this with the prospective increase of 180 per cent in the years 1950–2000 for the whole underdeveloped world. Each percentage point magnifies the problem, as the time available for adjustment is telescoped.

The above describes the general situation, the average for two-thirds of humanity. Within that general situation are to be found particular conditions considerably more critical in character. The current rate of increase for the less developed world, on the basis of recent estimates, appears to be about 1.8 per cent, as compared with 1.3 for the more developed societies. This means an excess of births over deaths amounting to 18 per thousand inhabitants each year. But the 1957 United Nations *Demographic Yearbook* gives much higher rates for a considerable number of countries. Rates of increase frequently run as high as 3 per cent and even reach 4 per cent. Be it understood that an annual increase of 3 per cent means a doubling of population within 24 years, and 4 per cent means a doubling under 18 years. Here are some examples, based on the period 1953–56:

Southern Rhodesia	3.1%	Laos	3.2%
Costa Rica	3.9	Malaya	3.1
Dominican Republic	3.4	Syria	3.8
El Salvador	3.4	Brunei	5.9
Venezuela	3.1	Papua	4.4
Taiwan	3.8	New Guinea	3.7

True, most of the populations here noted are rather small, and inadequate census information makes for uncertainty as to accuracy in several situations. But the upward trend is unmistakable. The cumulative meaning is plain. Rates of growth are becoming larger throughout the underdeveloped world. The present rate for Europe as a whole, apart from the U.S.S.R., is 0.8 per cent; for Northern America, 1.7. In contrast, the rate for Middle America is 2.7; for South America, 2.4; for South-West Asia, 2.5.

Reduced to its simplest element, the demographic situation is the relationship between birth rates and death rates. In a word, what is happening is that the traditionally high birth rates of Asian, African, and Latin American peoples continue, while the

traditionally high death rates are falling dramatically. It may help
to clarify the picture, however, to note some of the broad distinctions which characterize the demographic situation. The United
Nations Secretariat, in *The Future Growth of World Population*,
groups the regions of the world under four categories of demographic situation. Regrouping the four categories according to rate
of growth, on the basis of the 'medium assumption' projections,
gives the following picture in terms of 1950 and the year 2000:

A. *Low density, moderate growth.* Northern America, Temperate
South America, Australia and New Zealand, and the Soviet Union.
With 41 per cent of the land area of the world, the countries of
this group had 386 million people in 1950 or 15.5 per cent of the
total. While the projected population for the year 2000 is 768
million, the percentage of the world total is expected to drop to
12.3 per cent.

B. *High density, moderate growth.* The three European regions
and Japan. With some 4 per cent of the world's land area, the population is projected to grow from 477 to 721 million, which would
constitute a fall from 19.1 to 11.5 per cent of the world total.

C. *Low density, rapid growth.* The three regions of Africa, Central
America, Tropical South America, South-West Asia, and the Pacific
Islands. With about 39 per cent of the land area, the population
is calculated to grow from 384 million to 1,220 million in the
50 year period, from 15.4 per cent of mankind to 19.5 per cent.

D. *High density, rapid growth.* The Caribbean, Central South Asia,
South-East Asia, and East Asia except for Japan. With less than
16 per cent of the land area, the half of humanity now dwelling
in these regions is projected to grow from 1,250 million (50.1 per
cent) to 3,560 million (56.8 per cent).

This brief delineation indicates the anatomy of the population
explosion. The areas of moderate growth are the industrialized
societies of the temperate zones, whether densely or sparsely
populated. The areas of rapid growth are the pre-industrial societies
of the tropical and sub-tropical zones. As Dr. Egbert de Vries has
pointed out, the terms 'North' and 'South' describe the distinction
better than 'West' and 'East.' Further, as we distinguish groups
C and D, we find the regions of most dangerous population pres-

sures in the last category, where high density is rapidly becoming higher.

From the point of view of the demographic explosion, a major difference between groups A and B on the one hand, and groups C and D on the other, lies in the age composition of the populations. The peoples of the underdeveloped world are basically youthful, because of high birth rates and a heritage of low life expectancy. The peoples of the more developed societies, with lower birth rates and a longer life expectancy, have a much larger percentage of the aged in their population. A generalization which indicates this differential is that in Asia, Africa, and Latin America, according to the study, *Future Growth* . . . , those under 15 years of age will make up, in 1960, roughly 41 per cent of the population, while in Europe, the U.S.S.R., Northern America, and Oceania, they will account for only some 27 per cent.

To cite some concrete examples, here is the age distribution of five of the less developed countries of groups C and D, based on estimates in the 1957 *Demographic Yearbook,* in terms of percentages:

	Under 20	20–44	45 and over
Belgian Congo	45%	36%	19%
Ceylon	50	36	14
Philippines	55	32	13
Colombia	53	34	13
Peru	55	31	14

And here, for contrast, are comparable percentages for a few of the Western countries grouped under A and B:

	Under 20	20–44	45 and over
Denmark	34%	34%	32%
England & Wales	29	35	36
France	31	33	36
Switzerland	30	35	35
United States	37	34	29

As might be anticipated, some countries in this category show an age composition of intermediate character:

	Under 20	20–44	45 and over
Greece	36%	38%	26%
Japan	42	37	21

The significance of this breakdown lies in the fact that the youthful composition of peoples in less developed regions enlarges the increase of population when a decline in death rates opens the door. There are so many young parents and parents-to-be in the lands of rapid social change that any tilting of the birth-death balance in the direction of life means a boom in babies. True, a continued improvement in health conditions and in life expectancy will mean in time more older people past the child-bearing age. But that is a long-term consideration.[6] The immediate effect is acceleration of population growth.

To understand the present situation more fully, some consideration needs to be given to birth rates and death rates which in their interrelationship determine rates of growth. The youthful composition of populations in the less developed countries is but one of the factors in the current explosion. Clearly it is not the critical factor, since for centuries the young have predominated in the tropical and sub-tropical regions, where the population explosion is now centered, without producing the portentous multiplication of human beings which characterizes the world of today. The age distribution intensifies the accelerated growth, but it is not the primary fact. That must be sought among the rates of birth and death.

Nations and regions vary widely in regard to birth rates, as indeed do different groups and classes within the nations. Sweden, near one end of the scale, has 15 births per thousand inhabitants; Guam, at the other, has 60. Yet on the whole there is a notable stability in regard to birth rates. Drastic and sudden changes are rare. One outstanding recent exception is Japan, where the birth rate fell from 34 per thousand to less than 19 in eight years — 1948–56. The Japanese situation will be considered in another connection. At the moment it is noted as an unprecedented example of a rapid reduction in fertility.

That significant changes take place in regard to birth rates is undeniable. But they tend to be gradual and moderate. There has been, for example, a gradual lowering of the birth rate in some of the countries of southern Europe: during the past eight years, the Italian rate has dropped from 22 to 18, and the Portuguese from 27 to 23. In the Netherlands during this period the birth rate has dropped from 25 to 21. Venezuela, on the other hand, which had a birth rate of 30 in the 1932–38 period, has experienced a steady increase to 47 in 1955. As statistics improve and accumulate, no doubt many long-term changes of significance will be found. Scandinavian records, for example, show that birth rates which now run from 15 to 19 averaged 31 to 34 in the period 1735–1800.

For most of the underdeveloped world the information is very scanty, both in regard to complete coverage and time span. The authors of *The Determinants and Consequences of Population Trends* state:

> Though the data for the countries with high fertility are fragmentary, the available evidence indicates that the birth rate seems to be generally near or above 40 . . . In the few cases where available birth rates extend over several decades . . . there is no evidence of an upward or downward trend — with the possible exception of certain Latin American countries.

Birth rates in the more developed regions are little more than half those found in the less developed areas. The 1957 *Demographic Yearbook* gives these regional rates: Northern and Western Europe, 18; Central Europe, 19; Southern Europe, 21; Northern America, 25; Oceania, 25; U.S.S.R., 26. In contrast with these figures are the estimates for the rest of the world: Northern Africa, 42; Tropical and Southern Africa, 50; Middle America, 42; South America, 39; South-West Asia, 42; South Central Asia, 40; South-East Asia, 44; East Asia, 35. The scattered records for countries in these areas are consistent enough to justify such estimates. They go hand in hand with the youthful composition of Asian, African, and Latin American populations.

They do not explain the unprecedented growth of these populations, however, for the few records available indicate that birth rates were also high before the rapid expansion began. It is on the other side of the ledger, in the rates of mortality, that the dynamite is to be found. Here lies the key to the present explosion of population. As the 1957 *Demographic Yearbook* states:

> It appears that the dramatic declines in the death rate which some of the so-called 'underdeveloped areas' have experienced have no precedent in the history of mortality among the countries of the world which now enjoy the lowest rates.

Some of the reasons for this fact will be examined in the next chapter. At the moment, attention is focused on the fact itself.

And it is a stupendous fact. Never before has there been any comparable reduction of such magnitude in death rates throughout the world. There have been significant declines of a gradual character in areas of European settlement during the past century. But even the technically most advanced Western countries did not experience such a revolutionary reduction in mortality as has characterized recent years in large parts of the less developed world. Despite the dearth of good statistics in these regions, the conclusiveness of the evidence is unmistakable. The picture becomes more dramatic each year as the reduction in death rates is extended. In the short period between 1947 and 1956 the world death rate dropped from 22–25 per thousand to 18, according to estimates by the United Nations Population Branch. On the basis of simplified population models, which may be more correct than figures based on fragmentary statistics for Asia and Africa, the Secretariat would estimate a world death rate of 25 for 1950, indicating a still more rapid decline since then. Since mortality was already low in most of the Western lands, the main factor was the rapid decline of death rates in other parts of the world.

The 1957 *Demographic Yearbook* devotes special attention to mortality statistics. It includes a table showing average crude death rates for 84 countries and territories, for 1930–34 and 1950–54. For the sake of wider coverage, figures based on statistics deemed incomplete are included for 20 areas. Even so, Asia and Africa are inadequately represented. Nevertheless, practically all the data point in the same direction, 80 of the 84 areas showing a fall in death rates during the two decades. Here are a few of the figures, with the code symbols 'C' and 'U' to indicate whether the statistics are regarded as more complete or less so:

	Code	Average 1930–34	Average 1950–54	Per Cent Change
Singapore	C	23.8	11.0	−53.8
Mauritius	C	31.6	15.1	−52.2
British Honduras	C	23.7	11.5	−51.5
Taiwan	C	20.6	10.1	−51.0
Cyprus	C	15.3	7.7	−49.7
Ceylon	U	22.4	11.8	−47.3
Chile	C	23.9	13.6	−43.1
British Guiana	C	23.2	13.5	−41.8
Venezuela	C	17.9	10.6	−40.8
Mexico	C	25.6	15.5	−39.5
Thailand	U	16.3	9.9	−39.3
India	U	23.7	14.4	−39.2
Ecuador	U	24.8	16.6	−33.1
Yugoslavia	C	18.4	12.5	−32.1
Egypt	U	27.0	18.6	−31.1

While the more dramatic changes have been taking place in the less developed countries, the war against high mortality rates has also had its successes in the economically more developed societies. In these areas victories had been successively won over many decades, particularly in the early part of this century. Here are figures for some of the more industrialized countries:

	Code	Average 1930–34	Average 1950–54	Per Cent Change
Japan	C	18.1	9.4	−48.1
Italy	C	14.1	9.9	−29.8
Finland	C	13.6	9.7	−28.7
Poland	C	15.0	11.1	−26.0
France	C	16.0	12.8	−20.0
Netherlands	C	9.0	7.5	−16.7
United States	C	11.0	9.5	−13.6
Canada	C	10.0	8.7	−13.0
Australia	C	8.8	9.4	+ 6.8

What is striking in the two tables is the extent to which lands which have suffered high mortality for centuries are now approaching the relatively low rates of the more developed societies. This is true even when allowances are made for incompleteness of data. There is another table in this same survey showing death rates in 1956 for 63 countries and territories where data are reasonably adequate. Whereas a few years ago death rates below ten per thousand were regarded as suspect, half of the territories listed in this table show a death rate under ten. And about half of these are in the less developed sections of the earth.

Another way to envisage the changes in mortality levels is to look at the life expectancy tables. While the paucity of information on the less developed countries severely limits this approach, there are a few clues. In the years since World War I, life expectancy at birth has continued to grow in the Western countries: by seven years in Australia and New Zealand, eight in Denmark, ten in Sweden, 12 to 13 in England and Wales, 14 in the United States. While life expectancy in the less developed regions is still markedly below that of the more developed societies, the increase has been noteworthy. Ceylon is the prize example, even if not typical. Since 1920–22 life expectancy at birth has risen from 32.7 years to 60.3 years for males, and from 30.7 to 59.4 years for females. During this period, each year has practically added a year to the expectation of life.

And what of the future? It seems clear that, with the progressive aging of populations in Northern America, Europe, and the Soviet Union, at least, death rates will become stabilized or even rise slightly. For the rest of the world further declines are anticipated. A projected estimate for 1975 is given in *The Future Growth of World Population:*

	1950	1975
World	25	17
Africa	33	29
Northern America	9	9
Latin America	19	12
Asia	33	19
Europe	9	10
Oceania	12	10
U.S.S.R.	7	7

It seems clear that it is the upsetting of the ancient and tragic balance of high birth rates and high death rates, through the rapid reduction of mortality, that is the key to the present phase of the population explosion. Here is the factor which has initiated the chain reaction, though the presence of plentiful 'fissionable' material made it possible. Among such must be counted the youthful composition of Asian, African, and Latin American peoples, and the marriage and family patterns which foster high birth rates. It is the interaction of a rapidly declining mortality rate with such factors that defines the demographic problem of today and tomorrow.

Here then is the population explosion. As suggested above, it is a two-stage affair. Its first phase was an unprecedented expansion of population in the lands of the Industrial Revolution, the areas of European settlement — particularly in the New World, where natural increases combined with migration from Europe to make growth particularly rapid. In the areas of European settlement, including Latin America, the population virtually tripled between 1650 and 1850, and since 1850 has about tripled again, rising from 335 million to roughly one billion as of now.

While this first phase of the demographic revolution has greatly slowed down, it is not wholly spent — even when Latin America, which leads the vanguard of the second phase, is excluded. In the United States, for example, a birth rate of around 25 per thousand and a death rate under ten still augur considerable growth. The decline predicted for the present decades has not taken place. Instead, the Census Bureau has raised its forecast for 1975 from 206.9–228.5 million to 215.8–243.9 million. Students of urban development at Yale speak of an urban belt from Baltimore to Boston in the making. Two authors in the 1958 *Yearbook of Agriculture* state: 'Our population now increases at a rate that will give us 700 million people in 100 years and 2,800 million in 200 years.' While these figures do not take into account the factors likely to depress the rate of increase, they suggest the dynamic character of the population situation even in some of the countries of the first phase.

The second and current phase of population growth, however, makes the first seem mild because of the rate of growth and because of the much larger population base involved. Latin America is in the van, Asia is moving into high gear, and Africa moves at a slower pace but with great potential. According to the medium assumptions, the United Nations demographers anticipate that between 1960 and 1975 the annual rate of increase will rise in Latin America from 24 to 28 per thousand, in Asia from 17 to 23, and in Africa perhaps from 16 to 17. This would mean a net annual addition to the human race rising from 37–8 million in 1960 to nearly 64 million in 1975 for the underdeveloped world as a whole, compared with a rise from 10 to 11 or so million a year in the more developed regions. It should be noted, moreover, that the world-wide increase of 47 million projected for 1960 was already reached by the middle of 1956.

In this new and massive expansion of mankind lie international issues of the first magnitude. They have been more neglected by governments than any other of the major problems in the world crisis. The time when neglect was possible, however, is rapidly running out. The consequences of the population explosion are acquiring such an imperative character that statesmen and other leaders of opinion will no longer be able to shirk their responsibility. And churchmen, too, who have given too little attention to a great human dilemma, will see beyond the statistics the problem of the family in poor and desperate societies caught in this population explosion. The challenges have an inexorable quality.

Causes and Consequences

ह‍ If there are overtones of alarm in a description of the contemporary population explosion it is because of the grave chain of personal and social consequences which it is calculated to produce in our generation, and because there are serious obstacles to averting catastrophe. It is not because there is anything wrong *per se* in the increase of the human race. On the contrary, the Biblical injunction to Adam and Eve, repeated in the story of Noah, was to 'be fruitful and multiply, and fill the earth and subdue it' (Gen. 1:28, 9:1). 'I came that they may have life, and have it abundantly' (John 10:10) has quantitative as well as qualitative relevance. Human life and community, like the rest of God's creation, are in themselves indeed very good.

No, it is not the increase of the human race, the multiplication of candidates for salvation, which in itself causes concern in approaching the population question from a Christian perspective. It is rather what that increase, or more accurately the rate of increase, portends for the quality of life on this planet. From another angle, the question is the responsible use of the knowledge now available to man for making the conditions of this our earthly pilgrimage as worthy as possible.

Before turning to a more specific consideration of the causes of the population explosion, it might be well to pause momentarily for a word about Thomas Malthus and current demographic theory. Few writers have been more widely misinterpreted and

misunderstood than this amiable Anglican priest, who fathered
the science of modern demography perhaps more by the debate his
Essay on the Principle of Population stirred up than by what he
actually said.[1] The *Essay* grew out of some discussions he had had
with his father on human equality and perfectability, and the il-
lusions held by the social reformers Godwin and Condorcet. He
regarded himself less as originating than underscoring the proposition that population tends to increase more rapidly than resources,
unless checked. Later he found others beside David Hume and
Adam Smith who had pointed toward this conclusion. One was
Benjamin Franklin, who had written in 1775:

> There is no bound to the prolific nature of plants and animals, but
> what is made by the crowding and interfering with each other's
> means of subsistence. Were the face of the earth . . . empty of
> other inhabitants, it might in a few ages be replenished from one
> nation only; as for instance, with Englishmen.

Malthus took as his example of unchecked population growth
that of the United States where the population was doubling in
25 years,[2] and argued the impossibility of doubling the agricultural
output of his own island every quarter century. Thus he argued
that 'the power of population is indefinitely greater than the
power in the earth to produce subsistence for man':

> Population, when unchecked, increases in a geometrical ratio. Sub-
> sistence only increases in an arithmetical ratio . . . By that law of
> our nature which makes food necessary to man, the effects of these
> two unequal powers must be kept equal. This implies a strong and
> constantly operating check on population from the difficulty of
> subsistence.

Under the term 'positive checks,' Malthus referred, in the 1803
edition of the *Essay*, to 'every cause, whether arising from vice or
misery, which in any degree contributes to shorten the natural
duration of human life.'[3] In the second edition, he also placed
more emphasis on the 'preventive check' which he called 'moral
restraint,' by which he meant delayed marriage from prudential
motives, and premarital continence. Since there must be some

check, it is 'better that this check should arise from a foresight of the difficulties attending a family.' He denied any imputation on the goodness of the Deity in permitting beings to be born without the necessary means of subsistence. Virtue, rather than happiness, is the proper Christian concern, and this involves the 'subjection of the passions to the guidance of reason.' This, in brief, is the main argument.[4]

Undoubtedly, Malthus put his thesis in a formula that could not be defended in detail. Nassau Senior, in his correspondence with Malthus, indicated that food in fact could develop more rapidly than population. The classical economists did not follow him very far, though his idea of a law of diminishing returns in agriculture had influence. Karl Marx attacked the idea of a universal law of population: 'overpopulation' was a by-product of capitalist fetters on the means of production. Herbert Spencer developed an 'evolutionary' theory that as man became more intellectually developed and able to survive as an individual, his reproductive powers diminished, so that a balance would be arrived at. The rising standard of living in 19th-century Europe tended to put Malthus in the shade. But the collecting of census data and the like, which he helped to stimulate, went forward. And his stress on the tendency of population to outstrip resources was a permanent contribution.

Frank Lorimer has a good synopsis of current demographic theories in regard to primitive societies in his introduction to *Culture and Human Fertility*. Carr-Saunders concluded in *The Population Problem* that in various primitive societies there are factors, such as abstention from intercourse, abortion, and infanticide, which tend to maintain an 'optimum population' in relation to available resources and technology:

> The view put forward here is that normally in every primitive race one or more of these customs are in use, and that the degree to which they are practiced is such that there is an approach to the 'optimum' number.

A contrary theory has been advanced by Frank Notestein and other American demographers. As Notestein has stated it:

Any society having to face the heavy mortality characteristic of the premodern era must have high fertility to survive. All such societies are therefore ingeniously arranged to obtain the required births. Their religious doctrines, moral codes, laws, education, community customs, marriage habits, and family organization are all focused toward maintaining high fertility.

Lorimer also mentions a somewhat intermediate position advanced in connection with a 'Cross-cultural Survey' at Yale. From data on some 200 societies, Professor C. S. Ford notes both the universal concern over barrenness and pressures against childlessness, and the wide resort to abortion, infanticide, and contraceptive attempt. He states:

Emerging from this brief survey of the control of conception in cross-cultural perspective is the impression of a delicate balance between pressures toward bearing children and tendencies to avoid birth.

Professor Lorimer thinks none of the theories gives sufficient recognition to 'the diversity of cultural conditions influencing fertility in different societies.' The living space of most primitive societies waxes or wanes:

The record of famines, wars and migrations points toward recurrent maladjustment in the relations of people and resources. . . .

With this preliminary excursion, let us turn again to the present massive maladjustment of the population explosion, which means a sudden waning of effective living space for a good part of the world. The 'delicate balance' of social pressures has moved into a new setting. The 'high mortality' against which pro-fertility customs were developed is in rapid decline. Any 'optimum' level of population is more severely challenged than ever before. For one of the principal 'positive checks' has suffered a series of major defeats. The war against human disease has won unprecedented victories in our generation.

This is the great paradox in our situation. The chief cause of the mounting pressures of population is the beneficent and spectacular progress in modern medical science and its application to public health programs in the less developed countries. It is this which causes the dramatic declines in mortality, the main factor in the upsurge. Indeed, as we shall see, it has also had some effect in raising birth rates as well, though the changes here do not compare with the dramatic lowering of death rates.

In a few countries, like the United States, other factors have played a part in post-war growth. Pascal Whelpton finds that changes in marriage patterns form the largest influence on the higher U.S. birth rate since the war. More women, particularly in the better-off sectors, are having larger families, and more women are having at least one child. But the chief factors are earlier marriages and earlier child-bearing:

> Less than half of the rise in annual fertility from the depression low to the post-war high is attributable to more children per married couple, and more than half to the fact that women are marrying younger and having their first child at a younger age. The latter circumstance has moved to the past ten years some millions of births that would have occurred during the next ten years if the former pattern of age of marriage and the first confinement had continued.

The United States, however, is on the periphery of the population explosion. Its changing marriage patterns are not typical of the underdeveloped world at the center of the present expansion. In this world the overwhelmingly predominant factor has been what Kingsley Davis has called 'international disease control.' Unlike the Western countries which experienced a gradual decline in death rates from rising standards of living even before the medical advances of the past century, the less developed countries are experiencing rapid drops in mortality principally through the impact of new and relatively inexpensive preventive health measures on infectious and epidemic diseases. In some ways, the most successful technical assistance programs, and the quickest to produce results, have been the health campaigns aided by the World Health Organization (W.H.O.) and related bilateral agencies.

These campaigns are producing the dramatic results, though behind the current programs are decades of patient work on tropical diseases by missionary hospitals and foundation research. Likewise the training of indigenous medical personnel has been a major contribution by the voluntary agencies. Arthur March has compiled A *Directory of Protestant Medical Missions*, covering three-fourths or more of the total. Included in the survey are 1,602 medical units — hospitals, dispensaries, tuberculosis sanitaria, and leprosaria — 688 in Africa, 668 in Asia, plus 64 in the Arabic world and 60 in the Pacific islands, and 99 in Latin America, plus 23 in the Caribbean. If Roman Catholic medical missions and institutions supported by foundations are added, we can appreciate one of the underlying reasons why the contemporary campaigns have had such gratifying success — and such perplexing additional consequences.

Let us look first at the victories. Information summarized in a report submitted by W.H.O. to the U.N.'s Committee on Information from Non-Self-Governing Territories [5] gives the following picture:

Malaria — A major program of W.H.O. is that of global malaria eradication, a plan which grew out of the successful spraying campaign in Greece. In the struggle to liquidate malaria, before the carriers become immune to the sprays, 9 countries and territories with a population of 231 million have achieved eradication, 7 with 43 million are far advanced, 44 with 302 million are implementing the program, and 16 other countries are laying plans. Thus malaria which counts 300 million cases and 3 million deaths annually is being attacked in a concerted way.

Treponematoses — The technical policies recommended by W.H.O. aim at 'complete eradication' of this group of debilitating diseases which includes yaws. 'By the end of 1958 about half of the 200 million people affected with yaws will have been examined . . . and about 25 million persons will have been treated with long-acting penicillin . . . Clinically active yaws will have been reduced from about 15 million to less than half a million cases.'

Tuberculosis — In the W.H.O.-UNICEF campaigns, 162 million have been tuberculin-tested and 60 million given the BCG vaccination. The world total of victims is estimated at $\frac{1}{2}$ to 1 per cent of the world's adult population.

Quarantinable diseases — Six major killers of old — cholera, plague, smallpox, yellow fever, typhus, and relapsing fever — are grouped together, having been reduced, except for smallpox in some areas, to 'very modest proportions.' New insecticides kill the carriers of plague, and even pneumonic plague responds to new drugs: there were 514 recorded cases in 1957, the lowest since the beginning of the century. Cholera is confined to a few endemic areas, though an epidemic in 1947 caused 10,000 deaths. As for yellow fever, clinical cases are now 'extremely rare'; combined vaccination against yellow fever and smallpox is being applied on a mass scale in French Africa. The provisional 1957 figures for smallpox show a total of 136,000; vaccination does not yet cover the whole population. The newer insecticides permit the control of both typhus and relapsing fever, the first now limited to certain mountain areas in 3 continents, and the latter in sporadic form in some African territories.

Bilharziasis — This parasitic disease with 150 million victims remains difficult to control, without prospects yet for effective eradication; the newer molluscicides are fairly promising.

Helminthiasis — The parasitic worms which debilitate are widespread: round worm — 644 million cases; hookworm — 457 million; whipworm — 355 million. Most of the helminths are still a major challenge; one with 20 million victims now can be controlled.

Leprosy — Sulfones are effective in treatment of this disease with 10–12 million victims. Control programs in the foreseeable future may reduce its prevalence.

Sleeping Sickness — Human incidence has decreased considerably through the 'strenuous action of mobile teams for detection and treatment in French African Territories'; but the tsetse fly is hard to control.

Trachoma — This virus disease of the eye counts 300 to 400 million victims. 'Sulfanamide and antibiotic treatments have proved efficient and easily applied. For this reason it is considered that the disease can be eradicated.'

Cerebrospinal Fever — This type of meningitis, which can become a killing epidemic in the tropics, has in recent years been shown to respond 'easily to antibiotic and chemotherapeutic treatment.'

These rather dry and technical notes describe one of the great stories in man's age-old struggle against the ills of the flesh. If you translate them in terms of human lives saved, of potential achievement not cut off before its time, of suffering and disability brought to a halt, of grief and tragedy averted, one can only thank God for the mass of misery and death which has been lifted from mankind by these medical and public health conquests. In comparison, the great victory of the Salk vaccine against polio becomes a footnote in a really majestic chapter of the war against disease. There is, as indicated, the other side of the medal — the impact on rates of population growth. Whatever must be said about that, however, can hardly qualify our admiration and gratitude for this achievement.

While the weapons of this war have been many and varied, the new insecticides and antibiotics stand in the forefront.[6] The chief weapon of the antimalaria campaign, DDT, can be taken as the symbol of the current crusade against disease in the less developed world. It is relatively inexpensive, can be dusted by hand or spread from airplanes, and makes a heavy impact not only on the incidence of malaria but on other diseases spread by insects. Furthermore, it requires no major concomitant or antecedent changes in community life. As Kingsley Davis of the University of California, who recently served as Rapporteur of the U.N. Population Commission, has stated:

> The amazingly accelerated reduction of mortality in underdeveloped areas in recent years has . . . been accomplished by international disease control, not by economic development in these areas themselves. It required no essential change in the customs and institutions of the people, no advance in general education, no growth in per capita income.[7]

This, it seems to me, is a pivotal point. International disease control is not something that has emerged step by step out of indigenous culture and development. It is primarily the result of transference and application of Western medical and public health techniques. However significant the contribution of local doctors and health authorities, the main ingredient has been the contribution of Western science. Disease control is fundamentally an import from the West, subsidized in part by the West. It is not less valuable for this reason, but the leaders of the underdeveloped world are less prepared for the consequences. Reducing mortality in the less developed regions, with modern aids, has proved to be a relatively easy, inexpensive, and quickly successful sector of international development efforts. By a quirk of circumstance, the war against the killers has gone ahead somewhat faster than against the disablers. This disease control means in the long run for the needy societies more hands to help, and, even now, stronger hands to help. Yet its main initial economic effect, which also continues, is the rapid increase in mouths to feed. Three points are made in the U.N. population study, *Determinants and Consequences of Population Trends:*

1. The underdeveloped countries have had the benefit of techniques and knowledge which have evolved gradually in more advanced countries.
2. It has been possible to achieve a reduction in mortality in underdeveloped countries at relatively low cost.
3. The decline in mortality cannot always be attributed to improvement of the economic condition of the population.[8]

Two of the more dramatic examples of the impact of international disease control are seen in post-war Mauritius and Ceylon, where the vital statistics are relatively good. Between 1946 and 1952, when malaria campaigns were being conducted, the death rate in Mauritius declined from 28.6 per thousand to 14.8. The figure for 1956 was 11.8. The results in Ceylon were equally amazing. In the words of the U.N. study:

> In Ceylon, the crude death rate was 20.3 per thousand population in 1946 and had shown little change during the fifteen preceding years. In 1947, however, it was only 14.3 and in 1948 only 13.2. This decline of 35 per cent in two years has been attributed to the campaign against malaria, a disease which until 1946 was the chief cause of both morbidity and mortality. The use of DDT, which played an important part in the anti-malaria campaign, also brought about a considerable decline of the mortality from several other infectious diseases which are spread by insects.

In fact, the death rate in Ceylon was cut virtually in half in eight years after the war. While less dramatic in results, the use of the DDT technique against disease-carrying insects, according to Kingsley Davis, 'has achieved startling success in many other countries, such as Cyprus, Sardinia, India, Greece, Taiwan, Iran and the Philippines.' [9] The new methods appear to have made greater headway in regard to island populations than in the larger countries of the mainland. Yet it is the same international disease control which has cut death rates by a third or more in India, Thailand, and many more of the less developed countries. In several of these, as explained earlier, because of the youthful composition of the population the mortality rate has temporarily fallen below that of the Western countries. This is the revolutionary change wrought in ancient societies by the application of relatively inexpensive programs of public health.

International disease control has an additional if lesser impact on the rate of population growth which paradoxically is expressed in terms of higher birth rates. This is the effect on maternal health which reduces prenatal mortality and raises the percentage of live births. The war against malaria appears to be particularly important in this regard. As the W.H.O. report, previously cited, summarizes the point:

> Malaria . . . causes many abortions and stillbirths, through the predilection of malaria parasites for destroying red blood cells and for concentrating in large numbers in the placenta, thus affecting a country's birth rate. Figures published by W.H.O. show that in British Guiana, for example, the birth rate rose from 35.6 per cent in 1946 to 44.3 per cent in 1952, in the presence of malaria control. In Mauritius, during a country-wide eradication project, the birth rate rose from 38.4 per cent in 1946 to 48.1 per cent in 1952.[10]

While improved nutrition and related standards of living have no doubt played a part here and there, the evidence seems conclusive that the massive factor in the population explosion of the underdeveloped world is international disease control superimposed on societies full of young parents and parents-to-be.[11] Its full effect has by no means been reached. In large countries like India and China, health programs move more slowly than in more compact countries.[12] Moreover, the world-wide war against disease is being stepped up. The March 1959 issue of *Economic World* described plans for 'a spectacular international drive to raise health standards throughout the world,' a key element being the bipartisan bill in the U.S. Congress to appropriate $50 million to create a National Institute of International Medical Research. This is in addition to some $100 million a year currently spent on overseas health programs. The article reports:

> Experience in the current worldwide drive against malaria has convinced health authorities that international cooperation in the massive use of existing techniques can completely or nearly eradicate a number of prevailing diseases that have been mass killers throughout human history. And scientists are convinced that international pooling of research efforts will appreciably hasten new breakthroughs in medical knowledge.

The implications seem to me clear. The prospect is that throughout the underdeveloped world, where population growth has been held in check by high death rates, these rates can be expected to drop dramatically within the next few years. Because of the composition of the population they may even fall temporarily below the death rates in Western countries, as has already happened in some instances. Of course, the new insecticides and antibiotics are being used without knowledge of their long-term effects. Resistant strains of carrier insects may continue to develop. Resistant strains of germs such as staphylococcus may arise or multiply in the wake of the antibiotics. So the long-term results cannot be predicted with certainty. Yet the immediate prospect is one of a still further radical decline in death rates. Here is the TNT of the current explosion of population on the less developed continents.

To put it bluntly, the balance of nature has been upset — the old and tragic balance whereby population was kept in line with available resources through high birth rates and high death rates. Now the death rates have been tampered with, the death rates upheld by the death of so many babies, children, and young adults. The family, which needed a large number of offspring to have progeny survive, now finds itself blessed with many children —

and cursed with the difficulties of feeding them. The threat of premature death by starvation has been substituted for the ancient tragedy of premature death by disease. This is the bitter irony in the current demographic situation.

The one solution which is ruled out by every Christian and humanitarian impulse would be an effort to turn the clock back, to cut down on international medical assistance in the hope that the old balance of life and death could be restored. That the hope would be vain, in that the public health programs of the under-developed world are now too indigenous to be repealed, is beside the point. The argument that these programs, by reducing crip-pling diseases, also increase the productive capacity of the less developed societies, is valid but not determinative. The unassailable point is that improvements in public health are long overdue. Too long have mothers in the less privileged regions given birth to children destined for an early grave. Too long has early promise been snuffed out by preventable disease. Whatever else is wrong, conscience argues that the world-wide crusade for better health is right.

That other things are wrong, or at least inadequate, becomes clear when we look at the probable consequences of the present population explosion. For these consequences, so largely ignored in public discussions of world affairs, are grave in the extreme. No comparable threat to the stability, and hence to the peace, of this atomic age has been given so little attention in the counsels of governments. One would hardly guess from the debates in the U.N. General Assembly, much less from the aid programs of gov-ernments, that the population explosion was a reality. But the stark and stubborn facts refuse to be ignored, and the time when it was possible to hide in the sand rapidly runs out. The harsh time of public reckoning is close at hand.

Probably the least significant of the consequences of the popu-lation explosion is the one frequently mentioned: the shift in the balance of the races. The 'rising tide of color' is a fact rather than a prophecy. In 1950, the peoples of European descent accounted for roughly 30 per cent of the human race. By the year 2000, they will in all probability account for only 20 per cent of mankind. That this trend will increase tensions between the colored majority and the dominant white minority which controls most of the world's industrial power seems very likely. That it will put a world spotlight on racial injustice within a multiple society is even clearer.

But the sharpest cleavage in world society is not along racial lines. It is the Soviet-Western confrontation within the white sector which constitutes the main division of our divided world. The concentration of military and economic power in these antagonistic camps is such that the underdeveloped countries are inevitably drawn into one or the other — or walk a tightrope between them, hoping for support from both, or at least noninterference. But many are rather 'wobbly' from their rapid social change, in which the demographic revolution is a principal factor.

Instability is one of the important consequences of the new rise in population growth. As explained earlier, the youthful composition of the poorer peoples compounds the rate of growth, and the rate of growth compounds the youthful composition of the population. As the millions of new children grow up, swamping the highly inadequate schools and social facilities and pouring on to labor markets which have limited absorptive capacities, it does not require the gift of prophecy to predict trouble. Inadequate training or discipline combined with the frustrations of unemployment and limited opportunity form an explosive combination.[18] The same problem can be seen on a much smaller scale in some of the urban centers of the Western world. In many of the less developed countries, restless youth constitute a growing peril to political stability. The largest political force in the making is inexperienced, volatile, and increasingly frustrated — a mounting problem for the responsible politician and a temptation for the unscrupulous. In either case, an unstable, aberrant, and dynamic factor looms on the political and social scene, potentially creative or portentously destructive in accordance with the leadership provided.

From time to time a good deal of nonsense has been written about the relationship between population pressures and war, as if hunger and deprivation were direct causes of aggression. The plight of the 'have nots' was used in arguments for economic appeasement of pre-war Japan, Italy, and Germany. Yet they were 'have' countries in regard to standards of living, compared with the victims they attacked: Manchuria and China, Ethiopia, and Poland. Hungry nomadic tribes may roam and fight, but hungry peoples in the international society of today are likely also to be weak peoples, the pawns rather than the principals of power conflicts. Hungry men, if not disabled by their condition, may cause revolutions, but it takes a goodly food supply to make a war.

This is not to say that population pressures and concomitant political stresses and strains may not influence the leaders of densely populated countries to risky foreign policies, to find either a possible solution for the nation's plight, or at least a lightning rod for charged emotions at home. The campaign of Sukarno against the Dutch to secure control of West Irian (Netherlands New Guinea) may be a latter case in point. Even if sovereignty over this primitive and ethnically distinct territory were transferred, it would not provide any immediate easement of Indonesia's plight, but the issue provides a convenient drum for nationalism. Again, when the demographic situation of Egypt is considered, it is easier to understand the 'kinetic' foreign policy of Nasser, the seizure of the Suez Canal and the efforts to achieve hegemony among the Arab peoples, presumably to bring within reach some of the oil revenues which might ease the problems of national livelihood. A number of the tensions in the underdeveloped world may well have demographic roots.

Yet these are of consequence in the world situation primarily because of their impact on the major power conflict between the Soviet bloc and the Western concert. The less developed countries occupy a good deal of the middle ground between the 'lines,' where much of the struggle for global advantage takes place. Western policy has attempted to shore up those countries under most obvious Soviet pressure, as part of a strategy of containment, while trying to muddle through with inexpensive development assistance elsewhere. Soviet policy has belatedly discovered the propaganda advantages of small amounts of well-dramatized assistance in certain vulnerable countries, without weakening the ideological argument that development can succeed only under Communism.[14] Both policies add up thus far to 'too little and too late' in regard to the densely populated countries.

The danger to peace in the underdeveloped world lies in the weakness of countries imbued with the hope of escape from ancient poverty and beset by mounting population pressures. Often without adequate indigenous leadership or any really dynamic international assistance, they struggle to keep their heads above water. But problems grow more rapidly than solutions, and encourage the dream of Communist empire. The temptations to Communist expansion and the last minute efforts of the West to prevent such expansion constitute the real dangers of war to which the population explosion is a major contributor.

As matters now stand, with population growth rampant and tending to defeat even sacrificial efforts at economic development, the chief initial victim of the population explosion is likely to be the free society. No government in Asia can turn its back on the promise of economic and social progress which contacts with the West — including Christian missions — have helped to arouse. The level of international aid is thus far geared to a strategy which courts failure, at least in the densely populated countries. The amount of belt-tightening that is possible within the framework of a free society is limited, particularly in new democracies which cannot be expected to generate a high degree of self-discipline and sacrifice. Consequently, the tendency to abort and abandon the democratic experiment, in favor of a more coercive form of society, seems likely to grow, as indeed there is evidence in a number of countries. In most cases the authoritarian substitute may not take a Communist form. But the Soviet empire stands ready to harvest the failures. As I have argued before, the first issue in the lands of the population explosion is not economic and social development. The first issue is the free society.

Much has been made, and rightly so, of the competition between Communist China and the free society of India, the two biggest countries of Asia in process of development. Both are densely populated and growing rapidly. Both have limited resources, though China may be more favored by nature. While the price in human dignity and enforced sacrifice exacted by totalitarian procedures in China seems terribly high and may in the end prove a factor of weakness, it would be unrealistic, I think, to believe that the procedures of coercion cannot in the short run achieve a faster rate of economic modernization than the procedures of consent used in India.

The major potential advantage of India lies in the far greater development assistance which the Western powers could provide. Thus far, however, such assistance has been 'modest,' to put it mildly, bilateral and multilateral grants and loans providing roughly a 1 per cent supplement to India's national income in 1957–58,[15] though somewhat larger assistance has since been forthcoming in response to the crisis in the Second Five Year Plan. While the level of Soviet aid to Communist China is surrounded with considerable uncertainty, there is evidence that significant amounts of Soviet industrial equipment and 'know-how' have been exchanged for Chinese raw materials. I fear that the Western powers will wake up to find that the contest between India and China for economic development and Asian leadership has been waged under rather unequal material advantages. It is hardly necessary to spell out what this could mean to the hard-pressed lands of the population explosion.

One further possible consequence of the rapid increase of humanity in poor and crowded countries remains to be noted. The gap between fertility and mortality may be narrowed, as Irene Taeuber and other demographers have pointed out, by a new rise in mortality. The ancient 'positive check' of famine may recur in terrible form in a poor crop year. The United Nations and F.A.O. have co-operated in the idea of building up national food reserves to promote development needs and to provide against emergencies. But so far the scope of such undertakings has been on a fairly limited scale. No doubt, countries with food surpluses would respond as best they could to the tragedy of famine. Yet the story of Joseph still has relevance.

Some of the possible consequences of the population explosion have been traced in terms of the impersonal-sounding economic and social categories. Let us not forget, however, that each of these has a personal dimension, that 'the larger crisis of our time is reflected in families throughout the whole wide earth.' The shock waves of the population explosion 'buffet countless families.' It is in these effects on individual persons and families that the Christian concern is centered. The main issue is the family caught in the ferment and upheaval of social change, bewildered, frightened, subject to disruptive forces, tending to lose its spiritual and social moorings. Here is found the most fundamental cost of the new pressures of population.

From this short review of the dangers which threaten, we now turn to some of the possible ways out: in international and internal migration, in new food supplies and economic development, in population policy and family limitation.

IV

Migration and Population

ॐ Since the time when primitive man moved south ahead of the glaciers, migration has served as a safety valve for areas which became overpopulated in relation to available resources. Even then migration was not easy, for primitive man required a lot of living space to survive, and usually migration meant dispossessing others from their hunting grounds. The warfare among the American Indian tribes, despite the fact that they numbered but an estimated million persons at the coming of the white man, can help us visualize the difficulties of early migration.

While most movements of population have no doubt been accomplished by force of arms, as in the successive migrations from the Eurasian heartland which helped to submerge the Roman Empire, the modern world has seen substantial movements of settlers into relatively unoccupied territory — at least from the point of view of the settlers if not the indigenous inhabitants. The opening up of the New World, Australasia, and lesser regions paved the way for considerable emigration from more densely populated countries in Europe. The trickle grew into a stream in the 19th century. Since 1821, for example, immigration into the United States has totaled more than 40 million persons, with upwards of 35 million coming from Europe, one from Asia, and five or so from the other Americas. The rest of the New World received a comparable number, mainly from the southern European countries.

Perhaps 70 million Europeans all told over the past three centuries have found new homes in the Americas. This migration played a significant role in easing the population pressures consequent upon the decline of European death rates, and the lag in the reduction of birth rates. It reached a crescendo in the early years of the 20th century, ground to a virtual halt during the depression years, and was renewed somewhat after World War II, primarily to care for some of those uprooted by war and tyranny. Something like four million refugees and migrants from Europe have resettled in the Americas since 1946, if we reduce the gross imigration by one-third to account for the returnees.[1]

The main areas of European settlement outside of the Americas have been members of the British Commonwealth, Australia, New Zealand, and the Union of South Africa. Since 1821 roughly four million migrants have gone to Australia, less than one million to New Zealand, and about one million to the Union. The main source, understandably, has been Britain itself. The movement of Frenchmen to Africa perhaps also should be mentioned, although the main settlement in Algeria is regarded in France as a matter of internal migration. The post-war migration of Jews to Israel should also be noted.[2]

In contrast with the opportunities open to Europeans for overseas resettlement, which enabled perhaps 80 million in modern times to find new homes, the opportunities for Asiatics have been extremely limited. The chief openings have been in the relatively less densely populated regions of South-East Asia, some of which, like Indonesia, have rapidly been acquiring their own population problems. It is estimated that about $11\frac{1}{2}$ million Chinese are living outside of Chinese territory, mainly in South-East Asia, where about a million Indians have also found a home.[3] Carr-Saunders put the figure for Indians somewhat higher: 1.4 million in Ceylon and Malaya as of 1931. Practically all of these doors are now shut, for a variety of reasons, one of which is rapid growth of population throughout the region.

The very limited opportunities for Asian emigration outside of Asia appear to have stemmed principally from various importations of Asian laborers following the progressive termination, during the

19th century, of the African slave trade. This infamous trade, incidentally, while hardly designed to relieve population pressures in Africa, undoubtedly slowed down the African rate of growth and even more accelerated the increase in population in the warmer sections of the Americas, from the Mason-Dixon line to Brazil. Carr-Saunders says, 'there is reason to believe that as many as 20 million Africans were taken from their homes,' though it is doubtful that more than half that number survived the journeys in the abominable slave ships. In this time of dynamic population growth, however, no group in the world is increasing more rapidly than the New World descendants of the African slaves.

The chief origin of Indian settlements outside of Asia, as Carr-Saunders points out, was the emigration of Indians under indenture. This practice was prohibited by the government of India in 1915, to protect the emigrants, but many chose to remain, and they formed the core of Indian populations in Mauritius, South Africa, Trinidad, British Guiana, and Fiji. The figures given by Carr-Saunders come to about 800,000 persons, and the total is undoubtedly well over a million today. Even so, it should be noted that all Indians outside India do not exceed half of one year's annual increase in the motherland, which is now somewhere between five and seven million souls. The other Asian minorities overseas are even smaller. Most of the 400,000 Chinese migrants to the United States came in the period after the Civil War when the building of the railroads and related enterprises in the Western states created a demand for cheap labor. Chinese were excluded from the mainland beginning in 1882, from Hawaii in 1898, and from the Philippines in 1902. There was also a smaller influx of Japanese in the first quarter of the present century, until the Immigration Act of 1924 excluded Orientals.[4] The total Japanese emigration to the New World has been estimated at 750,000, the largest settlement being in Brazil. For every Asian who has found a home overseas, there are 300 to 400 still in Asia.

Practically all of the doors are closed to the crowded peoples of the underdeveloped world, or, if ajar, rather thoroughly stuck. While the United States law of 1952 offered Asians token quotas, access was reduced from another quarter: colonial dependencies in the Western Hemisphere were reduced to a quota of 100 each, to cut down British West Indian immigration which had taken advantage of the British quota. Doors in Africa under Western control have been closed to Asians, and the newly independent countries show no disposition to open theirs. In the case of Australia, immigration from Europe is facilitated, while immigration from Asia has been barred in fact by administrative devices such as the 'dictation test' requiring 50 words to be written in 'any' European language which the examining officer may specify — a device now terminated, I believe. Canada also has no quota system, but follows a restrictive pattern in regard to Orientals. Only in South America, chiefly in Brazil, is a thin trickle of Japanese immigration still permitted.

Thus at present the dense populations of Asia find no substantial opportunity for overseas migration, either in the less populated industrialized countries, such as Australia, Canada, and the United States, or in the less inhabited areas of the underdeveloped world, such as Brazil and territories south of the Sahara. The same spirit of nationalism which makes for restrictive policies in Asia is operative in the immigration policies of the governments which control the main opportunities for immigration. Racial and cultural prejudice is no doubt a factor in most policies, as is apprehension over economic conflicts expressed in racial tensions. The concern of both the industrialized and industrializing societies is more and more for the skilled worker, rather than the unskilled or the peasant. Recurrent unemployment, and the haunting memories of depression, make legislators and administrators cautious rather than generous. Consequently, even European migration is difficult. The Intergovernmental Committee for European Migration, for example, has struggled to resettle 854,000 Europeans in seven years, although its original goal was a quarter of a million annually.

Demographic considerations, moreover, provide a powerful argument for restrictive and conservative immigration policies. Let us look for a moment at the demographic situation of some of the

countries which have played the largest role in the resettlement
of refugees. If we compare the population figures for 1955 with
rough estimates for the year 2000 based upon the U.N. median
forecasts for regions, in terms of present agricultural area,[5] we
have the following picture for the selected countries:

	Persons per square mile of present agricultural area	
	1955	2000
West Germany	930	1,230
United States	96	163
Canada	67	123
Australia	6	11
Brazil	124	447
Argentina	35	66
Venezuela	85	324
Israel	817	3,100

Of course, such an exercise needs to be treated with considerable
reserve. The derivative population forecasts are very rough, though
it should be added that the specific impact of recent immigration
on population growth is not taken into account and might enlarge
some of the estimates. Furthermore, the medium-assumption population forecasts are not necessarily more correct than those based
on higher assumptions. On the other hand, present agricultural
area may change markedly in 40 years, particularly in a country
like Brazil, and in any case be made more productive. Nevertheless, these countries which have carried the main load in refugee
resettlement all confront in the decades immediately ahead a
considerable prospective increase of pressure on their agricultural
resources from their own population growth. Increasingly, they
will be occupying their own living space.

If we take a broader look at the implication of demographic
trends for migration possibilities, the same general conclusion
emerges. In *The Future Growth of World Population*, if you recall, the U.N. demographers grouped the regions of the world
under four categories. The most critically situated group is composed of regions with high density and rapid growth: the Carib-

bean, Central South Asia, South-East Asia, and East Asia except for Japan. If we speak of migration as a means of easing population pressures, here are the mass of potential candidates, for their already crowded populations confront a prospective increase of 185 per cent during the last half of this century. The second category, high density and moderate growth, includes Europe and Japan. Pressures here are much less severe — a prospective 51 per cent increase during the half century — but obviously there is little room for immigration.

So we come to the two remaining categories. The third, low density and rapid growth, includes Central America, Tropical South America, South-West Asia, the Pacific Islands, and all of Africa. A generation ago Latin America and Africa would have been regarded as providing large opportunities for immigration. Today they form a group of regions where internal growth seems likely to mean 318 persons in the year 2000 for every 100 living in 1950. The only kind of migration which the more favorably situated countries under this category can reasonably be expected to accept is a highly selective migration calculated to expand the available resources more rapidly than it intensifies the population pressures. In short, the immigrants needed are the engineers, technicians, and skilled workers, who are the very people the countries in the first category are least able to spare.

This brings us to the fourth category, that of low density and moderate growth. This final group is composed of Northern America, the southern tip of South America, Australasia, and the Soviet Union. From a demographic point of view, these relatively sparsely settled regions of the temperate zones offer the main technical possibilities for immigration, even though they are expected to double their population from internal growth during the current half-century. Political factors aside, the U.S.S.R. would appear to have the greatest need for settlers of the pioneer type to help develop Siberia and the vast reaches of Asiatic territory. The northern frontier of Canada is another potential area for pioneer settlement. The potentialities of Australia and Argentina depend very much on the possibilities of improving the supplies of water. Industrial expansion in all of these countries offers a different kind of frontier. The absorptive capacity of the United States appears to depend more on the strength of an expanding economy than upon any special geographical considerations.

It should be noted that, except for Western Germany, the four countries last named, together with Brazil, have in fact provided the main opportunities for migrants of all types during the post-war years. The order of magnitude of their combined rate of absorption may be put roughly at a half million persons a year. The Research Group for European Migration Problems (R.E.M.P.) puts the 'permanent migrant intakes' by the five countries from all European sources at 3.6 million for the years 1946–53.[6] Immigration from Latin America to the United States would raise the total by an uncertain amount,[7] while Asian immigrants, as previously indicated, constitute a negligible factor. Undoubtedly special humanitarian considerations helped to swell the numbers in the early post-war years. But at least the record shows what can be done.

To increase the rate achieved in the early post-war years substantially, say to one million settlers a year, does not seem impossible, but the obstacles impress me as stubborn. The migrants for the most part need to fit in to the development needs and plans of the admitting countries, and that means a much higher level of skills than migrants needed even a half century ago. The development and social capital required has also become more costly and complex. It is more than a question of transportation and housing, and much more than one of quotas and visas. A million settlers a year is more than 3 per cent of the present population of the major receiving countries, and migration today needs to be seen more in terms of the absorptive capacity of the economies involved than in terms of unused land. But the main point for our purpose is that even a doubling of the post-war rate would not open the doors to Asian immigration. The fact is hard but true.

Sometimes in church circles and even at the level of government, migration is discussed as if it were a right. Thus, Monsignor

Edward B. Swanstrom stated, in presenting a resolution to the Breda Conference of 1954:

> Man's right to move to parts of the earth where his productive capacities can be put to use stems from the Christian view of property. Where men cannot draw sustenance for their families in overpopulated areas, there exists the right of migration to areas of the earth's surface where less population pressure on resources is exerted.

The good Monsignor here seems to confuse a principle of Christian charity with the less noble principles of international law. One of the elementary functions of national sovereignty, which may be an antiquated institution but is still very much alive, is control of ingress and settlement in the national territory. It is one thing for the churches to urge upon their governments, on grounds of charity and justice and enlightened self-interest, the moral obligation to adopt more generous and less discriminatory immigration policies. It is quite another thing to say that men who need to migrate have a legal right to do so. At this stage of history it is hard enough to establish an international right to asylum, as a safeguard for human rights, and it would be foolhardy to attempt to promote an international right to migration.

This does not mean that national sovereignty may not eventually be modified in this direction. Indeed, I would argue that in the interdependent world of today, the question of migration is affected with an international interest, in the same way that tariff policy is involved. This means that governments have an obligation to consider the impact of immigration policies upon the welfare of other peoples before adopting and putting them into effect. To carry this a step further would mean procedures of international consultation through regular diplomatic channels and the United Nations. All this would not remove the ultimate right and responsibility of the national government to determine and implement its own policy in the light of the national interest. What it might accomplish is a broader view of what the long-term national interest really is. A practical result, I believe, would be to remove the more discriminatory bars to Asian immigration, those which add insult to injury.

The insult is clear, but is the injury real? Thus far we have looked at migration in terms of immigration possibilities, and it is time to look at the desirability of emigration in regard to the underdeveloped world. By now it should be clear that overseas migration offers the rapidly multiplying peoples of the less developed societies no real easement of their situation such as it offered the peoples of Europe during the past century — e.g. in helping Ireland to reduce her population, and Italy and Greece to buffer their population pressures through emigration and the remittances of emigrants. The empty spaces have become much more occupied and the potential occupiers vastly more numerous. More than a decade ago the American demographer, Warren S. Thompson, pointed out that 'the population needing outlets is five or six times that of Europe of 1800, and the lands available are relatively small and not so richly endowed as the Americas.' The logistics alone would be formidable. The Red Cross Commission to China on the famine conditions of 1928–29 said in its report:

> If all the ships that sail the seven seas were withdrawn from their regular routes and devoted henceforth exclusively to carrying emigrants out of China they would not keep up with the procession.

Translating this into contemporary terms, it would take a thousand crossings by goodly sized ships to transport enough Indians to reduce by one-fifth the increase of one year in India's population. Indeed, if the countries of immigration enlarged their post-war rate of admissions by half and admitted only migrants from the underdeveloped world, the total would be about equivalent to the annual *increase* in the annual increase of the lands of the population explosion. The Reverend William J. Gibbons, S.J., said, as rapporteur on migration at the World Population Conference of 1954, that while migration can help to relieve population pressures, 'it is not to be expected that under present circumstances, the population pressures of certain areas, especially those of continental proportions like India's, can be resolved by emigration.'

It is very clear that the pressures cannot be resolved by such means.[8] It is not even certain that the very limited overseas migration which might be possible would do more good than harm. The countries of immigration are all engaged in rapid economic development, and consequently place a premium upon the technician and skilled worker. The selective immigration processes designed to get 'the cream of the crop,' which trouble some European students of migration, would be applied equally to immigration from the less developed countries. Even without official screening, as Clarence Senior has pointed out in a paper on 'Migration and Population,' Puerto Ricans coming to the United States have a considerably higher level of education and occupational skill than the average for the island. The skilled worker and technician are precisely the people in desperately short supply throughout the less developed societies and even a small loss would be grievous.

There are additional considerations which supplement this point. The migrant most welcome is the young adult who has completed his training period. Any considerable emigration will consequently mean a reduction in the productive segment of society, and a relative increase in the non-productive — the young and the old. G. Beijer, the editor of the *R.E.M.P. Bulletin*, estimated in a background paper for the World Council study on migration that the 'costs of producing a man' in the Western world range from $3,000 to $8,000, i.e. the total for food, housing, clothing, medical care, education, and specialized training. The costs are obviously less in the underdeveloped world, but not negligible. Senior estimated in 1947 that raising a male child to the age of 18, or the start of his productive career, cost the Puerto Rican economy at least $3,000 to $3,500. The country of emigration loses this investment, offset by such remittances as the migrant may send back. More important may be the loss in terms of human initiative, aptly expressed in the colloquial phrase 'get up and go.' [9]

In short, in this day of increasingly selective and specialized migration, there is a real question whether the country of immigration is not the main beneficiary, and whether the cost to the country of emigration, particularly one limited in trained personnel, may not be larger than any slight palliative received through remittances. This is no argument, of course, for persistence by countries of immigration in discriminatory practices which are unjust and embitter relations with the excluded nations. Yet it would be a sad day for the latter, when immigration policies become more wise, if money spent on the resettlement of migrants from the less developed societies were regarded as a substitute for developmental assistance.

If overseas migration offers little or no prospect for easing the population pressures in the lands of rapid social change, there is another form of migration which merits some attention. This is internal migration, which is possible in certain countries with considerable territory and an uneven distribution of population.[10] In a number of situations, internal migration has provided an opportunity for both population and economic growth. Examples include the westward expansion of the American and Canadian peoples and their present much smaller movement northward; the Russian movement into Asiatic Russia which continues; the Chinese expansion into Manchuria and the outer provinces, which also continues. Less dramatic examples can be found in the cases of smaller countries.

The two clearest examples of possible benefit from internal migration are the island nations of Indonesia and the Philippines. The population pressures in Indonesia are concentrated in the fertile island of Java, while neighboring Sumatra, to mention the largest possibility, is relatively underpopulated. Likewise, the Philippine population is unevenly distributed and, as pressures mount, a movement to the less populated islands could help. India has some room for settlement in her northern provinces, and some of her neighbors in South-East Asia have similar opportunities for internal expansion. If the indefinitely large potential of the Amazon basin can be harnessed more successfully, Brazil, whose present development is concentrated largely in the southeastern section, has a great empire to inherit, and perhaps to share with other tropical races.

Internal migration can palliate local population imbalances in several instances. Yet the fact that international frontiers are not involved does not make such migration easy. The clearing of jungle, the equipment of settlers, and, not least, the translation of national needs into family decisions to move, can be formidable. It cannot be done successfully unless there is sufficient capital to give the new settlements a reasonable opportunity to prosper. A friend of mine, related some years ago to an international team working on problems of Javanese resettlement in Sumatra, indicated that one of the causes of discouragement was that, while strenuous efforts succeeded in resettling 80,000 people in one year, the net increase in the population of Java during the same period was several times greater. Internal migration, where the circumstances permit, can help somewhat, provided it is reinforced with economic development. But its beneficial effects are nullified so long as fertility is rampant.

Coming back to international migration, I find various arguments, from considerations of justice and wise expediency, for modifying immigration policies which are unduly restrictive. Larger allowance for Asian settlers, while not deluding Asia into thinking that Western doors were open, might temper some of the resentment and reduce one of the psychological barriers to understanding, on which hang so many hopes for the future of freedom and of peace. A certain amount of Asian immigration could serve the purpose of cultural enrichment, like the exchanges of professors and students. The demographic argument, however, is conspicuous by its absence. Even a cursory consideration of the facts convinces that migration offers no way out for the peoples of the population explosion.

If the movement of people to less densely populated regions offers only a minor and limited palliative in the present population explosion, the main positive alternative is to develop new ways to feed them where they are. We now turn to this question.

V

Food and Population

᠂᠊᠊ A second main line of approach to a solution of the population problem is offered by the struggle for economic and social
development of the societies long underprivileged. If migration
does not offer a propitious way out, then the main hope of easing
the pressures and of restoring a balance between population and
available resources appears to lie in the expansion of the food
supplies of Asia, Africa, and Latin America. Man does not live by
bread alone even at the material level, but in the tropical and sub-
tropical societies which compose the underdeveloped world, food
merits a larger share of attention than in colder climates where
clothing and shelter assert a stronger claim. The increase and distribution of food resources can be taken as a pivotal issue in the
war for development.

Before turning to the main argument, passing note might be
made of a more extreme thesis, advanced in *The Geography of
Hunger* by Josué de Castro, a Brazilian nutritionist and former
head of the F.A.O. Council. Arguing from some earlier experiments on rats by J. R. Slonaker, which suggested 'that in propor-
tion as the diet increases in protein content, reproductive capacity
drops,' de Castro argued the theory that 'specific hunger is the
cause of overpopulation.' In support of this notion, he drew up a
neat table of countries, ranging from Formosa with a 45.6 birth
rate and daily per capita consumption of 4.7 grams of animal
proteins, to Sweden with a 15.0 birth rate and 62.6 grams con-

sumption. In short, he argued, a better diet would directly reduce natality by making people less fecund.

While scholars have not found it difficult to show the factual as well as the logical hiatuses in the de Castro thesis, more sophisticated versions of the underlying idea persist. Lord Boyd-Orr, in his introduction to *The Geography of Hunger*, argued that 'the only real effective method of birth control is to improve the diet, raise the standard of living and education of the nations . . .' [1] These factors may indeed be favorable to a reduction in fertility, but they hardly cause or explain it. Diet and standards of living may have some slight impact on reproductive capacity, but it would still be ample for a high birth rate. No serious scientist, to my knowledge, asserts that lower birth rates in the West are caused by reduced fecundity. As is stated in the U.N. study: 'In recent years, there is almost universal agreement that the major part, if not all, of the decline in family size has been brought about by the practice of family limitation.' [2] Here is the missing link in the causal chain.

The main argument, however, does not claim that better food and general economic improvement will have a direct restrictive effect on fertility, but rather that it is possible to develop food and related resources more rapidly than the population increases, and thus maintain — or restore and maintain — a favorable population-resources balance. A few enthusiasts seem to hold that human ingenuity can maintain such a balance in perpetuity no matter how inflated the human sum may become, but most advocates of the economic way out are content with the prospects for the 'foreseeable future.' Thus the F.A.O., the bellwether of this flock, uses this term in its assurances against 'neo-Malthusian' pessimism; for example: 'The F.A.O. believes that technically it is possible to achieve the necessary increases in production of foodstuffs and basic raw materials to meet world needs for the foreseeable future. . .'

Actually, despite the brave front against the neo-Malthusians to reassure the faithful, the F.A.O. optimism does not go very deep. The possibilities are 'technical'; it is admitted that to keep barely ahead of equilibrium involves 'social, political and administrative problems . . . of immense magnitude.' And this struggle does not cover 'the further urgent need to make a real improvement in the inadequate subsistence levels' of the underdeveloped world. In fact, it is admitted elsewhere that even the status quo is not being maintained: 'So far, food production in the world as a whole has not been able to keep pace with the ever larger requirements of the increasing population of the earth.' The bold trumpet thus has a rather muted tone when put to the test. To put it another way, the F.A.O. program is considerably more realistic than some of its propaganda.

In any case, there can be no doubt as to the crucial importance of the war against hunger, whether or not it suffices as an answer to the population problem. To appraise the prospects of the crusade against the ancient enemy of famine and the ills which flow from chronic undernourishment, we need to start with a clear understanding of the present balance sheet in Asia, Africa, and Latin America. Let us look first at the level of nourishment in these continents, recent trends in the production of food, and the condition of land under cultivation. These form the terminus *a quo.* Then it will be feasible to examine the nearer and more distant technical possibilities, which form the potential terminus *ad quem,* without losing contact with present reality.

Adequate nutrition involves both quantity and quality, the calories which provide the necessary energy, and the proteins, vitamins, and minerals essential to health. Since the majority of people in the less developed societies live mainly on cereals — the protective value of which is often injured in processing — or on starchy roots, the 'hidden hungers' are undoubtedly vast, though difficult to measure. Protein consumption, which can be measured more readily, is generally low in the underdeveloped world, animal protein being the most expensive nutriment in the human diet.[3] The reason is that only some 10 to 15 per cent of the energy consumed by animals is recovered as food,[4] so that in many areas men must choose the 'original' calories produced by the available land rather than the reduced yield in the form of animal products.

Protein malnutrition, the 'illness with many names,' is particularly injurious to young children. According to the F.A.O. pamphlet, *Man and Hunger*: 'It is believed that in some parts of Africa every child suffers from it at some time of his life.'

The fact that protein deficiency is widespread does not, of course, mean that the rather wasteful protein levels of many Western diets, in which animal proteins constitute 40 per cent or more of the total, have to be achieved to provide adequate nourishment. By combining the calories in the plant foods consumed and the 'original' calories in the animal products consumed, Karl Sax, in the Foreign Policy Association pamphlet, *The Population Explosion*, puts the dietary level in Oceania, North America, and Argentina at more than 10,000 original calories as compared with little more than 2,100 for India and about 2,600 for China. He thinks 'it might be possible to provide a diet adequate in proteins and vitamins from cereals, vegetables and animal products without exceeding 3,000 original calories,' though 5,000 would be more likely to assure a complete and adequate diet. The current Western ideal may err on the side of wasteful excess, as present reality in other parts of the world is harmfully deficient.

Diets in the underdeveloped world are also widely deficient in terms of quantity. Calorie requirements per person per day do not offer too precise a yardstick for diet, but it is the best single means of measurement now available. Calorie requirements, as estimated by the F.A.O. Calories Committee, vary somewhat, the main factors of variance being climate, body size, and population structure in terms of age and sex.[5] Norway, for example, is given a requirement of 2,850 calories, and India 2,250. The U.N. *Report on the World Social Situation* for 1957 indicates that most of the less developed countries are below par in terms of elementary standards of calorie consumption. To cite the worst examples, the Indian diet is given as 24.4 per cent below the estimated requirement, the French North African at 20.9 per cent below, and the Mexican at 17.9 per cent below. In varying degrees, the diet of the underdeveloped world is at present tragically inadequate both in regard to quantity and quality.

In regard to trends in food production, despite the national and international efforts to date to aid development, the current picture is far from encouraging. The latest issue of the F.A.O. publication, *State of Food and Agriculture 1958*, which gives preliminary figures for the 1957–58 crop year, shows a rise in the index numbers of total food production for Latin America, the Far East exclusive of mainland China, the Near East, and Africa from 88 as the average for 1934–38 to 121 tentatively for 1957–58. But the index for *per capita* food production for the four regions during the same period shows a slight drop, from 108 to 106. Rises for the Near East and Africa are offset by declines in the Far East and Latin America. In spite of the plans, assistance, and local sacrifices of the past decade, food production in the underdeveloped world is hard pressed to keep its head above the mounting flood of population.[6]

There are a number of reasons for this state of affairs. The F.A.O. publication itself states that in the less developed countries 'agricultural expansion is more difficult [than in the developed countries] because of more primitive techniques, lack of investment capital and often unsuitable systems of land tenure and other institutions.' In addition to the social obstacles, there is the condition of the land itself, and the tropical or sub-tropical climate which is typical of the less developed sector of humanity. While the majority of mankind lives in the temperate zones, the majority of the underdeveloped world — roughly a billion people out of 1.8 billion — dwells in the tropics. And much less is known about tropical agriculture, with its uneven or all too copious or all too insufficient rainfall, than about agriculture in more temperate climates. The terrific leaching of soils inadequately fertilized to begin with, plus the lack of checks on competing growth, whether vegetable or animal, offset any advantages derived from the year-round growing season. The soils of the ancient societies are 'tired' from the centuries of use and misuse. Many have turned into deserts through the breakdown of social organization and of irrigation systems. It is a far from encouraging prospect.

Two of the post-war books with a strident concern for soil conservation, *Our Plundered Planet* by Fairfield Osborn and *Road to Survival* by William Vogt, were severe in their judgment of the end result of agricultural malpractices, particularly in the less developed regions. Osborn, arguing that it takes nature 300 to 1,000 years to build an inch of topsoil, pointed out how often the ancient pattern of 'cut, burn, plant, destroy, move on' had prevailed. Much of the Middle East had once been fertile, and was destroyed by man. China's land was eroded, India's wasted. Much land in North Africa, once fertile, was now desert. Man must recognize the 'necessity for cooperating with nature . . . the time for defiance is at an end.' Vogt similarly criticized the destruction of irreplaceable soils, particularly through 'the shattering of the hydrologic cycle,' which involves the destruction of plant cover followed by the washing or blowing of topsoil. He thought most of the Latin American countries were living by destroying their resources — 'over most of the southern continent soil erosion is all but universal on cultivated lands.' He noted the 'disastrous' lack of organic matter and soil nutrients in China; the 'bludgeoning' force of heavy rains in India; and the low carrying capacity of Africa, which has poor soils in its savannas and soils prone to destruction by leaching if forest cover is cut in the rain-belt. Even if the grim pictures are overdrawn they cannot be ignored.[7]

Here in brief, despite variations and local bright spots, are the dark aspects of the general food situation in the less developed countries: the inadequate diet, the stalemated production of food, the frequent occurrence of tired and abused soil. It is well to remember these realities when we look at the brave new world of what is possible in the way of new resources in the broad field of human nutrition. Too often the enthusiasts seize upon the manifold technical possibilities as if their achievement were assured, without reckoning the hard intermediate steps required to graft them onto the actual situation. On the other hand, I think the enthusiasts for family planning tend to downgrade or dismiss too lightly the wide variety of potentialities for sustaining larger populations, which can now be described.

One of the troubles with a number of analyses of potential food supplies is that they approach the problem in global terms, as if an improved production in one sector implied progress in consumption in another. Thus, there is discussion of the northward expansion of agriculture in Canada or Russia — where considerable effort is being made — or the development of mixed agriculture in southern Australia. These are parts of the more developed world, and it remains to be proved that an expansion in these areas will benefit more than temporarily or indirectly the lands of the population explosion. We need to give primary attention to possibilities within these less developed regions since, at the current stage of international relationships, they cannot count upon more than a relatively small amount of international assistance. This dominant principle was stated by F.A.O. in its submission to the Atomic Energy Conference of 1955: 'freedom from want must depend essentially upon the efforts made by each country on its own behalf.'

Let us look first of all at the soils of the underdeveloped world. The 1938 Yearbook of the U.S. Department of Agriculture, *Soils and Men*, gives a map of the primary groups of soils in the world, patterned after the work of Glinka, Marbut, and others. The map shows these broad groupings for the underdeveloped world:

Lateritic soils — The largest area is made up of the red and yellow soils, such as are found in the southeastern U.S. Included here are most of South-East Asia, Central Africa with its rain-belt, and the Amazon basin. These soils, particularly under the impact of tropical rains, tend to lose fairly quickly their nutrients, once their forest cover is removed, and generally require rather heavy fertilization and crop rotation to produce satisfactorily.

Sierozems and desert soils — The second largest category applies to South-West Asia and the Sahara, with smaller sections of South-West Africa, part of Argentina, and part of the west coast of South America. Some of these soils are fairly fertile, but the lack of moisture severely limits any use at present.

Chernozems, brown and chestnut soils — The highly fertile black and brown soils are mainly found across Middle Africa, between the Sahara and the rain-belt, in East Africa and a good part of southern Africa, in the basin of the Rio de la Plata, and in a large section of northwest India and Pakistan. These appear to be areas of high potentiality, limited in some regions by uneven rainfall.

Gray-brown Podzolic soils — Such soils, similar to those of the north-eastern U.S., are found in northern China and Korea. They vary considerably but are in general moderately fertile.

The lateritic soils of Asia already carry a very heavy load of human beings. They are soils which tend to 'tire' quickly and could benefit greatly from heavy fertilization programs. One of the reasons for low yields in India appears to be inadequate supplementary nutrients, a deficiency for which the government is trying to compensate. These soils apparently are not propitious for large increases in production, though irrigation in some areas can greatly mitigate the effect of the dry seasons. The lush vegetation of the Amazon basin and Central Africa has frequently led to great expectations about the potential breadbaskets to be found in these tropical jungles, when converted to food production. The character of the underlying soil, combined with the extremely heavy rainfall, however, is not encouraging.[8] If trees or other perennial crops, which will hold the soil and humus, can be utilized for human consumption then the hopes surrounding these areas may be realized. No one has a right to dismiss out of hand the food potential in these fountains of verdure; yet no one, I gather, has discovered how they can be harnessed to nutritional needs.

The savannas beyond the great African rain-belt appear to have greater possibilities, as does the basin of the Rio de la Plata. The main obstacle in the dark-soil areas of Africa seems to be the seasonal droughts which, along with the tsetse fly, inhibit even grazing. In time, no doubt it will be possible to irrigate part of this area from inland waters, and to develop an insecticide to cope with the 'ruler of Africa.' Neither, however, offers an immediate prospect. The basin of the Rio de la Plata also has a sub-humid climate, but the rainfall in this predominantly temperate region is more evenly distributed. With better drainage in low-lying areas, the additional food potential of this area seems very considerable.[9] Its present production lifts Argentina and Uruguay measurably above the level of the underdeveloped world.

The utilization of fertile desert and semidesert areas depends upon the possibilities of developing inexpensive water supplies for irrigation. J. O. Hertzler, in his excellent summary on 'Increasing the World's Food Supply' in *The Crisis in World Population*, points out that 'no world survey of lands both good as to quality and potentially irrigable by natural waters has been made.' It is conceivable that sea water, desalted by ionization or some new process, can eventually be used in certain areas, provided atomic development makes power sufficiently cheap for the processing plants and pumping stations. Supplementary irrigation in regions like the African savannas could also be facilitated by such means. The prospect, however, seems remote and uncertain, and leaves unanswered the question as to how less developed countries are to finance the atomic installations and pipelines.

The expansion, then, of tropical agriculture into new areas of the underdeveloped world seems beset by many tough obstacles. In most potential areas, the combination of fertile land and even, adequate rainfall is lacking. R. M. Salter thought that a billion acres of cropland could be added, 900 million in South America and Africa, and 100 million in the islands south of the Asian mainland.[10] A billion new acres of tropical cropland would mean a 40 per cent increase in the world total of land under cultivation and conversion of 20 per cent of all the unused land in the tropics, according to Director-General B. R. Sen of F.A.O. It seems a very large order, not impossible to do in time, but hardly possible to do quickly or without large capital expenditures. The relative want of knowledge about tropical agriculture is a further handicap. Also, it should be noted that Asia, the continent which needs new food supplies most critically, has the least room for agricultural expansion.

The better utilization of existing cropland appears to offer a brighter short-range prospect. The improvement of seed through hybridization and selection, and of livestock through scientific breeding and artificial insemination, offers a major advancement. Hybrid corn (maize) has increased United States yields by 20 per cent, and even more may be accomplished in the less developed societies by the application of Western methods in this field. The introduction and development of new crops especially suited to tropical conditions is another field worthy of research. [11] The successful first steps betoken the promise of the future.

Fertilization is one of the great agricultural needs throughout the underdeveloped world. The leaching of lateritic soils under the impact of tropical rainfall makes replenishment of plant nutrients such as phosphorus especially needful. The whole underdeveloped world in 1953–54, however, consumed less than 4 per cent of the world's supply of commercial fertilizers. F.A.O. specialists think that better soil fertility practices, such as crop rotation and the use of fertilizers, could increase production 'by at least 50 per cent, and in many countries by 100 per cent.' Good fertility practices also involve soil conservation, be it noted, and rehabilitation of land that has been abused 'invariably means a reduction in the areas available for crops or livestock.' [12] This need for soil conservation, incidentally, provides an argument against plans to utilize marginal land in many instances.

The extension of irrigation is another major resource for the increase of food production, which is doubly important for the tropical world in view of the seasonal rainfall and the long growing season possible if moisture is available. The irrigation systems of ancient civilizations were one of their crowning achievements and even today it is estimated that one-fourth of the world's food supply is grown on irrigated land.[13] Important opportunities for extension remain. For example, an F.A.O. study of the lower Ganges-Brahmaputra basin, where 130 million people live, has shown, as B. R. Sen put it, 'that the number of acres cultivated per annum could be doubled if full use were made of water which is at present mainly running to waste, quite apart from the possibilities of increasing yields.' Irrigation dams, although costly for underdeveloped economies, can help to control floods, provide electric power, and increase the supply of fresh water fish.

Improved tools can also help to increase yields by making possible deeper or quicker plowing. This can be important in a country like India, where prompt action is necessary if a second crop is to be planted between the harvest and the monsoon rains. By improved tools is not meant mechanization of agriculture, which the small plots and inadequate industrial base as well as the available draft and manpower make unsuitable in most of the less developed countries.[14] By improved tools is meant the substitution of the scythe for the sickle, as in Afghanistan, or the practical metal plow designed by Leigh Stevens for use in India, simple enough to be made in a village smithy and small enough to be pulled by an Indian bullock, yet increasing considerably the area a man can plow in a day. The development of improved tools especially adapted to existing conditions is a combined challenge to Western and indigenous technicians.

The war against plant and animal diseases and pests, as well as against insect and rodent depredators of food in storage, is another important consideration. Some of the Western fungicides and insecticides are proving useful, and the development of additional aids is being worked on. The F.A.O., in its submission to the Atomic Energy Conference of 1955, stated that the estimate of a 25 to 50 per cent loss to stored grain and pulses in Central America from insect pests is 'probably generally applicable in most of the less advanced countries.' For the world as a whole, F.A.O. has estimated that rats probably destroy as much grain as moves in international trade.[15] The depredations are undoubtedly particularly severe in the less developed countries, where suitable storage facilities are often lacking. Other nonagricultural factors are involved in wastage, namely inadequate means of transportation and lack of storage and marketing facilities. As a friend of mine at the U.N. who is engaged in technical assistance has pointed out, food may be spoiling in one section and badly needed in another near by, but the lack of roads and transport prevents distribution.

Taking these various possible means to improvement together, it seems entirely reasonable to regard a 50 per cent or even a 100 per cent increase in food production in many sections of Asia, Africa, and Latin America as possible within two or three decades, even when the handicaps to desired changes in underdeveloped societies are taken into account. To accomplish such a goal would require a considerable concentration of dedicated effort by local governments, and wise and substantial assistance by the more developed

countries. It is true, as a P.E.P. report said in relation to goals set
by F.A.O. in 1951, involving a world food production increase of
from 2.3 to 3.3 per cent annually, that 'there is nothing in modern
experience to suggest that such increases are practicable for any
length of time.' Yet we are living in an age of unprecedented
change, and if the nations respond to the call of F.A.O. Director-
General Sen for more concentrated effort, symbolized by a 'Freedom from Hunger' Campaign, a much more radical advance seems
to me possible. This does not mean that the chances for accom-
plishing such a result are bright. It certainly cannot be achieved by
halfway measures. But a really determined and persistent campaign
might enable most of the less developed countries to stay ahead
of their population pressures for several years.

There are also important nonagricultural potentialities which
need to be taken into account, particularly for the longer pull. The
seas around us, more than twice as capacious as the dry land, offer
many resources which are hardly tapped. The U.N. Conference on
the Conservation and Utilization of Resources in 1949 pointed out
that 98 per cent of the fisheries are concentrated in the northern
hemisphere, and held that an expansion of fishing operations
might well increase the catch of 20 million tons by 20 per cent.[16]
The F.A.O. has given a good deal of attention to fish farming as a
supplement to diet in less developed countries. It is possible to
stock rice paddies with a fast-growing fish such as tilapia, and
secure important additions of protein for the Asian table.

Since fish in the oceans are near the apex of a nutritional pyramid, it is conceivable that the more abundant plankton, the
minute marine life which is more than half protein, can be
harvested and processed for human or animal food.[17] Or again,
there is the bottom of the pyramid, the algae which use photo-
synthesis to capture the sun's energy. The green algae, Chlorella,
for example, if grown in tanks with carbon dioxide, can absorb 2
per cent of the available solar energy, as compared with 1 per cent
in average agriculture. From these, foods rich in proteins and
vitamins can undoubtedly be produced for man or beast. Hertzler
states that experiments are being made to produce an artificial

milk. There is also seaweed, if it can be harvested economically enough, which offers a source for fertilizer, animal feed, or a mineral additive in the human diet. The aquatic resources, which at present supply a tiny fraction of nutritional needs in most countries, are clearly considerable in the longer view.

There are also terrestrial possibilities for enlarged food supplies apart from agriculture. Certain yeasts can be put to work on carbohydrate materials, such as sugar cane, to produce a nourishing product high in protein — as nutritious as beef, if not as tasty. It may be possible to synthesize carbohydrates, in turn, from sawdust. Leaves contain proteins and it may become possible to extract the nutrients from this abundant source. It is now possible to manufacture amino acids, the key elements in animal protein, as well as vitamins. This led Dr. G. Sankaran to propose that countries like India concentrate their agriculture on the most productive calorie staples, and manufacture the necessary vitamins and proteins.

It is extremely difficult to estimate the possible benefits which the underdeveloped world can derive from the marine and chemical processes here described, assuming that their promise is attained. Some of the procedures may be adaptable without undue expenditure, but in general these prospects of modern technology can be geared into technologically developed societies more easily than into those which are backward in this respect. The poorer countries lack the far-ranging fleets to capture the more distant fruits of the sea, and the industrial plant to produce food through the miracle of chemistry. The richer countries which are best equipped to take advantage of the new resources have at present the least need of them.

It is one of the ironies in the present situation that the 'have' countries together have much brighter immediate possibilities for expansion of food supplies than the 'have-nots,' quite apart from the marine and chemical divisions of future food production. They have most of the good temperate lands with well-distributed rainfall, the hybrid and disease-resistant seed, the fertilizer plants and mechanized tools, the agricultural experts and educated farmers.

If surplus-producing countries, like the United States, Canada, Australia, New Zealand, and Argentina, really unshackled their agricultural production, even within the framework of good soil conservation practices, the increase in world food supplies would be marked. Even now, with various restrictive factors, warehouses are bulging, and finding storage facilities is a problem. This productivity is at the core of many of the optimistic forecasts as to future food capabilities.[18]

To those who believe in the universal fatherhood of God and hence regard all men as brothers, and particularly to those who see these brothers as men for whom Christ died, the idea of curtailing crop production in the privileged sections of the earth and of hoarding the 'surpluses' when at least half of mankind suffers from malnutrition, has a fundamentally immoral character. The fact that the agricultural 'surpluses' cannot at present be distributed to the needy by the normal procedures of the world market does not lessen the challenge to human ingenuity, rooted in motives of social justice and solidarity. Surely devices can be found for transferring available foods in a larger way to the more necessitous underdeveloped countries without ruining the price structure on which free world farmers depend for a livelihood. The U.S. program for disposal of surplus agricultural commodities which in fiscal 1958 transferred 26 per cent of the $4 billion total of U.S. exports of farm products, is a beginning capable of extension.[19] The crisis confronting a number of the densely populated countries calls for considerably more than a 'business-as-usual' approach.

The case for a more imaginative and enlightened response to emergency food needs by the countries in a position to help is strong from every angle. There must be hope, however, that the emergency is not permanent, that the teeming societies of Asia will, with international assistance, succeed in achieving a balance between mouths to feed and their own food supplies, grown at home or purchased by trade. Neither the existing ethos of international society nor the higher requirements of Christian morality justify the idea that some peoples should become the perpetual wards of charity. The claims of past injustices may be weighed. The larger humanitarian claims press an insistent appeal. But the responsible leaders of the less developed societies are the first to hope that assistance will be geared to a strategy which will enable their people to stand on their own feet, in regard to food and the other elements of decent material existence.

This is the dream of economic and social development which has captured the expectations of societies long stagnant or steeped in fatalism. How can modern technology be applied in these pre-industrial societies to give substance to this hope? How can the machine be harnessed to ease the ancient burdens and lift standards of living to a more worthy level? Space does not permit more than the briefest indication of the dimensions of this problem, and their bearing on the possibilities for a better balance between nutrition and population in the lands of demographic pressure.

In the West the accumulation of capital for industrial development was accomplished by domestic savings, by foreign trade, and by borrowing, processes which still grow as economies expand. All three of these routes to capital are difficult for most of the countries which now seek industrialization. They have the important ingredient of abundant manpower, if largely untrained, but find it hard to acquire the machines. One reason is that the manpower is so abundant and so impoverished, that domestic savings become a euphemism for grim taxation. The U.N. Report, E/3255, lists the less developed areas in three groups according to per capita income: there are 19 countries in Group I, with an income of less than $100 per person a year; 17 in Group II, with a per capita income between $100 and $200; and 11 in Group III — nine Latin American countries plus Israel and Lebanon — in the over $200 category. A Special Studies Project of the Rockefeller Brothers Fund put the per capita gross national product for the underdeveloped world, not including China, at $118 as of 1956. Even allowing leeway for differences in purchasing power, we can see that the amount which can be squeezed out of such incomes for capital development is extremely limited, at least within the framework of a free society.[20]

The borrowing possibilities of the pre-industrial economies are also highly restricted, except for the very few which have things like oil or uranium to offer. 'The total capital investment in the less developed part of the free world came to $17 billion in 1956 compared to $146 billion in the industrialized part.' The latest U.N. Secretariat Report on long-term private international investment indicates that it 'appears to have averaged $2 billion a year' for the 1955–58 period, in respect to the underdeveloped countries, this constituting about half of the total outflow. The Report also indicates that much of this investment has gone to the relatively 'have' countries in Latin America, the largest item being U.S. oil investments in Venezuela. To this private investment should be added governmental and intergovernmental loans totaling about $1 billion net in 1957–58.[21]

In addition to the level now reached — the $3 billion a year in loans — bilateral and multilateral grants of slightly more than $2 billion in nonmilitary aid in 1957–58 should be noted.[22] Thus the world total of assistance may be regarded as roughly $5 billion a year for the non-Communist sectors of the underdeveloped world. It constitutes more than one-half of 1 per cent of world income. This is a substantial accomplishment, and a measure of considerable growth in a sense of international solidarity. Nevertheless, while experts disagree as to present absorptive capacities in the three continents, most agree that a higher rate of investment and/or grants is needed. The same judgment is found among church leaders. As was urged in the statement on 'Christian Concerns in Economic and Social Development,' commended to the churches for study and appropriate action by the Central Committee of the World Council of Churches in 1958:

> Far more grants and generous loans are essential . . . If at least one per cent of the national income of countries were devoted to these purposes, the picture would become much more hopeful.

In this connection, the statement also said that 'international private investment has an important role to play, and both receiving and contributing countries have to follow constructive policies so that such investment can be stimulated to share responsibility in the common task.' In view of losses suffered in connection with local government bonds during the depression years, private investors are still somewhat 'gun shy.' Stimuli, such as agreements against double taxation, or governmental insurance against loss of principal through arbitrary expropriation, can help to make capital today more venturesome. What seems to be the biggest obstacle, however, cannot be overcome. This is the competition offered by investment opportunities in the more developed countries in these days of automation and potential atomic power. The 'Rockefeller Report' projects recent growth rates in total production of goods and services, to show 'the general dimensions of the economic prospects for the next 10 to 20 years.' The rate of annual growth for the free world industrial nations is given as 4.5 per cent; the same rate is seen for the Communist bloc as a whole; the rate for the less industrialized nations of the free world is projected as 2.5 per cent. The lands of rapid social change are changing less rapidly in terms of production than the industrialized countries. This is one of the hard facts of the situation.

Consequently, the arguments which place the main stress on governmental aid seem impressive. Governments can afford to give more weight to longer-range interests than bankers who hold funds in trust for clients promised steady returns. Even the governments have neglected unduly the larger considerations in their stress upon disarmament as a precondition for large-scale assistance; for unless greater stability is achieved in the areas of social ferment, the temptations and dangers of such instability will tend to undermine the conditions for disarmament. Indeed, they pose a major threat to an all-too-fragile peace. One of the particular blind spots has been neglect of the need for more vigorous assistance in regard to the social infra-structure of the less developed countries, the public services such as education which do not yield immediate profits but which are essential to development. The perennial challenge to help meet this need through SUNFED or a better alternative has not yet been answered.

The third and in many ways most important road to development is through international trade. This is the main resource through which the less developed countries can hope to purchase the capital equipment they need to modernize their production. In 1956, for example, according to the U.N. *Statistical Yearbook*, their imports came to $25 billion and their exports to $24 billion. A 20 per cent increase in their trade would consequently be equivalent to the present total of grants and loans of all kinds. One of the obstacles to such an increase is the failure of the major creditor nation, the United States, to pull its weight as an importer. The same *Yearbook* indicates that whereas in the three years 1954–56 United States developmental assistance amounted to $3 billion, during the same period U.S. imports fell short of exports by $15 billion. The gap between imports and exports has since been narrowed, one reason being that foreign purchasers are presently less dependent on American sources of supply. In fact, the drain on U.S. foreign exchange from larger expenditures for overseas military installations and foreign aid, in the face of reduced surpluses in exports, has led to 'Buy American' pressures on recipients of aid. Greater attention to multilateral assistance and trade would seem to make more sense.

Yet there are also limitations in the available trading resources of the pre-industrial countries. According to the 'Rockefeller Report,' for this group as a whole, save China, the combined imports and exports in 1956 were equivalent to about 37 per cent of the total value of their goods and services. A few of these lands, like Venezuela and countries around the Persian Gulf with their oil, Bolivia and Malaya with their tin, Chile and Rhodesia with their copper, and the Congo with its uranium, have significant underground resources to exploit. The Germans call this use of the national patrimony *raubwirtschaft*, or 'plunder economy,' and various commentators speak of the amount of the world's resources going down the maw of Western industry.[23]

Yet such nations, which have mineral raw materials to trade, seem to me often better off than the others who must depend upon plant or animal materials for foreign exchange.[24] These latter materials, in varying degrees, tend to cut into the agricultural area available for the local food supply — obviously so in the case of crops like cotton, sugar, and tobacco; probably less so in regard to bush crops like tea and coffee, or tree crops like rubber and palm oil. The organic raw materials have the advantage of being replaceable, but on the whole they have a lower trading value; for some of the densely populated countries they represent a present belt-tightening to secure the equipment to facilitate a more adequate larder in the future.

For most of the pre-industrial countries, dependence on the sale of one or two primary commodities for their foreign exchange constitutes a major handicap. Widely fluctuating prices tend to upset economic plans and to precipitate financial crises, even though much of the economy may be independent of world markets. Diversification of produce is, of course, part of the answer, though much easier in theory than in practice. The failure of Western leaders thus far to come up with acceptable means to cushion the shocks of primary price fluctuations is one of the black marks on their record.[25]

When we consider these various indications together, can there be any doubt about the grave obstacles to industrialization as a means of assuring the less developed countries a more adequate food supply and higher standard of living? The impact of mounting population pressures has already forced countries like India to defer some of the economic goals in order to buy food. One by one the densely populated nations seem slated to fail in their struggle for development, unless they can quickly curb the human pressure on their means of subsistence. The hope exists that rising standards of living will, one way or another, lead to reduced fertility: 'eventually the birth rate falls, balancing the lower death rate, and the growth of population slackens,' according to one U.N. report. For countries like India, Indonesia, and Egypt, however, there must be a fall in the birth rate to offer a minimal existence, let alone a rising standard of living and the benefits of a free society.

Monsignor Irving De Blanc of the U.S. National Catholic Welfare Conference wrote at the end of an article on 'Birth Control and the Population Problem,' released in June 1958 by the N.C.W.C. Bureau of Information: 'We may have to find another planet.' This, indeed, seems to be the chief remaining alternative to facing up to the question of family limitation. We now turn to this question of family planning.

Population Policy and Family Limitation

  If in the regions where population growth has a long 'head-start' over economic and social development, vigorous pursuit of the latter, however essential, cannot suffice to restore an adequate balance, and voluntary migration offers only the most limited kind of safety valve, then some means of curbing population growth is indispensable. At the very least, the survival of free societies in Asia depends upon it. Even totalitarian regimes cannot escape the inexorable either-or, although a wider range of desperate choices are open to them than to governments dependent upon popular consent — such as compulsory redistribution of popula-tion, or attempted migration by force of arms. No matter how much the demographic problem is ignored, it cannot be escaped.

  Aside from drastic measures like an attempted forced separation of the sexes in labor battalions which could be adopted only by a fanatical tyranny, the antifertility alternatives to war, famine, and pestilence are not very great, so far as governments are con-cerned. They can facilitate the availability of means to family planning. They can strive to improve them. They can try to per-suade parents to use them. And they can reinforce their arguments with economic pressures through tax and social security legislation. But the fact remains that parents have a good deal more to do with determining the birth rate than governments, as Mussolini and Stalin, for example, found when they pursued pro-natalist policies. Despite Fascist cajolery and financial penalties and inducements, the Italian birth rate continued to fall. Despite Stalin's clamp-down on abortion and contraception in 1936, there is some evidence of a continued decline in fertility.[1]

A few years ago Hope Eldridge compiled an interesting survey of governmental population policies.[2] Most of the data relate to Western governments and to policies designed to encourage population growth or prevent population decline. The French government, for example, following earlier pro-natalist measures, adopted in 1939 a co-ordinated population policy in the 'code de la famille,' which includes 'economic aid to the family, protection of maternity and infancy, the suppression of abortion, the encouragement of marriage and parenthood, and the restriction of the traffic in contraceptive devices and of birth control propaganda.'[3] Several of the other European countries follow some of these measures, although few have a consistent population policy — e.g. the Netherlands, under population pressures, had a family allowance scheme in which payments per child increased with the size of the family, while the U.S.S.R., with a pro-fertility concern, generally followed a regressive scheme.

As the English demographer, D. V. Glass, says in a foreword to Miss Eldridge's survey: 'We may take it as axiomatic that social policy is never single-minded and rarely fully consistent.' This seems to be particularly the case in so far as the demographic implications are concerned, since they are often ignored. For example, three different U.S. population 'policies' could be deduced from the following: the survivor clauses of the Social Security Act provide maximum benefits for a survivor with two children and no more for a third, except as payments may be prolonged; the Federal Income Tax provides a flat-rate exemption for dependents; local school taxes are usually based on the value of real property, without regard to the number of children. It appears dubious, however, that the legislators looked at any of these in relation to a population policy. There is no reason why the demographic implications of social legislation should not be considered, except that the subject is clothed with ignorance and controversy.

Dr. Eldridge lists three countries with policies designed to modify the rate of population growth: Japan, India, and Italy. Several more could be added if the survey were made today. Italy is included because of post-war revision of Mussolini policies: the substitution of flat-rate family allowances for progressive allowances, and the resumption of aided emigration. In India, the Panel on Health Programmes of the Planning Commission recommended in 1951:

1. That the state take steps to provide facilities for sterilization or for giving contraceptive advice, especially where either is indicated on medical grounds.
2. That the state assist in the study of methods of birth control and problems of dissemination of information.
3. That provision be made for the improvement of population statistics and the study of population problems on a permanent basis.

Provisions for giving effect to these recommendations were included in the First Five Year Plan, and have since been given greater emphasis in the administration of the Second Five Year Plan.

The third country, Japan, merits particular attention in view of the unprecedented reduction in the birth rate achieved since policies to reduce fertility were instituted beginning in 1948. The crude birth rate has fallen from 34.3 per thousand in 1947 to 18.5 in 1956, and will fall further if the objective of 13.0 is pursued. This dramatic reduction in nine years compares with the German experience of a decline from 32.9 to 20.3 in 20 years in the early decades of this century, and the Dutch experience of a decline from 35.0 to 20.3 in the 55 years preceding World War II. While crude death rates have also been nearly halved in Japan since the war, the net increase of population has fallen to less than 1 per cent — 820,000 for a population of 91 million in 1957 — betokening a stationary population before the end of this century if the trend continues.

How was this sudden reduction in fertility achieved? There can be no doubt that the main factor was the legalization of abortion on social grounds. Despite the sanctions for both contraception and sterilization, and efforts to promote the former, authorized abortions rose to more than one million a year. Japanese colleagues tell me that unauthorized abortions may be as numerous.[4] If so, the grim fact is that abortions considerably exceed live births in Japan. Nor is Japan the only country where this ancient and tragic method is a major factor of fertility control. The authors of a U.N. Secretariat 'Survey of Legislation on Marriage, Divorce and Related Topics Relevant to Population,' issued in March 1956, made the following comment:

> Nowhere is the evasion of law as striking as in the case of abortion. For instance, although abortion is a crime in all forty-eight states of the United States, estimates of the number of legal abortions performed in the United States every year range from 700,000 to more than two million. Similarly, it has been said that the number of abortions in France greatly exceeds the annual number of registered births.[5]

When the import of the Japanese experience for the plight of Asia, Africa, and Latin America is assessed, the fact that Japan is a developed country needs to be remembered. Medical technique is relatively advanced, and medical facilities fairly widespread. The literacy level is higher than in many Western countries, and the disciplined attitudes of the people in regard to official leadership are exceptional. The popular understanding of the demographic implications of the loss of war and empire, and the succeeding economic crisis, was undoubtedly rather general. In short, even if the moral and medical objections to abortion as a means of fertility control are overlooked, Japan's success in reducing her birth rate so much and so quickly cannot be regarded as proof that the underdeveloped countries can do likewise. Both the technical and social obstacles need to be reckoned realistically.

Apart from abortion and the still older method of family limitation, infanticide,[6] what are the available and prospective means for family limitation in the less developed countries? Such methods must not only meet the test of effectiveness but also be sufficiently congruent with the mores to be acceptable, as well as adapted to the level of economic and social development to be feasible. Of course the customs and attitudes vary enormously, but some generalizations, at least about Asiatic mores, can be made. As for the limitations imposed by the stage of development, the predominant illiteracy rules out methods involving complicated instructions, the inadequate medical facilities prevent methods requiring much professional attention, and the low level of income forbids any procedures that are costly. There are other limitations, such as lack of privacy or of running water, but these are the main ones.

THE LIMITATION OF MARRIAGE

One approach to the reduction of fertility is through the limitation of marriage, by postponement of the age of marriage — the 'moral restraint' of Malthus — and/or by an increase of celibacy. Both reduce the number of fertile years in a given society, and in fact it is a combination of the two which largely accounts for the moderate birth rate in Eire. Carr-Saunders pointed out [7] that in 1926 53 per cent of the Irish women aged 25 to 35 were unmarried, and 29 per cent of the 35 to 45 age group. The average age at marriage for women was slightly over 29 years. Late marriage and nonmarriage are regarded as mainly responsible for the moderate birth rate, which had dropped to 19.4 per thousand by the 1930's.

While male celibacy is a factor in Buddhist culture, and to a minor degree in Hinduism, it is completely foreign to the mores of Islam; and feminine celibacy is uncommon throughout Asia, and, indeed, the whole underdeveloped world. In a French study cited by Father de Lestapis, the small percentage of celibate women in certain of these countries is indicated for the 30–34 age group: Algeria (1948) — 5 per cent; India (1931) — 1.5 per cent; Ceylon (1946) — 6.5 per cent; Formosa (1930) — 2 per cent. Celibacy tends to be looked upon as unnatural, and for a woman as a missing of her vocation. High rates of maternal mortality, as well as polygamy, have no doubt been contributing factors in the opportunities for exercising this vocation. An Indian bishop tells me that one of the practical obstacles to the extension of family planning lies in the tendency of married folk to lack confidence in the instruction of unmarried nurses. As the Indian student of population, S. Chandrasekhar, has stated: 'The major factor in Indian demography is the universality of the married state in India.' This applies to a large part of the underdeveloped world.

Later marriages seem to offer a larger possibility for reducing the fertile years in underdeveloped societies. Opposition to child marriages and legal restrictions are growing. For a tiny fraction of the girls, higher education is a factor in delaying marriage. Yet the kind of postponement which serves to reduce fertility in Eire is not here in view. The shift that is taking place is one from the early teens to the later teens, and there is some evidence that such marriages may be *more* fertile than the child marriages. A study by J. H. Sinka in Lucknow and Kanpur, for example, showed that wives whose marriages were consummated at ages 16 to 18 were somewhat more fertile than either those whose marital relations started at an earlier age or those married later. Thus in countries like India, later marriages might in practice mean a higher birth rate. Only a rather fundamental change in the status of women, with large-scale increases in feminine education, is likely to make later marriages into a restraining influence on fertility.

THE LIMITED USE OF MARRIAGE

Turning to efforts to limit fertility within marriage, we consider at the outset abstinence and periodic continence as methods. Complete sexual abstinence, the only marital method of family limitation sanctioned in Orthodox Christian statements, is an obviously effective method, and is expensive only in terms of human values in the normal marriage. The failure of Gandhi's personality to win many adherents for this solution suggests that less persuasive proponents would have a very dim chance of success. It can be argued that in the austere or harsh conditions of life in many sectors of the underdeveloped world, marital relations play a larger role in ameliorating the human lot than is the case in the diversified cultures of the more developed societies.

Abstinence, it should be added, plays an important part in the spacing of children in a number of African societies. The taboo against sexual intercourse with a woman nursing a child, combined with a long — or prolonged — period of nursing, enables the mother to avoid too frequent pregnancies. The custom is undoubtedly a mainstay of polygamy, since the taboo limits the nursing mother rather than the father. On the other hand, a colleague found in one discussion with African women that polygamy was regarded as necessary to birth control — without it, how would a woman space children? The health of mother and child, rather than the number of offspring, is frequently the major concern in Africa.

Periodic continence or the 'rhythm' method, sanctioned for right motives in both modern Roman Catholic and Protestant teaching, was known to some extent in the ancient world. In recent years more has been learned about the ovulation cycle; and periodic continence of from one to two weeks in each cycle, depending on individual variations, is a fairly effective method of family limitation except where cyclical irregularity makes it too unreliable.[8] The late Abraham Stone, who conducted some tests of this method in India, found that this last was a particular problem since inadequacies in the Indian diet seemed to make for cyclical irregularity. Another difficulty proved to be in making the calculations required for effective periodic continence. The beads he introduced for this purpose were used in various ways, as charms and talismans. Part of the trouble stemmed from the relative complexity of the method; part from a lack of education about reproduction which would hamper most methods of family limitation. I doubt that it would be justified to rule out this method in the underdeveloped world — for the couples it suits physically, temperamentally, and morally — on the basis of Dr. Stone's unsuccessful trial.[9]

In the West, efforts are being made to increase the reliability of this method. Temperature charts help to indicate the time of ovulation which aids the calculations for the following month. New glucose tests developed independently by Dr. Joseph Doyle and Dr. Charles H. Birnberg offer promise of another means to determine more accurately the time of ovulation, thereby reducing at least the post-ovulation period of continence required to prevent conception. There is the possibility that the temporary use of new drugs to suppress ovulation might be followed, in some cases, by a more regular ovulation pattern. Such procedures to make periodic continence more reliable, however, are also likely to make it more complex and more costly, and these are obstacles in the less privileged societies, apart from the element of self-denial involved.

THE LIMITATION OF CONCEPTION BY DIRECT MEANS [10]

In turning to the mechanical and chemical means to prevent conception by blocking in some way the union of sperm and egg, we part company with Roman Catholic teaching, which condemns all such methods as contrary to 'nature.' Passing reference should at least be made to two 'natural' methods, which are probably the oldest and still most widely used methods of contraception: namely withdrawal or *coitus interruptus*, and efforts to expel the semen after coitus. Effectiveness is said to be variable in regard to the first and generally low in regard to the second — if the methods are otherwise acceptable.

The mechanical and chemical methods of the West include the sheath or condom, the diaphragm and cervical cap, and various spermicidal jellies and creams. The most frequent recommendation of the doctors and clinics is a suitable feminine appliance, fitted and refitted professionally, and used with one of the spermicides. Cultural antipathy and physiological ignorance in many of the densely populated areas, however, offer serious obstacles. At least as serious is the cost involved. S. Chandrasekhar writes in terms of Indian conditions:

> The cost involved in setting up the necessary clinics and providing them with doctors and equipment would be prodigious. Even after this initial expenditure, there is no guarantee that the needy mothers could afford the cost of the necessary equipment, even if the clinical consultation were free. Shocking as it may seem, in many rural areas the cost of having a baby would be cheaper than the price of the birth control equipment.

In view of such considerations, some attention has been devoted to the question of cheaper and simpler contraceptives. A piece of rubber sponge dipped in a strong saline solution is one: its effectiveness seems somewhat uncertain, and its acceptability not too wide. Perhaps the most promising in this category for the underdeveloped world is the foaming tablet containing one or another spermicide. The tablet is relatively inexpensive (under one cent), simple to apply, and reported to be rather high in effectiveness. Preliminary tests on a new vaginal foam in an aerosol dispenser are also said to offer promise of effectiveness at potentially low cost. Yet even a contraceptive costing a fraction of a cent poses a financial problem for the impoverished peasant.

The Long-Term Prevention of Conception

At present, the lack of readily available, cheap, simple, and acceptable contraceptives in Asia is giving sterilization the inside track. Severing the *vas* in the man is an office procedure. Sterilization of the woman is a more serious operation, often performed after and in conjunction with childbirth. Surgical sterilization is completely and permanently effective, though some work is being done on laboratory animals with a view to improving surgical procedures to restore male fecundity, and thus lessen the finality of the sterilizing operation. As the population pressures mount, interest in and support for this solution continue to grow. Some states in India are offering bounties to parents agreeing to sterilization after the third or fourth child. Unless a technical 'breakthrough' is achieved in regard to a really suitable and acceptable contraceptive, an increase of pressure for sterilization seems to me virtually certain.

New Biological Methods [11]

Ever since our early ancestors tried to find some magic drug to replace the anguish of infanticide as a means of family limitation, people have hoped for an oral contraceptive. The *Medical History of Contraception* by Norman Himes abounds with references to ancient and medieval potions designed to prevent pregnancy by rendering the woman temporarily or permanently sterile, or to destroy the embryo at an early stage. Recipes persist in folk lore. Deputy Shao Li-tsu, who called the Chinese population problem to the attention of his fellow deputies, later passed on the formula of 'advanced herbalist' Deputy Yeh Hsi-chun: twenty-four fresh tadpoles swallowed in two days in the spring would 'prevent conception for five years.'

The very number of recipes which have circulated argues that none or practically none of them has been effective. Two plants emerging from folk experience, however, are the subject of contemporary research. A U.S. government agent found that the Soshone Indians used an infusion of a weed, *Lithospermum ruderale*, to limit fertility. For nearly two decades scientists have been working in the United States and Britain to extract and test on laboratory animals compounds from this plant. If successful, the drugs would temporarily suppress ovulation by inhibiting the secretion of certain hormones. But success, without serious side effects such as shortening the life span, is still uncertain, and research continues. The other plant is the East Indian field pea, 'mantar' or *Pisum sativum*, on which Dr. S. N. Sanyal is working in India. In Calcutta, incomplete clinical tests of its active ingredient suggest that it may reduce conception by 50 per cent, which is not promising from the point of view of effectiveness.[12]

Most of the work on oral contraceptives, however, has stemmed not from work on plant extracts, but from work on physiological processes and particularly the hormones, the secretions which govern various functions. Research to find drugs which simulate the hormones, or which counteract their activity, has led to the now publicized 'pill.' In this relatively young and open field of hormone research, the possibilities for developing antifertility agents are theoretically very wide. Dr. Nelson has listed some two dozen 'vulnerable points' in reproduction which might offer an opening for the physiologic control of conception.[13] Many new types of drugs for the limitation of fertility seem likely to emerge in the course of time.

From the point of view of technical research the reproductive process appears as a continuum, beginning with ovulation and spermatogenesis on through implantation of the fertilized ovum. From the point of view of nontechnical categories, however, there is an important line of division between drugs designed to prevent conception by inhibiting or otherwise affecting ovulation or spermatogenesis, and those directed at the ovum after it has been fertilized.

The publicized steroid compounds, Norlutin and Enovid, are of the first type. When taken daily for 20 days of the feminine cycle,[14] the pills inhibit the secretion which brings on ovulation, so that it does not occur. The pills are then stopped so that menstruation occurs, and the artificial cycle is then resumed. Tests in Puerto Rico have thus far demonstrated this type of oral contraceptive, or more accurately temporary sterilizing agent, to be highly effective, and comparable with the most effective of the older techniques. Tests in Los Angeles so far do not give the steroid pill quite as high a rating for effectiveness, and place more stress on undesirable side effects, such as headache and nausea in some cases. The possibility of any longer-range harm cannot finally be determined except by years of testing. The steroid pills may eventually become a highly important means of controlling fertility. For the present, at least, the cost is prohibitive for the underdeveloped world — several dollars for a month's supply.

The other drug which should be mentioned, since human tests are in progress, is MER-25, investigated by Dr. Nelson and Dr. Segal at the Rockefeller Institute. This compound is of the second type mentioned above. In tests on rats, the newly fertilized ovum, while in the tube, proved highly susceptible to the drug's selective action, so that implantation did not occur. Dr. Nelson writes:

> As far as we know, the egg is affected while it is in the tube only. Once it reaches the uterus, there is no effect whatsoever, the embryo proceeding to implant and develop in a normal fashion.[15]

MER-25 thus appears a potentially effective means to prevent — or interrupt — a pregnancy within the first two or three days of conception. Harmful side effects are not anticipated. It may prove to meet more of the criteria of the economically less developed societies than the steroid pills. But it may also pose a difficult moral issue for the religious conscience, since it involves the destruction of a fertilized ovum, even though not yet implanted, and hence is the expulsion of the product of conception, i.e. abortion as traditionally if not precisely defined.

Here then is the technical picture insofar as I understand it. The immediate prospect is not propitious for the lands of population explosion and rapid social change. There is no single cheap, simple, effective, acceptable, and available contraceptive that provides a 'solution.' The foaming tablet or aerosol vaginal foam may come closest to meeting the criteria at present. The availability of inexpensive and safe oral pills seems some years off. Nor are research and testing being pushed in a substantial way. Aside from sums spent by the pharmaceutical companies, and research on broader aspects of reproduction, the world budget for research in the field of fertility controls probably does not exceed half a million dollars from private donations. The myopia of Western governments in this area is nowhere more clearly indicated.

The technical problems are by no means the only, or perhaps even the primary, obstacle. At least as important is the need for educational undergirding to provide the necessary knowledge and sustain the essential motivation. The education required is partly general — the struggle against illiteracy and for the larger view of national development, described in an earlier chapter. The educational task is also specific: to visualize the family in its relation to national development, to gain a new appreciation of the quality of family life as against quantity, to understand enough about the human body and reproduction to make family planning effective.[16] These are enormous challenges, in terms of any short-range timetable. As Sir Solly Zuckerman has said in a wise discussion of the fertility question in the UNESCO publication, *Impact of Science on Society*:

> Women have to be persuaded that the larger their families, the greater the burden they have to bear, and the less the care they can

give to each child. It is extremely difficult to spread such views as these in agricultural communities, where for hundreds of years children have been regarded as a source of labor, and therefore as a blessing and not a burden.

A whole range of pro-fertility elements in culture are here involved. The tendency to regard procreation as a woman's main destiny, the desire for sons to pursue filial piety, the view of the large family as a kind of old-age insurance, as well as the exploitation of child labor, all stand in some measure athwart the kind of population policy which can restore a tolerable balance and reinforce the hope of a free society. To modify such attitudes, like the other basic tasks in development, is a responsibility of the peoples in the underdeveloped world.[17] Yet the Western governments and international agencies could help in important supplementary ways, through various types of educational assistance in the broad sense of the term, if they were not so inhibited by fear of the religious issue in the whole area of family planning.

It needs to be repeated that the governments of the densely populated societies in Asia are more ready to be helped in this area than the West is ready to help.[18] As anyone who follows intergovernmental affairs knows, the actual requests of recipient governments are adjusted to the intimations from assisting governments as to the kinds of aid they are prepared to extend. There is no sign that such intimations are forthcoming.[19] The only discernible reason is the fear lest religious controversy be engendered by any projects in the field of family limitation. It is primarily apprehension over Roman Catholic reactions that causes a failure of nerve, since Protestant views have not been clearly formulated and firmly expressed. Consequently, we need now to turn attention to religious views of the family, and particularly to Christian doctrines on parenthood.

VII

Parenthood and World Religions

&❧ Anything as fundamental, mysterious, and awesome as the birth of new life is inescapably related to man's religious instinct. The miracle of birth links the living with the dynamic, the creative in the universe. Fertility in the natural world is essential to individual survival, and human fertility is essential to social survival. Thus it is understandable that anthropologists should find fertility rites common in primitive religion in all parts of the world.[1] The uncertainties of the flock and the harvest, and the uncertainties of high mortality surrounding the family, made propitiation of the fertility gods important for daily bread and progeny. In some societies ignorance of the physiology of generation made parenthood doubly mysterious, and where the relationship between sexual intercourse and procreation was dimly understood, there were still the baffling questions of successful pregnancy, of safe childbirth, of healthy babies, of sons. The fertility cult was a normal fact in primitive society.

Apparently, the major religions of today had to struggle in their infancy in varying degrees against such cults and the sex mores related to them. Hinduism, in its characteristic syncretistic fashion, absorbed a fertility cult in the worship of Shiva, who among other things is the god of reproduction.[2] Buddhism is an ascetic revolt against the passions of this life, yet in the Buddhist literature can be found the imprint of older pro-fertility patterns.[3] Judaism had a struggle to oust the local fertility gods, the *baals*. Early Christianity was concerned with the corrupting influence of Greco-

Roman license, in which the worship of Venus was a factor. And Islam came onto the scene in this field as a reform movement, elevating somewhat the low status of women and curbing somewhat the unrestricted polygamy in the Arab culture of the time.

At the same time the major religions, except perhaps Buddhism, preserved the nearly universal concern for fertility in their doctrines and practices, and Buddhism offered a compromise way for the married laity. In addition to Hindu syncretism, there is the strong fertility element in Judaism, which continued in the Old Testament heritage of Christianity. And the moral and marital reforms of Mohammed stopped far short of any hostility to fertility. The persistence of pro-fertility attitudes may represent to some extent the impact of the vanquished faiths, or the compromises contributing to victory. In either case, the mystery of new life is a basic question for all religion, and since for most of man's history the struggle for life has been waged against heavy natural odds, a generally strong pro-fertility emphasis in the major religious traditions is wholly comprehensible.

Our concern, however, is primarily the contemporary bearing of the main religions on the question of responsible parenthood, particularly as they affect attitudes and policies in the underdeveloped world, rather than the historical evolution of their teachings. The succeeding chapters deal with Judaism and Christianity. But these are not the predominant faiths in Asia, the largest sector of the underdeveloped world. Consequently, in this chapter brief and tentative note will be taken of the positions of Hinduism, Buddhism, Islam, and Communism, that hybrid of secular faith and political expediency which currently rules policy in China. The notes are perforce tentative in view of the need for more adequate information and analysis of the non-Christian religions in this respect. The available data are limited and inconclusive.

HINDUISM

The attitude toward parenthood in Hinduism, which counts a total community of perhaps 300 million souls and is the predominant faith in the most densely populated large region on earth, is obviously important if a limitation of fertility is to restore a balance between population and available resources. Hinduism is such a conglomeration of different religious beliefs and folkways that the answer is complex. The amoral behavior of the Hindu pantheon, reminiscent of the Greek deities, gives little or no ethical guidance, and the wide range of cults existing side by side offer quite divergent norms for conduct.

There are strong pro-fertility elements in Hinduism beyond the rites associated with Shiva and his consorts, with the *lingams* or phallic symbols, Nautch girls, and all that. The male-centered view of life, combined with the belief in reincarnation, makes sons important to pray for their ancestors and deliver them from hell, and tends to relegate woman chiefly to her childbearing function. The 'seed and soil' concept of procreation seems to be common in the Hindu tradition and, with the *ahimsa* or noninjury doctrine, would appear to indicate a predisposition against any form of contraception.

On the other hand, there is a strong ascetic element in Hinduism. Kenneth Saunders has pointed out in *The Ideals of East and West* that the early thinkers held out as 'the ideal man the *muni*, or wandering friar, who has "risen above the desire for sons, for wealth and for domination." ' Later the religious ideal is the *yogi*: 'aloof, benevolent, detached, severe in mystic contemplation.' This ideal was diluted for the layman in the favorite book of devotion, the *Bhagavad Gita*, but it offers some counterweight to the erotic and fertility elements in Hinduism. Probably more important, in regard to present-day issues of contraception, is the fact that the Hindu approach places more emphasis on spiritual attitudes than on ethical rules. The head of the Ramakrishna Mission in New Delhi wrote a friend in Chicago, stating that the Mission had 'no official opinion on social problems like birth control,' having faith in enlightened social opinion:

> Swami Vivekananda held the view that social evils are like diseases in the body politic whose radical cure is through purifying and strengthening the life blood of the body through fundamental

spiritual education of man; social reforms remove only the surface symptoms; this is also important and necessary; but he desired his movement to concentrate on the first while saying godspeed to all well-meaning social reformers.

The problem of special population pressures in India is comparatively recent.[4] One factor was high rates of infant mortality. Carr-Saunders in *World Population* points to three other factors. One was maternal mortality: the census of 1931 showed that the average Indian mother had four children born alive and slightly less than three survive; the partial explanation is that many mothers died before reaching the end of the reproductive period. A second factor was child marriages, with 181 per thousand married 'women' under the age of 15 in 1931. Carr-Saunders points out that intercourse shortly after puberty is 'inimical both to health and fecundity.' The third factor was the Hindu ban on the remarriage of widows. The health programs have since reduced infant and maternal mortality and the reform spirit of modern India has reduced the number of child marriages and relaxed the prohibition on remarriage. Another antifertility factor was the various and numerous ritual restrictions on sexual intercourse. It seems probable that this factor, too, has been modified in the growth of secularism in the new India.

Thus both the natural and unintended religious and social restrictions on fertility have been reduced during the past generation, inexorably raising the question of other means to keep the birth rate in check. I say 'inexorably,' though it is evident that Gandhi's opposition to birth control, apart from complete abstinence, considerably delayed a more realistic approach to the problem. Gandhi regarded contraception as morally equivalent to prostitution, and, as Father de Lestapis has recorded, told Mrs. Sanger that he regarded periodic continence in the same category. But his successors have felt compelled to initiate birth control measures, starting rather gingerly with the promotion of contraception in the First Five Year Plan, and stressing more energetically both contraception and sterilization in the Second. At the Third All India Conference on Family Planning in January 1957, a government spokesman declared the intention to equip 2,000 rural planned parenthood clinics. The desperate character of the situation is indicated by the fact that in at least one state bounties are now offered to parents who undertake sterilization after the third or fourth child.

While the statement that 'all the great Hindu social reformers' in recent years have been in favor of family limitation may give too optimistic a picture, it seems true that Hinduism presents no sharply defined doctrinal obstacle to curbs on parenthood. The fundamental doctrine is on a different level. Moreover, Indian opinion is moving toward support of family limitation. A poll in several communities in the states of Mysore and Uttar Pradesh indicated that from 60 to 78 per cent of the parents expressed the desire to limit progeny. Yet this does not mean that the cultural obstacles, partly rooted in religious belief and custom, are no longer formidable. Nor does it mean, especially in view of the lack of suitable and ready available methods of contraception, that social inertia is not still a major obstacle to India's most critical problem.

BUDDHISM

Buddhism like Hinduism, as Frank Lorimer and colleagues have pointed out, appears rather 'passive' in regard to efforts to control fertility. 'Passive' seems particularly appropriate for the faith that counts from 300 to 350 million Asians, for Buddhism appears to have very little doctrine of parenthood in the sense used in this review. The whole point of view seems calculated to discourage fertility.

A central tenet of Buddhist doctrine is that the origin of suffering is desire. In his final words under the *sala* tree, the Buddha said:

Consider your body; think of its impurity; how can you indulge its cravings as you see that both its pain and its delight are alike causes of suffering? . . . You must break the bonds of worldly passions and get rid of them as you would a viper.

Buddhist literature abounds with references to renunciation of earthly love for the free mind and spirit. A man, for example, sees his fair wife approaching, his son upon her arm; but he sees in her 'a subtle snare' — such bonds have lost their hold, because his mind is free.[5] Passions accumulate the *karma* or just reward of further troubles in later reincarnations. This asceticism applies to love of children as well. In the tale of Prince Wessantara, whose vow of self-abnegation is tested, the Prince gives his children away 'that I may have perfect insight,' whereupon legions of gods exclaim: 'Wondrous is he whose mind is unshaken even at the loss of both his children!' The hierarchy of values is indicated in this teaching, the last point bringing us back to the primacy of individual salvation:

> One should forget himself for the sake of his family;
> one should forget his family for the sake of his village;
> one should forget his village for the sake of his country;
> one should forget all the world for the sake of enlightenment.

Under Buddhism, the married man is definitely a second-class citizen, tied down by worldly desires and cares, who may ultimately achieve enlightenment — by leaving his family to become a 'homeless brother.' In the meantime, he should learn to live with wife and child in harmony, train and provide for his children, and follow the rules of detachment so far as possible. The family should work as 'busy as bees' — partly to support the 'homeless brother,' the ascetic beside whom the benedict is a 'common man.' In all this there is precious little sanction either for marital relations and procreation or against family limitation. Parenthood seems to begin after the children are born.

There is in Buddhism a strong compassion for all sentient life, one of the points in the 'noble eightfold path' being to harm no living creature. This presumably constitutes a ban on abortion as well as infanticide.[6] In the tale of Kālī there is a reference to the use of an abortifacient given by the barren wife to the pregnant wife, but the point of the tale is the evil of hatred rather than the immorality of abortion. Thus far I have found no evidence that the 'seed' is regarded as a living creature, and the legislative situation in predominantly Buddhist countries, mentioned below, supports the view that it is not so regarded.

From the point of view of actual practice, it appears that Buddhist belief gives a certain spiritual tone to the culture of its adherents, rather than any kind of detailed ethical system. Referring to the Buddhist ideal of compassion and awareness of common creaturehood, Professor Philip Ashby of Princeton wrote in an unpublished paper:

> While it cannot be denied that the precepts did succeed to some degree in furthering this ideal, yet the moral patterns which predominate among the masses of the people in Buddhist areas are more to be identified with the indigenous pre-Buddhist cultures and general custom morality of the specific area than with a system of ethics or morals which are peculiarly Buddhist.

ISLAM

The followers of Mohammed, who constitute the largest religious group in the underdeveloped world, with a total of 350 to 400 million persons, form an obviously key sector not only in Asia but also in northern Africa. Two of the gravest population problems are found in Egypt and Indonesia, or, more accurately, Java. The Population Reference Bureau estimated in 1958, on the basis of admittedly inadequate statistics, that the population of the Middle East was growing at the rate of 2½ to 3 per cent a year, a rate of growth exceeded only by that of Tropical South America. While the Muslim world is not growing proportionately as rapidly as it did in those astounding decades of the 7th century, it is no doubt growing more rapidly today in terms of numbers. The cradle is proving more potent than the sword.

Islam has important roots in the Old Testament, but in regard to parenthood, they grow chiefly in the soil of patriarchal history. In contrast with the unrestricted marital opportunities for Arab males in his time, Mohammed limited his masculine followers to four wives at a time, an austerity tempered by permission to sup-

plement the quota with such slaves as they could afford. Also
wives that did not suit could be replaced at the cost of the *mahr*
or marriage settlement. 'Consecutive polygamy' consequently has
been a common pattern.[7] One of the conveniences of the Mo-
hammedan heaven is that a righteous man may have his favorite
wives with him, or opt for the 'large-eyed maidens' if he did not
fare too well on earth.

Actually, this is not the full picture. Mohammed recognized
some reciprocal marriage rights and urged men to 'admonish
your wives with kindness, because women were created from the
crooked bone of the side.' He tolerated rather than approved
divorce: 'the thing which is lawful but is disliked by God is
divorce.' Also, impartial treatment of wives was a moral obligation:
'When a man has two wives and does not treat them equally he
will come on the day of resurrection with half of his body fallen
off.' [8] Contemporary Muslim reformers argue from this that the
Prophet was basically opposed to polygamy, since it is obviously
impossible for a man to treat two wives equally.[9]

In regard to parenthood, the ethos of Islam might be generally
described as procreation unlimited. The Koran echoes Genesis
1:28 in the injunction, 'marry and generate,' and 'marry a woman
who holds her husband extremely dear, and who is richly fruitful.'
The description of family conditions in Egypt appended to the
Warren Report, *The Family in Contemporary Society*, indicates
some additional pro-fertility factors that operate and have operated
in the past in other Muslim countries as well as in Egypt. Children
are employed on the land at an early age, and hence are economically useful. Muslim (as well as Christian) opinion attaches high
prestige to the parents of large families. Further encouragement to
the large family is given by the Muslim law of inheritance.

Despite the generally strong pro-fertility pattern in Islam, there
is some evidence that efforts may have been made to limit conception in sexual relations with slave girls. Norman Himes notes,
for example, that the *Encyclopedia of Islam* speaks of '*azl* or *coitus
interruptus* being frequently used with slave girls.[10] The purpose

in such practices probably lies in the following from Professor George Foot Moore:

> If such a slave bears a son who is acknowledged by her master, she becomes a 'mother of a child'; thereafter her master cannot sell her, and at his death she becomes free without further formality. A son thus acknowledged is free and shares in his father's inheritance with the sons of the wedded wives.

Dr. Himes also cites the varied contraceptive knowledge held by Al-Rāzī of Persia in the late 9th century, the 'greatest physician of the Middle Ages'; Avicenna in West Africa in the early 11th century; and Al-Jurjānī in 12th century Persia. The 'rational element' in their knowledge, he points out, was remarkable for the period, and far ahead of European knowledge. How widespread was such knowledge is hard to guess. In any case, it does not answer the question of a religious sanction. All it suggests is that there was no clear ban on contraception in the Koran; in the Sunna or tradition somewhat comparable to the Talmud in Judaism; or in the Ijma, the Islamic consensus which defines the authoritative.

With the explosive population pressures of the past decades, Islamic scholars have been making a fresh search of their traditions to find clues favorable to a doctrine of voluntary family limitation. They find a reference by a companion of the Prophet to the need to watch out for too many children; they are difficult to raise. Another reference suggests that birth control may be permitted when a woman is too feeble, a man too poor, or a woman fears the loss of her beauty. Such arguments are supplemented by demographic and nationalistic reasons.[11] In March 1953, the Fatwa Committee of Azhar University in Cairo, an influential group of scholars on Muslim 'canon law,' stated in response to a query:

> The use of medicine to prevent pregnancy temporarily is not forbidden by religion, especially if repeated pregnancies weaken the woman due to insufficient intervals for her to rest and regain her health. The Koran says, 'Allah desireth for you ease; He desireth not

hardship for you' (2/185); 'And hath not laid upon you in religion any hardship' (22/78). But the use of medicine to prevent pregnancy absolutely and permanently is forbidden by religion.

This statement indicates, I think, that there is little specific sanction for contraception in the tradition of Islam, and also that the contemporary leaders are determined not to let that fact impede the current efforts for voluntary family planning. The Minister of Social Services in Egypt spoke of birth control as a social necessity. The Minister of Food and Agriculture in Pakistan said: 'The senseless race between increase of food and increase of population must not continue any longer.' The governments of both countries have established a number of family planning clinics. Despite the pro-fertility elements in Islamic culture, the leaders of some Muslim countries, at least, do not find serious doctrinal obstacles in the way of a necessary population policy.

COMMUNISM

When Karl Marx attacked 'Malthusianism' as a by-product of a decadent capitalism, since overpopulation was wholly a consequence of private ownership of the means of production, he hardly envisaged that a century after the *Communist Manifesto* Communism would come to power in precapitalist China, a country whose most abundant product is babies. In connection with the 1953 census, sample surveys in 16 *hsien* showed a birth rate of 41.6 per thousand, and a death rate of 21.0. Applied to a population of 600 million that would mean some 25 million babies a year, with 12 million constituting the net increase. And the base today, of course, is higher — in the neighborhood of 650 million. China is contributing its full share to the population explosion, at least one-fourth of the total — possibly very much more than that.

Despite the Communist propaganda attacks on 'cannibalistic Malthusianism,' population policies in countries under Communist control have followed a varied and changing pattern. In the first years of the Russian Revolution, Lenin adopted a very 'neo-

Malthusian' policy, with abortion made easy and contraceptives gradually made available. The harsh conditions of life and the lack of housing no doubt made a doctrinaire approach impolitic. In 1936, Stalin suddenly reversed the policy, cutting down drastically on aids to family limitation. He may have been shocked by unpublished census data revealing the effects of forced collectivization, or concerned over future military and economic manpower needs.

Apparently there has been a further shift since Stalin's death. Father de Lestapis notes that the current Plan provides for the production of contraceptives, and that the renewed legalization of abortion is explained as a step to avoid the deaths caused by illegal abortions. While Khrushchev states that a doubling of the Soviet Union's 200 million will still be 'little,' de Lestapis thinks he is actually concerned over the housing shortage due to concentration on heavy industry. The countries of Eastern Europe under Soviet control seem to follow diverse convolutions of this changing line.

Our main concern, however, is with China, one of the densely populated countries of the underdeveloped world. In September 1954 after the regime had discovered from the 1953 census (as Clement Attlee was told) that the Chinese population was increasing at a rate of 12 million a year, one of the deputies to the National People's Congress, Shao Li-tsu, stated: 'It's a good thing to have a large population, but in an environment beset by difficulties it appears that there should be a limit set.' He urged a campaign to spread medical theories and give practical guidance on birth control. Two years later this plan was put into effect. Premier Chou En-lai, in introducing the Second Five Year Plan, stated:

> For the protection of women and children, for the upbringing and education of the rising generation and for the health and prosperity of the nation, we are in favor of the appropriate regulation of reproduction. We entrust the Ministry of Health with the task of working out an effective program of birth control with reference to publicity and practical applications.

The Party apparatus was mobilized for graphic propaganda in the villages. Sterilization and abortion were facilitated. The Chinese demographer, Ta Chen, told the International Statistical Institute in August 1957 that the state manufacture of Western-type contraceptives had as its immediate objective sufficient production to supply the needs of 25 million couples. While the official propaganda tried to dissociate the birth control program from 'Malthusian' ideas, the new emphasis was obviously embarrassing to the Russian Communists who had been arguing vehemently, as a doctrine of scientific certainty, that population was a problem only under capitalist conditions, and that socialism ended fears of overpopulation.

A shift occurred in Chinese Communist propaganda, and perhaps in policy, in 1958. In February attacks were made on 'the new theory of population' as contrary to Marxist 'science.' Dennis Bloodworth, in dispatches to the London *Observer* from Singapore after a visit to Red China, stated in September 1958 that the birth control program had not been terminated but had apparently lost some impetus. The ideological difference with Moscow had been overcome by the assertion that population growth is always an asset under socialism. But birth control was still necessary to prevent injury to 'socialist reconstruction' through too frequent incidence of pregnancies among working mothers. Radio Peking, Father de Lestapis notes, boasted in August 1958 that China would have a population of 700 million by 1962 and probably 800 million by 1968; under the Marxist regime there would never be too many people.

What lies behind this new tack, beyond a propaganda adjustment to the Moscow line, remains far from clear. The most sinister possibility is that, finding the cultural and social obstacles to contraception much more stubborn than foreseen,[12] the regime now looks to external expansion as 'a way out.' Subsequent actions in Tibet can be cited in this connection. Belief in the inevitability of an atomic holocaust, which China might best survive through weight of numbers, has also been mentioned as a possible explanation. Or it may be that preoccupation with the attempt to organize the villages into communes has reduced the priority given the effort to limit population. A fourth possibility is that, in view of obstacles to limitation by normal methods, the regime adopted the commune program partly as a measure of population control, through compulsory separation of the sexes for a large part of the time.

With these notes on the position of major non-Christian religions and Communism, it is time to turn to the Judeo-Christian tradition in its various manifestations. Before doing so, however, it might be of interest to observe the relation between religious predominance and differing patterns of national legislation in regard to methods of birth control. The available data are not complete, and now several years old,[13] but may still be generally indicative. The data cover laws regarding contraception, sterilization, and abortion.

By grouping the countries listed according to religious dominance, including Communism as one of the categories for this purpose, but omitting the non-Communist lands in which religious loyalties are too divided to give a clear indication, I find the picture roughly as follows:

Eastern cultures — On the whole, the least legislative restrictions are found today in areas of Hindu and Buddhist predominance. Contraception is legal, sterilization for the most part permitted on social as well as eugenic grounds, and abortion permitted for economic reasons under medical sanction in Japan.

Islam — The picture is mixed, with contraception legal in Egypt and Pakistan and illegal in Turkey — apparently on political rather than religious grounds. The penalties for abortion in Turkey are less severe than in many countries.

Communism — Because of shifting policies, the data here may be misleading. As of 1951–54 contraception was forbidden in Hungary and the U.S.S.R., and not restricted in Czechoslovakia or Yugoslavia — though state control of the means in the latter instance maintained restraints. The Yugoslav Penal Code authorized courts in exceptional cases to acquit persons inducing abortion on social grounds.

Judaism — Contraception is legal in Israel, but there are heavy penalties for induced abortion — 7 to 14 years imprisonment.

Roman Catholicism — The sale of contraceptives is illegal in most of the countries listed, Puerto Rico being the one clear exception, though Honduras and Argentina are said to lack legislation. In Austria and the Philippines, medical reasons provide an exception. In a number of European countries which formally ban contraception, however, it is stated that condoms are freely sold as prophylactics — e.g. in Malta they are issued to single men in the Navy, but not to married men. Sterilization is illegal in Italy and Paraguay; permitted in Puerto Rico and Panama; and for several other countries the indication is no legislation. Abortion is generally banned except for medical reasons.

Eastern Orthodoxy — Contraceptives are not restricted by legislation in Greece, although the availability of contraceptives appears in fact to be limited to the urban centers. Induced abortion, except for medical necessity, is subject to heavy penalties, particularly for professional practitioners.

Protestantism — In none of the predominantly Protestant countries listed is contraception prohibited, though the sale of contraceptives is variously regulated, and in the U.S. formally banned in eight states. Voluntary sterilization does not appear to be banned by any of the governments noted, though limited to eugenic and medical cases in Denmark and the Union of South Africa. The penalties against induced abortion are particularly severe, ranging up to life imprisonment, in most of the predominantly Protestant countries of the British Commonwealth; from 7 to 14 years in most of the states in the U.S.; lesser penalties in the Scandinavian countries.

It would be misleading to give undue weight to this very rough and incomplete legislative picture. But it offers one of the clues to the actual mores of the different cultures, at least in respect to government policy.

VIII

The Old Testament, Judaism, and Parenthood

&⤾ The story of Israel's life and beliefs, under the impact of God's progressive revelation of His righteous will, is important in a consideration of the question of responsible parenthood. The Old Testament record is significant as the formative influence on the ethos of the Jewish people. Historically, it has wider significance in its influence on the shaping of the Christian ethos. Consequently, we now turn to a brief examination of Old Testament doctrine which bears on the issue of responsible parenthood.

To understand this doctrine it is helpful to envisage the circumstances which confronted the Jewish tribes as they struggled to establish themselves in Palestine. The land was the crossroads of empire, with powerful neighbors waxing or waning to the north and south. There were also hostile communities to the west, in the coastal cities, and to the east. Without strong or clear natural frontiers, existence as a people was precarious. The exile in Egypt and the Babylonian captivity were reminders of the dangers of foreign dominance. These memories added poignancy to the prophetic dream of 'every man under his vine and under his fig tree, and none shall make them afraid' (Mic. 4:4).[1]

Also, the land itself had its hostile features. Archaeology indicates that the deserts have encroached on the usable land since Biblical times. The repeated ravaging of the country by hostile armies, and the resultant impact on the level of agriculture, has taken its toll. Walter Lowdermilk recorded in his *Palestine, Land of Promise* the estimate that 'over three feet of soil has been swept from the uplands of Palestine since the breakdown of terrace agriculture.'

Even so, it seems unlikely that Canaan in Biblical times was a 'land of milk and honey,' except in comparison with less fertile areas adjacent and in the enthusiastic eyes of the immigrants. The many Biblical references to water, and the lack of it, indicate that rainfall was a problem then as now. 'I will pour water on the thirsty land, and streams on the dry ground' (Isa. 44:3). At best, earning a livelihood from the land was a hard struggle. It illustrated the curse upon Adam: 'cursed is the ground because of you; in toil you shall eat of it all the days of your life' (Gen. 3:17). Nor was the older way of life, that of nomadic herding, any kind of idyllic existence. The vicissitudes facing the flocks made herding difficult and hazardous.

Consequently, as in many early societies, there were strong reasons in the environment for a major concern in fertility. No other concern affecting the family appears so often in Biblical literature. Both economic insecurity and international insecurity served to elevate the value of large families and large flocks. The challenge to survival for the tribes of Israel was seen as a call to growth and expansion. Underpopulation, rather than overpopulation, was the dominant reality.

It is true that the followers of Yahweh waged a victorious struggle against the fertility cults, the worship of the Baalim (cf. Num. 25:1–3; Deut. 4:3; 23:17). But it was a long and hard struggle and continued into the time of Josiah, who 'broke down the houses of the cult prostitutes which were in the house of the Lord' (2 Kings 23:7). The persistence of the fertility cults indicates, it can be argued, popular concern with fruitfulness.

The indignation of the prophets against the fertility cults, it should be noted, was directed against their idolatry and licentious rites rather than their preoccupation with fertility. It was the idolatrous aspect of the fertility cult which incensed Jeremiah: the leaders of Israel 'who say to a tree, "you are my father," and to a stone, "you gave me birth." For they have turned their back to me,' the Lord God (Jer. 2:27). Harlotry, in fact, became a common term for idolatry in prophetic preaching. Hosea, for example, after referring to the sins of the men who 'sacrifice with cult prostitutes,' speaks of Israel and Ephraim playing 'the harlot,' being 'joined to idols' (Hos. 4:14–15, 17; 5:3). The penalty, suggests Hosea, will be infertility: 'they shall play the harlot, but not multiply' (4:10).

Part of the prophetic indignation over the worship of the Baalim stems, no doubt, from the conviction that Yahweh is the true author of fruitfulness. His injunction, 'be fruitful and multiply,' to Adam (Gen. 1:28), repeated to Noah (Gen. 9:1,7) and to Jacob (Gen. 35:11), is also seen as a divine promise and blessing. The covenant with Abraham included the promise 'I will make you exceedingly fruitful' (Gen. 17:6). The pledge is repeated both for Ishmael (Gen. 17:20) and for Isaac (Gen. 26:24). Leah speaks of her 'good dowry' from God, her six sons (Gen. 30:20). The Psalmist sings: 'he raises up the needy out of affliction, and makes their families like flocks' (Ps. 107:41). The examples of fruitfulness as a blessing could be greatly extended.

While Hebrew thought, like that in many other societies, regarded sterility as strictly a feminine affair, it did not press the logic of its pro-fertility faith too far. Sterility could be a form of divine punishment. Hosea envisaged the penalty for Ephraim — which means 'to be fruitful' — to be 'no birth, no pregnancy, no conception' (Hos. 9:11). Yet for the barren woman her condition is described as a 'reproach' or 'affliction.' For example, when God finally 'remembered Rachel . . . and opened her womb' she said, 'God has taken away my reproach' (Gen. 30:22–3; cf. also Lk. 1:24–5). Hannah asked the Lord to 'look on the affliction of thy maidservant' and 'the Lord remembered her' (1 Sam. 1:11, 19). The removal of barrenness was seen as a fit subject for prayer (e.g. Gen. 25:21), but the fact of barrenness apparently was not regarded as a clear sign of personal sin.

The stress, in any case, is on God's power to grant the fruit of the womb. The barren woman does not stay barren, but becomes fruitful in the end. Sarah, Rebekah, Rachel — God finally blessed them all, in accordance with His promises. As the Psalmist sang: 'He gives the barren woman a home, making her the joyous mother of children' (Ps. 113:9). This is the main theme in regard to sterility.

In Old Testament thought human fertility is closely linked with that of nature. Families increase 'like flocks.' Joseph is a 'fruitful bough' (Gen. 49:22). The wife will be like a 'fruitful vine' and children like 'olive shoots' (Ps. 128:3). More significant, the injunction to 'be fruitful and multiply' as given both to Adam and Noah was closely connected with similar injunctions to the lesser creatures (Gen. 1:22; 8:17). Indeed, the injunction to Adam was connected with dominion over the lesser creatures, and followed by the promise of seed plants for food (Gen. 1:28-9). In days to come, prophesied Jeremiah, the Lord 'will sow the house of Israel and the house of Judah with the seed of man and the seed of beast' (Jer. 31:27). This link between human and natural fertility, commonly found in other religions concerned with fertility, is understandable in view of man's dependence on nature for survival. There is here in essence a concern for the balance of nature, for the balance between man and available natural resources.

It is not a static balance, however, that is sought. Rather it is one that is dynamic, rapidly expanding. The dream might be called the abundant society: one in which a man is able to surround himself with many children to comfort him in his old age, and to tend the growing flocks and fields; one in which the tribe advances toward a pre-eminent position by reason of its numbers and prosperity; one in which the whole people of God become a great nation, strong and secure.

The distinguishing feature of Old Testament thought in this matter, however, is insistence on the ethical and religious preconditions for human expansion, for the fulfillment of God's promises. The requirement is stated thus: 'if you obey the voice of the Lord your God, keeping all his commandments which I command you this day, and doing what is right in the sight of the Lord your God' (Deut. 13:18). Then, and then only, 'Blessed shall be the fruit of your body, and the fruit of your ground, and the fruit of your beasts, the increase of your cattle, and the young of your flock' (Deut. 28:1–4). If you had 'hearkened to my commandments,' said Isaiah, then 'your offspring would have been like the sand' (Isa. 48:18–19).

In addition to the dream of the abundant society, the Hebraic concern for posterity has another major source; the concern for preservation of the family name, for what might be called social immortality. Personal survival after death did not loom very large in Jewish tradition. One reason for this was no doubt the view of man as a unity of flesh and spirit, without the dualism characteristic of Greek thought. A great prophet like Elijah might be transported bodily by a whirlwind into heaven (2 Kings 2:11). But this obviously did not happen to the general run of men. For them there was Sheol, a rather dreary and Stygian underworld, the world of the grave. Existence in Sheol was shadowy, indistinct, diluted. The survival that really mattered was in this world, in posterity. The intense sense of belonging to a community, of group solidarity, so attenuated in modern man, must be appreciated to grasp the satisfactions found in this social immortality.

Preservation of the family name before the Lord was the way this concept was expressed. Thus Jacob blessed his grandsons: 'bless the lads; and in them let my name be perpetuated, and the name of my fathers Abraham and Isaac; and let them grow into a multitude in the midst of the earth' (Gen. 48:16). Or again, 'May his posterity be cut off; may his name be blotted out in the second generation' (Ps. 109:13).

Preservation of the family name through progeny was both a sign of God's blessing and a religious duty, for the continuance of 'the name of my fathers' as well as one's own name was at stake.[2] Presumably behind this concept was a view of the living God as primarily lord of the living, though a larger understanding began to take hold (cf. Ps. 139). In addition, names had a special importance in Jewish thought, as in other early societies. To have a name 'blotted out' was a family and personal catastrophe — indeed, a social peril.

Family duty and the ideal of the abundant society combine to

give the Old Testament ethic its strong pro-fertility bent. As the
Psalmist exults:

> Lo, sons are a heritage from the Lord,
> the fruit of the womb a reward.
> Like arrows in the hand of a warrior
> are the sons of one's youth.
> Happy is the man who has
> his quiver full of them!
> He shall not be put to shame
> when he speaks with his
> enemies in the gate.
>
> (Ps. 127)

The childless marriage is a calamity, and virginity is of value only
as a preface to marriage. Jephthah's daughter asked a stay of exe-
cution to bewail her virginity, for 'she had never known a man'
(Judges 11:37–9). A man with mutilated sex organs 'shall not
enter the assembly of the Lord' (Deut. 23:1). The obligation to
marry and procreate applied to the priesthood as much as to the
laity, though the priest was more restricted as to choice of wife:
'He shall take to wife a virgin of his own people, that he may not
profane his children among his people' (Lev. 21:14–15). Celibacy
had no place in the Hebraic scale of values.

Polygamy, on the other hand, had such an established place in
Old Testament culture that it is neither sanctioned nor criticized,
been accepted as part of the given: 'And Lamech took two wives'
(Gen. 4:19). Obviously, economic and social status placed limitations on the exercise of polygamy, and only kings could afford the
elaborate establishments of wives, concubines, and slaves of a
David or Solomon. But no obloquy attached to the man who chose
a multiple marriage as a means to fill his 'quiver' and keep his
name before the Lord, provided he did not steal another man's
wife or marry a near relative. Sarah, Rachel, and Leah during times
of barrenness transferred handmaids or slaves to their husbands
to satisfy the need for progeny and their own desires for at least
foster motherhood (Gen. 16:2; 30:3,9).

Some restrictions, however, entered into the tradition. A king is to show some restraint, for harem-building could lead to tyranny and idolatry as Solomon's reign had shown (1 Kings 11:1–13). So, 'he shall not multiply wives for himself, lest his heart turn away' (Deut. 17:17). Also, in the ordinances for the protection of the Hebrew slave, the Israelite who has a Jewish concubine, if he takes another wife, is enjoined not to diminish the first's food, clothing, or marital rights (Ex. 21:10). This principle, if applied, would disrupt the best-regulated harem.

Another institution even more closely related to 'preserving the name' is that of levirate marriage, a term derived from *levir*, a Latin term for brother. If a man died without progeny, it was his brother's duty to marry the widow and beget children to carry on the name of the deceased. The denouement of the story of Ruth hinges on whether the next of kin will 'do the part of the next of kin' or assign his obligations to Boaz. The next of kin decides that a levirate marriage might impair his own inheritance and Boaz takes over, 'to perpetuate the name of the dead in his inheritance, that the name of the dead may not be cut off from among his brethren and from the gate of his native place' (Ruth 4:5,10). Onan, in a similar situation, decided he did not want to give off-spring to his dead brother, and when he went in to the widow, Tamar, 'he spilled the semen on the ground' (Gen. 38:8–10). Deuteronomy describes the levirate duty: to provide a son to suc-ceed to the name of the deceased brother, 'that his name may not be blotted out of Israel.' The procedure to be followed when the duty is spurned suggests that evasion was a common problem (Deut. 25:5–10).

The special evasive action of Onan has been generally inter-preted as signifying *coitus interruptus*, although onanism has also been given broader connotations. The case of Onan is the one clear example of an act with contraceptive intent in the Old Testament, and it is understandable that it should involve *coitus interruptus*, undoubtedly the most universal and commonly practiced method of averting conception down the ages. It is also understandable that much subsequent attention and debate should have been focused on this example, because of its singularity. Efforts at family limitation were hardly in keeping with the ethos of Israel.

Was the sin of Onan, for which the Lord 'slew him,' his refusal to honor his levirate duty — his unbrotherly and selfish attitude — as the proponents of birth control tend to argue; or was it spilling his seed intentionally, as the opponents contend? To this we must return later. The immediate question is the conviction of Israel in this matter. And the weight of argument here, it seems to me, supports the thesis that Onan's guilt was thought to be primarily his practice of *coitus interruptus* — his repeated practice, apparently, since Genesis 38:9 actually says 'when[ever] he went in.'

The levirate duty was regarded as important. The unfortunate Tamar, who, in the guise of a *kedeshah* or cult prostitute, seduced her father-in-law to secure progeny, was judged to be 'more righteous' than the father-in-law who had delayed in providing his third son for the purpose (Gen. 38:26). Yet the penalty for refusing the duty seems relatively mild: a public shaming and a label attached to the guilty person's family name (Deut. 25:9). It is also true that the penalty for a nocturnal emission of semen is light: when it occurs in an army camp, because of cleanliness necessary in God's presence, the man is to leave the camp for a day, bathe, and return (Deut. 23:10). But this occurrence is an involuntary act. Onan spilled his seed by intent.

As Sherwin Bailey has pointed out, the word translated as 'spill,' *shāchath*, means 'to spoil, ruin, corrupt, or destroy' and not simply 'to spill.' It is, indeed, the same word translated as 'destroy' in the account of the Flood (Gen. 6:13). Dr. Bailey argues that the act was regarded as a heinous crime because in antiquity semen was regarded as 'virtually a human being in fluid form,' as seed in the full sense, having the 'properties of the fertilized ovum.' The uses to which the Hebrew words usually translated by *spérma* are put tend to reinforce this argument, for they are rendered both as seed or semen and as child or children (Lev. 18:21; 22:13). Also in the *Schulchan Aruch*, or Code of Jewish Law, which embodies the oral traditions and rabbinical interpretations of Judaism, the nonprocreative effusion of semen is linked with the phrase 'your hands are full of blood' (Isa. 1:15), and the act is said to be 'analogous to the killing of a person.' It seems consistent with the strong pro-fertility bent of Old Testament religion that the willful destruction of viable human seed should be regarded as a dreadful crime.

There is no evidence that contraception or periodic continence were known or used for the spacing of pregnancies in Israel. There was a strong taboo against intercourse during menstruation (cf. Lev. 15:24). There are also references to abstinence for religious reasons. In preparation for the presence of the Lord on Sinai, Moses 'said to the people, "Be ready by the third day; do not go near a woman"' (Ex. 19:15). And David, when he sought bread for his soldiers from the priest, Ahimelech, and was told that only holy bread was available, said, 'of a truth women have been kept from us as always when I go on an expedition' (1 Sam. 21:4–5). The point here is that sexual intercourse was regarded as causing a ceremonial uncleanness, since it involved a bodily discharge. Consequently, both the man and woman were ritually unclean until the following evening and after bathing (Lev. 15:18). There is no hint of continence for contraceptive purposes.

A major method of population control in many primitive societies has been infanticide. That this tragic approach to keeping a population in balance with its resources was known in Israel can be gathered from a reference in Ezekiel, where he speaks picturesquely of sinful Jerusalem: 'You were cast out on the open field, for you were abhorred, on the day that you were born' (Ezek. 16:5). But I find no evidence of this abomination being practiced for purposes of family limitation or population control. The worship of Moloch, with its grisly child sacrifices, made some headway among the Jewish people, as we can tell from the prophetic denunciations (cf. Jer. 7:31; 32:35; Deut. 12:31). J. H. Hertz in his edition of *The Pentateuch and Haftorahs* says, 'the story of the Binding of Isaac (Gen. 22) opens the age-long warfare of Israel against the abominations of child sacrifice which was rife among the Semitic peoples, as well as their Egyptian and Aryan neighbors.' This story, incidentally, reinforces the evidence that Moloch worship did not involve family limitation as a purpose — Isaac was an only son. Child sacrifice to Moloch, it is written in Leviticus, profanes 'the name of your God.' Those that practice it 'shall be cut off from among their people'; they shall be stoned to death (18:21, 29; 20:2). As Rabbi Hertz points out, the name of the valley in which the fearful rites were performed, Ge-Hinnom, came to be used as a synonym for Hell.

This summary of the Hebraic approach to parenthood has thus far stressed the strong religious, social, and cultural factors which favored a high level of procreation, and the probability that family limitation was neither known very much nor sought. But there was another dimension of Old Testament thought about the man-woman relationship which was to have an important influence on subsequent Jewish and Christian doctrine. This is the concept of marital companionship and union as themselves a blessing from God.

In the account of the creation in chapter two of Genesis, which critics hold to be earlier than the 'increase and multiply' account in chapter one, 'the Lord God said, "It is not good that the man should be alone; I will make him a helper fit for him"' (Gen. 2:18). The Hebrew term k'negdo, here translated 'fit for him,' Rabbi Hertz explains, 'may mean either "at his side," i.e. fit to associate with; or, "as over against him," i.e. corresponding to him.' The passage goes on, with its reference to 'bone of my bones and flesh of my flesh,' to assert the principle: 'Therefore a man . . . cleaves to his wife, and they become one flesh' (Gen. 2:23–4). Companionship and union, the two in one flesh — here is a major Old Testament insight into the reality of true marriage.

While the principal motif in the Biblical record is the concern for procreation, for building up the family and society, so that parenthood, and particularly the wife — or wives — is seen rather as a means to an end, the concern here for man and wife as an end in themselves under God is a secondary theme which helps to elevate the whole ethos. Despite the tradition and environment of polygamy and the other customs which put the woman in an inferior role, the concept of companionship worked as a leaven in Israel, disturbing the conscience over marital injustices and directing the hearts of men toward a higher view of marriage. The Old Testament provides considerable evidence of a greater appreciation of woman as a person and as a mate, and not solely as a mother, than obtained in other ancient societies.

Thus the seed of monogamous marriage based on genuine love was planted among the tares of ancient custom and masculine selfishness. The visible plants from the true seed found in the Old Testament record are not too numerous but they bear the promise of the future. There is, for example, Isaac's love for Rebekah, which comforted him after his mother's death (Gen. 24:67). There are Boaz and the widowed Ruth. There are the touching words of Elkanah seeking to comfort Hannah's grief over her barren state: 'Hannah, why do you weep? And why do you not eat? And why is your heart sad? Am I not more to you than ten sons?' (1 Sam. 1:8). There is the humane provision in Mosaic law exempting the newlywed from military service: 'he shall be free at home one year, to be happy with his wife whom he has taken' (Deut. 24:5). There is the rich love poetry in the Song of Solomon, which may be a collection of wedding songs. 'Enjoy life with the wife whom you love' (Eccles. 9:9). 'And rejoice in the wife of your youth, a lovely hind, a graceful doe. Let her affection fill you at all times with delight, be infatuated always with her love' (Prov. 5:18-19). Such citations may not seem very impressive when seen through modern glasses colored by romanticism. Seen through the spectacles of the ancient world, the picture is bright with deepened insight into the meaning of true marriage.

The 'one flesh' concept meant in essence a new status for woman. She is a partner, and not a brood mare or plaything. The corollary of this principle is a new attitude toward children, as persons in their own right. There are many signs of affection for children in the Old Testament, as in David's grief over his dead sons. But the main emphasis is on parental pride and filial duty. It is perhaps symbolic that the last verse in the Old Testament, according to the Christian canon, speaks of Elijah's returning: 'And he will turn the hearts of fathers to their children and the hearts of children to their fathers, lest I come and smite the land with a curse' (Mal. 4:6).

POST-CANONICAL JUDAISM

Thus far we have been considering the Judaic heritage common to Judaism and Christianity. It seems fitting, before turning to the New Testament, to continue with a brief examination of subsequent Jewish thought, both as a factor in the contemporary situation and for the possible light that the oral tradition imbedded in the Talmud may throw on the Old Testament itself. Post-canonical Judaism does not speak with a clear and common voice. But it is of interest and significance nonetheless.

The main primary sources here, in addition to the Torah or Pentateuch, are: the Talmud, the core of which is composed of the Mishna, or teachings compiled by Rabbi Judah the Patriarch in the 3rd century but published much later; the Midrash, or expositions of Scripture of varying dates and completed about the 13th century; the *Schulchan Aruch*, or Code of Law, a systematic summary of the 16th century; and contemporary actions by Rabbinical bodies. This material merits a fuller examination than is possible here. Yet a short summary may be useful.

The pro-fertility orientation of the Old Testament is continued in Judaism. 'Be fruitful and multiply' is the first of the 613 *Mitzvoth* — precepts or commandments. The repeated injunction to Noah to be fruitful and multiply (Gen. 9:1,7), says Rabbi Hertz, was the basis of the Talmud's 'strong condemnation of him who does not fulfill the command to found a family.' Willy Hofmann, describing the Orthodox Jewish point of view in *Orthodox Jewish Life* for January–February 1952, cites Isaiah 45:18 in support of the thesis that God created the world to be populated. The injunction, 'be fruitful and multiply,' was addressed to all mankind. He quotes a Jewish proverb as indicative of the attitude: 'Each child brings his own *b'rochah* (blessing) into this world.' Morris Kertzer in his *What Is a Jew?* similarly states that 'A home without children, Jews believe, is a home without blessing.' The *Jewish Encyclopedia*, however, indicates that as Judaism became urbanized the injunction regarding procreation was modified. Two children might meet the requirements of the *mitzvah*. Rabbi Kertzer gives a summary formula: 'According to Jewish law, every man and wife have a solemn obligation to bring at least two children into the world.'

On the obligation to marry and procreate, Judaism is agreed. Celibacy, says Rabbi Hertz, is 'contrary to nature.' The differences come in regard to limiting the size of families, the Orthodox tending to restrict severely both the reasons and the means, the Reformed and Conservative taking a less strict position. There is also considerable variety of interpretation among the Talmudic teachers.

In the Midrash (*Genesis Rabbah*) it is stated that both Onan and Er were killed by the Lord for spilling their seed. The *Niddah* section of the Talmud states that the 'wasteful discharge of seed is forbidden' (13a). Consequently, the Code of Jewish Law, or *Schulchan Aruch*, says that it is forbidden to 'cause in vain the effusion of semen,' the crime being more severe than any other mentioned in the Torah. Likewise the Mishna *Ketubbot* (7:5) forbids the expulsion of semen after coitus. Again, the *Genesis Rabbah* (23:2) explains that, in the time of Lamech, men often took two wives, one for procreation and one for pleasure; the latter would take a cup of roots to make her sterile and thus preserve her beauty. The Flood, it is suggested, was a punishment for this kind of behavior. Thus, both *coitus interruptus* and contraception are condemned. This is the rigorous tradition.

There is, however, another and more humane or realistic tradition. I am indebted here to the references collated by Dr. Himes. According to the *Yebamot* section of the Talmud (34b), during the 24 months in which a child is nursed, a man 'must thresh inside and winnow outside,' a euphemism for *coitus interruptus*. The Talmud also speaks of cohabitation with a *mokh*, or spongy substance, for minors, pregnant woman, and nursing mothers (*Tosephta Niddah*, 2:6). The *Tosephta Yebamot* refers to a woman being allowed to drink a cup of roots to become sterile (7:5). While abstinence is not part of the philosophy of Judaism, there are examples of abstention. Willy Hofmann, in the article cited earlier, refers to the Midrash statement that all on the Ark were forbidden intercourse during their stay on the Ark, and also to the Talmud teaching (*Taanith*) about abstinence during a famine. Even abortion (embryotomy) was permitted, when the life of the mother was in danger (Mishna *Oholot*, 7:6).

The composite picture is one of a tradition which permits, if it does not encourage, certain measures of family limitation at least after the second child. From the Orthodox viewpoint, according to Willy Hofmann, 'Jewish tradition and viewpoint cannot consider planned parenthood for social or economic reasons.' The Conservative and Reformed Rabbis do consider such reasons.[3] The resolutions of 1929 and 1930 of the Central Conference of American Rabbis, the Reformed group in the United States, 'urge the recognition of the importance of the control of parenthood as one of the methods of coping with social problems,' and support 'intelligent birth regulation.' 'We are aware,' said the Conference, 'of the many serious evils caused by the lack of birth control.' The Rabbinical Assembly, the Conservative body in the United States, stated in 1935:

> Careful study and observation have convinced us that birth control is a valuable method for overcoming some of the obstacles that prevent the proper functioning of the family under present conditions. . . . Proper education in contraception and birth control will not destroy, but rather enhance, the spiritual values inherent in the family and will make for the advancement of human happiness and welfare.

It should be added that the practice of the Jewish laity has outstripped the debate among the Rabbis. As Moses Jung has stated in *Judaism in a Changing World* (ed. Leo Jung), 'the practice of birth control seems to have become almost universal among the Jews.' This is borne out by census statistics, indicating the low birth rate of Jewish groups in Western countries. One is reminded of the fact that polygamy was not finally outlawed until the 11th century although monogamy, favored in the oral tradition, had established itself as the norm much earlier.

We find in Judaism, despite the legalism which has played such a large part in Jewish thought, the continuing ferment produced by the leaven of the 'one flesh' concept. 'Named "covenant" in the Bible,' writes Professor Jung in the symposium cited, 'marriage became in the Talmud "*kiddushin*," sanctification — the hallowing of two human beings to life's noblest purpose.' A similar concept is expressed by Sidney Goldstein in *The Meaning of Marriage and Foundations of the Family*: 'The sanctity of marriage does not depend upon conception or contraception but upon the spirit of consecration with which men and women enter the marriage bond.' A good conclusion is provided by Rabbi Eugene Mihaly in *Marriage and Family Life* (ed. A. B. Shoulson):

> Procreation is undoubtedly a fulfillment in marriage, but the love and companionship is no less a primary purpose. Eve was created to be a 'helpmate' to Adam since 'it is not good for man to be alone' and only later were they commanded 'to be fruitful and multiply.'

IX

The New Testament and Parenthood

ટ۶ The teachings of the New Testament which bear on the question of parenthood are best understood when seen in a dialectical pattern. There is a thesis and an antithesis, a yes and a no, and the complex synthesis of the two is more implied than worked out. This is true both of the Gospels and the Epistles. Moreover, since very little attention is devoted to the specific question of parenthood, the answers must be sought in the broader context of the approach to marriage and family life. Let us then turn to the yes and the no regarding the man-woman relationship, first in the Gospels and then in the Epistles. This division is not only convenient but useful, in that the teachings of Jesus were directed in the first instance at disciples and listeners imbued with the Judaic ethos of their Old Testament heritage, while the writings of Paul were sent to struggling churches surrounded by Hellenistic culture, even though a number of these churches grew out of Jewish synagogues. Thus, however much the inner content may be the same, the formulations differ as the audiences differ, and justify separate consideration.

THE GOSPELS AND PARENTHOOD

A good place to begin a consideration of the yes elements in the teachings of Jesus concerning marriage and family life is to remember what little is recorded of his own family life. Luke tells us that he was initiated into Jewish family life in the normal fashion, with circumcision and the rite of presentation for the first born (Lk. 2:21f.); and that when he was 12 years old he accompanied his parents on their annual trip to Jerusalem for the Passover, where they searched for him 'anxiously' for three days among 'their kinsfolk and acquaintances' before finding him in the temple (2:41f). The reference suggests that he took an active part in the family's social activities. Both participation in family economic life and the closeness of family ties are indicated in the saying quoted by Mark: 'Is not this the carpenter, the son of Mary and brother of James and Joses and Judas and Simon, and are not his sisters here with us?' (Mk. 6:3). The fidelity of Mary is one of the touching strains of the New Testament. The brothers of Jesus were also in the upper room in the testing days before Pentecost (Acts 1:14). And James became a leader of the Christians in Jerusalem, consulted by Paul (Gal. 1:19). All these evidences bespeak an extraordinarily warm family relationship.

This positive experience of family life which testifies to Christ's full humanity, to the completeness of the Incarnation, is of a piece with the positive attitude of Jesus toward the family. The story of the 'prodigal son' (Lk. 15:11–32) is a beautiful description of parental love, which taught the nature of divine love. The healing of the daughter of Jairus in response to the father's faith (Matt. 9:18ff.), and the son of the widow of Nain in compassion for her sorrow (Lk. 7:11–16) are additional clues. The abundant love of Jesus for children (e.g. Matt. 18:1f.; Mk. 10:13–16) is another indication. No saying of his on the specific question of the values of parenthood was preserved in the Gospel record, but there can be little doubt as to his positive attitude.

The evidence is even more conclusive concerning the high evaluation placed by Jesus on the institution of marriage. To start with a minor point: he had an obvious interest in wedding feasts. John states that 'the first of his signs' was done at a marriage in the village of Cana (John 2:1f.). In at least four of his parables there are references to wedding feasts: the parables of the marriage of the king's son (Matt. 22:1f.), of the wise and foolish virgins (Matt.

25:1f.), of the wakeful servants (Lk. 12:36f.); and that concerning places of honor (Lk. 14:7f.). In response to the question, 'Why do not your disciples fast?' Mark and Luke record the saying: 'Can the wedding guests fast while the bridegroom is with them?' (Mk. 2:18f.; Lk. 5:34f.). In John there is a passage in which John the Baptist compares the Christ to 'the bridegroom' and himself to 'the friend of the bridegroom' (John 3:29).

These references to Christ as the 'bridegroom' are undoubtedly related to the prophetic utterances about the betrothal or covenant between God and His people Israel. Said Hosea: 'And in that day, says the Lord, you will call me, "My husband" . . . and I will betroth you to me for ever' (Hos. 2:16f.). Likewise Isaiah said: 'As the bridegroom rejoices over the bride, so shall your God rejoice over you' (Isa. 62:5; cf. also Isa. 54:5; Jer. 3:14, 20). This concept of covenant or betrothal was no doubt part of Jesus' Messianic consciousness, as it was in Paul's insight into the relation of Christ and His Church. Paul writes to the church in Corinth: 'I betrothed you to Christ to present you as a pure bride to her one husband' (2 Cor. 11:2; cf. also Rev. 19:6–16). And there is the great passage in Ephesians (5:21–31), to which we will return, comparing Christ and Church with husband and wife. Marriage serves to symbolize a spiritual reality, a 'great mystery' as Paul calls it. For this inquiry, the important corollary is that the great mystery also reveals the spiritual potentiality of true marriage.

Jesus himself pointed to the heart of the matter when the Pharisees asked him concerning divorce. He replied:

> But from the beginning of creation, 'God made them male and female.' 'For this reason a man shall leave his father and mother and be joined to his wife, and the two shall become one.' So they are no longer two but one. What therefore God has joined together, let not man put asunder.
>
> (Mk. 10:6–9; Matt. 19:4–6)

Here the 'two in one flesh' concept, which played a significant but subordinate role in the Old Testament, is moved into the center of Christian doctrine on marriage. Also the theological dimension implicit in the idea now is made explicit — 'what therefore God has joined together.' True marriage is a spiritual and physical union of which God Himself is the author. Here indeed is the 'great mystery,' helping us to understand both the nature of God and the essence of genuine marriage. Here is the bedrock of Christian teaching on the man-woman relationship.

From this understanding of marriage as a God-given union, Jesus set forth the implication for the question of divorce. The Pharisees pointed out that only a certificate of divorce was required under Mosaic law. Jesus attributed this as a concession to 'your hardness of heart.' But this was not originally the plan — 'from the beginning it was not so.' 'Whoever divorces his wife and marries another, commits adultery against her; and if she divorces her husband and marries another, she commits adultery' (Mk. 10:11–12). The Lucan version agrees with Mark, while Matthew adds the qualification, 'except for unchastity' (Lk. 16:18; Matt. 19:7–9). The qualification suggests an attempt by the Christian community to adapt the saying of Jesus as a substitute for the Mosaic law. But Jesus was not erecting an external code of behavior; he was dealing with the inner heart of the matter, as he was when he identified adultery with lustful intention (Matt. 5:28) — which implies, incidentally, that nondivorce may also constitute adultery. All this, however, is by the way. The point here is that the reply of Jesus to the Pharisees underscores his stress on the God-ordained character of marriage.

All this forms part of the yes to marriage and family life. But there is also an important no in the teachings of Jesus, a no which stems from the overriding claims of the Kingdom and the sense of imminent divine judgment. It would be a very incomplete view of the matter if we did not take the antithesis into account. The theme is set in Luke's story of the youthful Jesus in the temple. To his anxious parents comes the reply: 'Did you not know that I must be in my Father's house?' (Lk. 2:49). There are, then, obligations which take precedence over family ties.

One important element in this no is the conviction that the end of the age and a radical transformation by a righteous God are at hand. The prospect of a fearful and yet glorious winnowing of the sons of men by the Almighty seems imminent. It is a time of divine revolution, and revolutions of any kind tend to be disruptive of family life. They are particularly hard on the women and children. Thus we find in the Synoptic Gospels the phrase, 'alas for those who are with child and for those who give suck in those days' (Mk. 13:17; Matt. 24:19; Lk. 21:23). 'The days are coming when they [the daughters of Jerusalem] will say, "Blessed are the barren, and the wombs that never bore, and the breasts that never gave suck"' (Lk. 23:29). It should be noted that Jesus does not himself call the barren blessed. In John, the approaching time of troubles is compared to childbirth, and the return of the Son to the post partum 'joy that a child is born into the world' (John 16:21).

Yet the time of troubles will be grim, with brother betraying brother, and father child, and children rising up against parents (Mk. 13:12). It is no time for normal family life. In fact such life may be an ominous sign. Just as in the time of the Flood, when 'they ate, they drank, they married, they were given in marriage,' so it will be in the time of the Son of man (Lk. 17:27). In the parable of the guests who made excuses (Lk. 14:16–24), there is the suggestion that marriage may be an impediment in regard to readiness for the Kingdom. One excuse for refusing the invitation to the banquet was: 'I have married a wife, and therefore I cannot come.'

The Lucan version seems particularly concerned with establishing celibacy as a norm, and this puts a certain question mark over sayings bearing on this issue not found in the other Gospels. When some Sadducees asked Jesus which of the brothers of successive levirate marriages would be the husband at the resurrection, Matthew records his reply thus: 'In the resurrection they neither marry nor are given in marriage, but are like angels in heaven' (Matt. 22:30). But the reply given in Luke is quite different:

The sons of this age marry and are given in marriage; but those who are accounted worthy to attain to that age and to the resurrection from the dead neither marry nor are given in marriage, for they cannot die any more, because they are equal to angels and are sons of God, being sons of the resurrection.

(Lk. 20:34–6)

The impression of embellishment is strong.

Some critics have suggested that the passage in Matthew about 'eunuchs for the sake of the kingdom of heaven' (19:10–12) may be a later interpolation in the interest of celibacy, one of the grounds being that the spirit of the passage is Greco-Roman rather than Jewish. Yet the idea is no more radical in its departure from traditional Judaism than many other teachings about the Kingdom, or indeed more radical than our Lord's personal life. The introductory phrase of this passage is: 'Not all men can receive this precept, but only those to whom it is given.' Incidentally, Sherman Johnson, in *The Interpreter's Bible*, questions the RSV translation of the term *logos* as 'precept,' rather than 'saying' or 'counsel,' since the former has a more binding connotation. The point seems well taken. Apparently, there was no particular emphasis on celibacy among the disciples, to judge from their practice. Paul asks the church at Corinth: does he not 'have the right to be accompanied by a wife, as the other apostles and the brothers of the Lord and Cephas?' (1 Cor. 9:5; cf. Matt. 8:14–15). We can conclude that there was no undue stress on celibacy in the teaching of Jesus.

Rather, his emphasis was upon the fact that the claims of the Kingdom transcend those of marriage and family life. The keynote is obedience to those transcendant claims. When Jesus was told that his mother and brothers were waiting outside to see him, he pointed to his disciples and said: 'Here are my mother and my brothers! Whoever does the will of God is my brother, and sister, and mother' (Mk. 3:35, etc.). Similarly, when a woman cried out, 'Blessed is the womb that bore you . . .' Jesus replied, 'Blessed rather are those who hear the word of God and keep it' (Lk. 11:27–8). Those who have forsaken home and family 'for my name's sake, will receive a hundredfold, and inherit eternal life'

(Matt. 19:29). 'He who loves father or mother more than me is not worthy of me; and he who loves son or daughter more than me is not worthy of me' (Matt. 10:37).[1]

This is the crucial point in the no of Jesus toward marriage and family life. He presents the claims of the Kingdom in dramatic fashion, but his own life indicates that he is fully appreciative of the lesser claims of home and family. It is the 'more than me,' the putting of family ahead of the will of God in regard to witness or service in society, the giving of supreme loyalty to one's own family circle, against which Jesus is giving timeless and timely warning. Jesus does not in any specific way deal with the question of parenthood. What he does provide, in his yes and no to marriage and family life, is a spiritual and moral frame of reference essential to truly sound answers.

The Epistles and Parenthood

When the Good News moved out from the harassed but inspired little community of believers in and around Jerusalem into the wider reaches of the Mediterranean world, the missionaries had to show its relevance to the condition of men in the predominant Greco-Roman culture of that world. Before turning to the writings of Paul that bear on the question of parenthood, a few comments on this Hellenistic culture seem in order. The differences in the moral environment required new approaches on the part of the Christian mission.

There was a considerable contrast between the Hebraic and Hellenic worlds in their attitudes toward the man-woman relationship. As has been indicated, sex and, more particularly, procreation were serious matters for the Jews, involving religious and social duties of the highest order. Any misuse of the sexual instincts was abhorrent. Perversion, as associated with Sodom, was utterly evil. The Greeks and Romans took sex much less seriously, regarding it as one of the baser pleasures, hardly related to the social duty of procreation. As Edwyn Bevan says in his little classic, *Christianity*, 'in practice, sexual indulgence (natural and unnatural) was thought very lightly of in ancient pagan society . . .' On the other hand, 'marriage was a civic arrangement for a utilitarian purpose, the "procreation of legitimate issue," as the Greek formula ran.' Little moral distinction was made among the varieties of sexual indulgence, which was regarded as 'playing the fool' in any case.

No doubt it is possible to exaggerate the depravity of Greco-Roman culture, especially from the perspective of contemporary society, with an erotic beam in its own eye. Not only the philosophers but also large numbers of ordinary folk undoubtedly led decent lives by later standards. The point is that the public standards were low. The moral dikes against licentiousness or any of its aberrations were weak. Unlike the righteous God of Israel, the gods of Greek mythology were all too human, indulging in most of the practices found in society.

In the urban centers, at least, prostitution was rife; much of it centered around the cult of Venus. Hans Licht states, in *Sexual Life in Ancient Greece*, that the seaport of Corinth was particularly notorious in this respect, a thousand 'priestesses' or cult prostitutes being associated with the temple of Venus. Both slavery and the exposure of infants were factors in maintaining the supply of prostitutes, the customs in regard to exposure permitting exploiters as well as foster parents to appropriate abandoned babies. The more elevated courtesans or *hetairae* took a much more active part in social life than married women, as was the case in several Oriental cultures. 'In the life of almost every more important personality, prominent in the history of Hellenism,' Licht asserts, 'the influence of well-known *hetairae* can be proved.'

Apparently male prostitution also was fairly common. Homosexual practices were regarded simply as one form of love. Licht traces *paiderastia*, as it was called, back as far as the *Iliad*. He attributes the propensity to male dominance in the culture, and it can also be described in terms of the low and unequal status of women. Plato in the *Phaedrus* and *Symposium* (178c) spoke at least tolerantly of homosexuality, primarily impressed by the mutual intellectual stimulation of brilliant young men. Later, in the

Laws (836f), he spoke in condemnatory terms, but the extent to which public opinion was opposed by the Christian era is uncertain. Certainly, Paul, with his training as a Pharisee and as a Christian, finds homosexual practices particularly repellent. Because the Gentiles worshipped idols, he wrote,

> God gave them up to dishonorable passions. Their women exchanged natural relations for unnatural, and the men likewise gave up natural relations with women and were consumed with passion for one another, men committing shameless acts with men and receiving in their own persons the due penalty for their error.
>
> (Rom. 1:26–7)

Now, it is true that the philosophers in general disparaged sexual indulgence and license as unworthy of the disciplined man and harmful to the life of reason. Plato, in the passage cited in the *Laws*, says that the man who puts soul first, 'reverently worshipping temperance, courage, nobility and wisdom, will desire to live always chastely in company with the chaste object of his love.' He proposes that sex indulgence 'be hemmed in by three kinds of force . . . that of godly fear, and that of love of honor, and that which is desirous of fair forms of soul, not fair bodies.' Other civic penalties are also proposed to give these reinforcement. Bevan quotes a saying of Epictetus that 'nobody was ever better for the carnal act, and a man may be thankful if he was not definitely the worse.' He also cites the Stoic Musonius, a contemporary of Paul's, who would have extramarital intercourse stamped as evil and marital intercourse limited to procreation. The calm arguments of the philosophers, however, did not make a wide impact on the practices of Greco-Roman society. For the mass of the people there was a moral as well as religious vacuum, which gave Christianity a practical challenge and opportunity.

In responding to this challenge, Paul brought the same Good News presented in the Gospels. The yes and the no of Paul in regard to marriage and family life are at the root, I think, the same as those of Jesus. But the form and emphasis are different, corresponding to the differences in their social setting, and no doubt compounded by differences in temperament, training, and experience. On the surface, at least, there is more of the negative and less of the positive in Paul's approach to the complex of questions which bear on the concept of parenthood. In considering his writings and the later New Testament materials, it seems useful to reverse the order and to look first at the no.

It was perhaps inevitable that Paul's main treatment of sexual matters should occur in a letter to the congregation in Corinth, with its large transient population, its major cult of Venus, and its notoriety for loose living. The problem of helping the little colonies of heaven to avoid becoming of the world was difficult enough in any case. In such an environment it was doubly difficult. Word had come to Paul that a member of the church was 'living with his father's wife,' presumably his stepmother, and not only had the congregation done nothing about it, but it was 'arrogant.' After urging the man's expulsion, Paul corrects a misunderstanding created by a previous letter. When he said 'not to associate with immoral men' he meant 'inside the church.' He had not been talking about going 'out of the world' (1 Cor. 5).

A bit further on he returns to this concern. Among those who will not inherit the Kingdom are the fornicators, adulterers, the effeminate, and homosexuals. The body is meant for the Lord; it is a member of Christ, a temple of the Holy Spirit. 'You are not your own; you were bought with a price. So glorify God in your body.' Paul here uses the 'one flesh' concept in a rather startling way. 'Do you not know that he who joins himself to a prostitute becomes one body with her? For, as it is written, "The two shall become one."' Paul's point is that such behavior obviously precludes becoming one spirit with Christ (1 Cor. 6:9f.). Johannes Weiss, in his *Commentary on First Corinthians*, developed the thesis that Paul uses *soma* (body) and *sarx* (flesh) here to mean one personality, since Greek was lacking in a specific term for this idea. This is a useful conjecture, for Paul can hardly mean that physical union alone constitutes the 'one flesh,' the 'great mystery' of marriage described in Ephesians. Much less can he intend that marriage precludes union with Christ. It is, of course, possible that the theological implications here are quite secondary

to Paul's passionate concern to extirpate sexual immorality from
the church.

Corinth is also believed to be the scene where he wrote his
famous indictment of immorality in the pagan world in his Letter
to the Romans, part of which has already been cited. As a Christian Jew, albeit a Roman citizen, who had devoted years to theological study in Jerusalem, it is understandable that Paul should
have laid particular stress upon the sexual sins of the Greco-Roman
world. Both adultery and homosexual practices were punishable
by death for all parties under Mosaic law (Lev. 20:10–13). But
the term used most frequently by Paul is *porneia*, the term for
extramarital intercourse in general, which the Authorized Version
translates as 'fornication,' and the RSV usually translates less precisely as 'immorality,' although 'fornication' is allowed to remain
in the saying of Jesus (Mk. 7:21). In Hebrew thought this was a
much lesser sin than the illegal and thieving union of adultery, and
the term occurs infrequently in the Old Testament although harlotry is often denounced. Yet in Paul, *porneia* normally heads the
list of vices or receives special attention (cf. 1 Thess. 4:3–8; Col.
3:5; Eph. 5:3; Gal. 5:19). Here is a broadening of the concept of
sexual sin.

In Galatians, Paul introduces the vices to be guarded against as
'works of the flesh,' with which he contrasts the 'fruit of the
Spirit,' stating that 'those who belong to Christ Jesus have crucified
the flesh with its passions and desires' (5:16f.). In Colossians he
introduces the list with the phrase, 'put to death . . . what is
earthly in you,' and contrasts this with 'the things which are above'
(3:1f.). In connection with the list in Ephesians, he contrasts dark-
ness and light (5:1f.). *Sarx*, or flesh, however, is the term most
commonly used in the Epistles in connection with sins and lusts,
and is usually contrasted with spirit, though mind is used on one
occasion (Rom. 7:25). This concept of flesh, which is especially
Pauline (cf. John 3:6 for a similar use), needs to be looked at
briefly for its possible bearing on the Pauline attitude toward
marriage and parenthood.

Paul uses *sarx* with a number of different though related connotations. In addition to carnality, it stands for bondage to sin, materiality as opposed to spirituality, the seat of passion and frailty. It leads to sin, corruption, death. It is particularly to be denied because 'the night is far gone, the day is at hand.' Therefore, 'put on the Lord Jesus Christ, and make no provision for the flesh, to gratify its desires' (Rom. 13:11–14). While the Hellenistic and Hebraic elements in this dualism of flesh and spirit can be debated at length, the contribution of Paul's own genius and temperament, and sense of inner tension and conflict in his religious life, should not be overlooked. 'I see in my members another law at war with the law of my mind and making me captive to the law of sin which dwells in my members' (Rom. 7:23).

Now it is clear that 'flesh' means more than the carnal principle, the sum and source of bodily appetites. William Cole in his *Sex in Christianity and Psychoanalysis* conceives of the Pauline dualism of 'flesh' and 'spirit' as a constant choice between an idol and God. The substitute for God may be carnal, but 'it may also be entirely "spiritual" in character, having nothing whatever to do with bodily appetites.' For example, Paul writes to the brethren in Corinth: 'While there is jealousy and strife among you, are you not of the flesh, and behaving like ordinary men?' (1 Cor. 3:3). 'Flesh' means the sinful element in human nature, the personality or ego of natural man, that which leads to 'behaving like ordinary men.' Yet, must it not also be said that Paul's concept of 'flesh' most definitely and particularly includes the fleshly 'passions and desires'? These must be denied, purged, mortified, to lead the life of the spirit. The fact that sexual sins stands in the forefront of the 'works of the flesh' cannot, I think, be attributed wholly to the low sex mores of Hellenistic society. The ascetic element in Paul is real.

It would be wrong to exaggerate this ascetic strain in Paul's make-up. But I think it would be equally incorrect to attribute his belief in celibacy as the 'better' way to the interim elements in his ethic. The eschatological note is particularly strong in his advice on marriage in 1 Corinthians, since at that time he still believed that he would live to witness the Lord's return.

> So, brethren, in whatever state each was called, there let him remain
> with God . . . I think that in view of the impending distress it is
> well for a person to remain as he is. Are you bound to a wife? Do
> not seek to be free. Are you free from a wife? Do not seek marriage.
>
> (1 Cor. 7:24, 26–7)

This is an argument for the status quo, for undertaking no new
obligations, when the divine revolution calls for concentrated alert-
ness, when 'the form of this world is passing away' (7:31). Paul
goes a step further in proposing an abrogation of certain existing
obligations, apparently on the ground that they distract from the
kind of watchful waiting required: 'the appointed time has grown
very short; from now on let those who have wives live as though
they had none' (7:29). Abstention is the rule in regard to anything which constitutes a distraction.

The eschatological motive influences but does not explain Paul's
belief that 'it is well for a man not to touch a woman' and that
'he who refrains from marriage will do better' than he who marries
(7:1,38). The key phrase, it seems to me, is in Paul's concern 'to
secure your undivided devotion to the Lord' (7:35), an obligation
not dependent upon the timetable of salvation. Marriage involves
'worldly troubles' and 'anxieties.' A man's interests are divided. A
widow will be happier if she remains as she is. Consequently Paul
wishes that 'all were as I myself am' — single and self-controlled.

The main requirement for the celibate life, Paul indicates, is
having one's 'desire under control.' It is well for the unmarried and
widows to 'remain single as I do' unless 'they cannot exercise self-
control' (7:37, 8–9). The similarity between this stress on self-
control and the counsel of Greek philosophy is clear. Indeed there
is a striking parallel between a statement of Paul's and one of
Plato's. Paul writes:

> Every athlete exercises self-control in all things. They do it to receive
> a perishable wreath, but we an imperishable.
>
> (1 Cor. 9:25)

Plato, after describing how Iccus, like other athletes, 'spurred on
by ambition and skill, and possessing courage combined with

temperance in his soul' had remained continent throughout his period of training, went on to say:

> Well then, if those men had the fortitude to abstain from that which most men count bliss for the sake of victory in wrestling, running, and the like, shall our boys be unable to hold out in order to win a much nobler victory . . . victory over pleasures — which if they win, they will live a life of bliss . . .
>
> (*Laws*, 840b)

The disciplined life of the spirit, free from the lusts of the flesh and the entanglements of marriage, and the Pauline ideal his letters portray, makes him superficially akin to the Greek philosophical tradition. But the purpose of this disciplined life immediately sets him apart. The purpose is whole-souled, complete, 'undivided devotion to the Lord.' It is Paul's concern that nothing stand in the way of this dedication that constitutes his no to marriage. In some ways it is more complete than that reflected in the Gospels. But, fundamentally, the criteria are the same: the demands of the Kingdom and the service of the Lord come first.

Since the extant letters of Paul, acknowledged by New Testament critics to have been dictated by him, say nothing specific about his attitude toward procreation or family life, we are forced to conjecture from comments on other topics, and from his silences. He makes no reference to the Old Testament injunction to 'increase and multiply' in his discussion of marriage, although he uses the terms in another connection — his appeal for contributions to the fund for the saints in Jerusalem (2 Cor. 9:10). The fruit of which he speaks is fruit of the Spirit. He refers to childbirth, but as a simile for the 'sudden destruction' when 'the day of the Lord' comes (1 Thess. 5:2-3). In fact his references to children are very few, except in expressions of his paternal concern for his children in Christ. He adjures children to obey their 'parents in the Lord,' and fathers to bring up their children in 'the discipline and instruction of the Lord' (Eph. 6:1-4; cf. Col. 3:20-21). He urges the Christian member of a mixed marriage to avoid divorce, to 'consecrate' the spouse, and adds: 'Otherwise, your children would be unclean, but as it is they are holy' (1 Cor. 7:12f.). He refers to

the family in speaking of the Father, from 'whom every family in
heaven and on earth is named' (Eph. 3:15), but by *patria* he evidently was thinking of tribe or nation.

The main composite impression one gains from these fragments
is that Paul must feel that the time is too short to be concerned
about the begetting and rearing of a new generation. He has some
interest in the spiritual status and welfare of existing children, but
the future belongs to a different dimension of reality. Certainly,
the pro-fertility traditions of Israel come to an abrupt halt in the
Epistles. Paul seems considerably less concerned about children
and family life than was Jesus.

The positive statements of Paul with regard to marriage are also
diluted as compared with the sayings of Jesus. The one major exception is a passage in Ephesians, and if the critics should succeed
in detaching that letter from the writings of Paul,[2] the resultant
yes would be faint indeed. In this passage (5:21–33), Paul likens
the love of husband and wife to the relationship of Christ and the
Church. Wives should be subject to their husbands as the Church
is to Christ, and husbands should love their wives as Christ loves
the Church. Indeed husbands should 'love their wives as their own
bodies,' as Christ nourishes and cherishes the Church, for 'we are
members of his body.' Paul then quotes Genesis 2:24, that 'the two
shall become one.' This is a 'great mystery' (*mysterion*) or, as
Moffatt translates it, 'profound symbol,' which reveals, Paul believes, the relationship of Christ and the Church. He closes with
a summary injunction regarding love and respect. This passage
gives noble expression to the 'one flesh' concept of marriage, and
is of a piece with the teaching of Jesus that true marriage is a
union given by God.

Paul was a man of his times in reflecting male dominance as the
proper pattern for the marriage relationship (cf. Col. 3:18–19),
while stressing the husband's responsibilities. Elsewhere, however,
the leaven of the Gospel is at work, producing a greater sense of
equality regarding those for whom Christ died. In Christ, 'there is
neither male nor female; for you are all one . . . and heirs according to promise' (Gal. 3:28–9). There are reciprocal rights to

marriage, and to conjugal relations within marriage, for both husband and wife rule over the body of the other (1 Cor. 7:2-4). The implications of Paul's teaching here and elsewhere are thoroughly monogamous. We see a similar sign of the leaven at work in 1 Peter, where wives are urged to be submissive to their husbands so that some may be won to Christian obedience 'when they see your reverent and chaste behavior'; husbands are urged to 'live considerately with your wives, bestowing honor on the woman as the weaker sex, since you are joint heirs of the grace of life' (3:1-2,7).

The only reference to marriage in Paul's writings that approaches the high view expressed in Ephesians is in 1 Thessalonians, and the significance of this passage hinges on the meaning attached to *skevos* or 'vessel.' Does it mean 'wife' in the way that woman is spoken of as the weaker 'vessel' in 1 Peter, or does it mean a man's own body? The RSV and most modern translations, though not all (e.g. Phillips), accept 'wife' as the right meaning. In this case Paul is saying that it is God's will and a man's sanctification that he abstain from sexual vice, and learn 'how to take a wife for himself in holiness and honor, not in the passion of lust like heathen who do not know God . . . For God has not called us for uncleanness, but in holiness' (1 Thess. 4:3f.). Here Christian matrimony is seen as a holy estate, somewhat as in Ephesians. In fact, it stands between that high plateau and the lower level of the injunction in Hebrews (13:4): 'Let marriage be held in honor among all, and let the marriage bed be undefiled; for God will judge the immoral and adulterous.'

While Paul denied himself the 'right to be accompanied by a wife, as the other apostles and the brothers of the Lord and Cephas,' pommeling and subduing his body, 'lest after preaching to others, I myself should be disqualified' (1 Cor. 9:5, 27), his reference to these eminent benedicts among the saints justifies the conclusion that Paul always regarded marriage as an honorable estate. Yet in his main treatment of the subject, other than the passage in Ephesians, he speaks of it with faint praise — 'it is no sin.' Each man and woman should marry 'because of the tempta-

tion to immorality,' i.e. sexual vice. If the unmarried cannot exercise self-control, they should marry: 'it is better to marry than to
be aflame with passion.' If a man is 'not behaving properly toward
his betrothed, if his passions are strong . . . let them marry —
it is no sin.' A widow likewise is free to remarry and does not
become thereby 'an adulteress' (1 Cor. 7:2ff.; Rom. 7:3). This
view of marriage as a remedy for concupiscence is a far cry from
the 'great mystery' of Ephesians.

At the same time it is a far cry from the passage in Revelation
which speaks of the 144,000 redeemed spotless from the earth as
first fruits of God and the Lamb: 'It is these who have not defiled
themselves with women, for they are chaste,' i.e. virgins (14:3f.).
Paul regards celibacy as the better, the preferable way, but only
for those like himself with a 'special gift' for celibate living, and
only for the purpose of giving 'undivided devotion to the Lord.'
For the generality of mankind, marriage is the proper mode; and
married Christians, Paul indicates, can have their own 'special gifts
from God' (1 Cor. 7:7). Moreover, despite his advice — in view
of the 'impending distress' — to those with wives to 'live as though
they had none,' in the same passage he counsels married couples
— 'by way of concession, not of command' — not to refuse conjugal relations except for a brief season of prayer, 'but then come
together again, lest Satan tempt you though lack of self-control'
(1 Cor. 7:29, 5–6). Marriage is a legitimate remedy for concupiscence, and the remedy should not be neglected unduly.

It is noteworthy that Paul, in the letters generally acknowledged
to be his, says nothing about procreation as an end of marriage.
But some attention needs to be given to the Pastoral Epistles, and
1 Timothy in particular. These letters, though traditionally attributed to Paul except by the Gnostics, have been increasingly
questioned as to Pauline authorship by New Testament scholars,
although a number believe genuine fragments to be imbedded,
particularly in 2 Timothy. The authenticity is questioned on
grounds of style and vocabulary; the degree of concern with ex-
ternals rather than the inner life of the will and spirit; the relatively high level of church organization revealed, as compared

with the primitive church.[3] Certainly in the field under review, the Pastorals do not sound like the rest of Paul. But some verses of 1 Timothy, given the weight of Paul's authority, played an important role in later Christian doctrine.

The author of 1 Timothy is exercised about proper order in the church and the rise of false teachers, who among other things 'forbid marriage' (4:3). A bishop should be the husband of one wife and keep his children 'submissive and respectful in every way.' Likewise deacons should not be married more than once, and should 'manage their children and their households well' (3:2f.). The older widows should be enrolled as such, but not the younger widows, who tend to become wanton and to idle and gossip. 'So I would have younger widows marry, bear children, rule their households, and give the enemy no occasion to revile us' (5:3f.). It seems obvious that we have here quite a different temper, outlook, and situation from what we find in the major Epistles.

The key text historically in 1 Timothy occurs in a discussion of the place of women in the church. They should dress modestly, not teach or have authority over men, but keep silent; for Eve, not Adam, was deceived and became a transgressor. Then comes the verse: 'Yet woman will be saved through bearing children, if she continues in faith and love and holiness, with modesty' (2:15). Not only does she have to lead an exemplary life in other respects, but she also has to bear children in order to be saved. This seems a bit hard on the feminine heir according to promise. Did Paul mean that only the male is 'justified by faith' (Rom. 3:28)? Of course not.

Spiritual salvation through childbearing is not only the traditional interpretation of this verse, but also the predominant one today, appearing as cited above, in the RSV. Since the term for childbearing can also be translated 'by the birth of the child,' some critics have argued a reference here to the Incarnation. Some of the modern translators, however, give quite a different meaning to the phrase. Weymouth, Moffatt, and J. B. Phillips all translate this as meaning to come 'safely through childbirth.' In a letter to the author, Prebendary Phillips points out that the Greek word *sozo* basically means 'save, keep sound.' He cites various New Testament examples indicating that 'the word *sozo* does not necessarily carry any theological flavor.' He adds:

> The differences in sense are most clearly brought out in the case of the Philippian jailor. When he cried, 'What must I do to be saved?' I myself believe that he was mainly concerned with his own physical security, seeing that he had failed as a Roman officer and was likely to be executed. But Paul, in his reply, points to a higher security in his famous words, 'Believe in the Lord Jesus Christ and thou shalt be saved . . .'

To the modern mind, at least, 'safe childbearing' makes more sense theologically than 'salvation through childbirth.' The immediately preceding reference to Eve suggests the penalty of increased pain in childbirth imposed upon her (Gen. 3:16). Perhaps the author meant that, despite this penalty, a woman of Christian virtue would come safely through childbearing. The weight of scholarship, however, seems to be against this sensible and charitable interpretation. The construction of the phrase as well as the early traditions appear to stand opposed to it. *Sozo* in a spiritual sense is used in the preceding chapter (1:15). And it must be admitted that a man with as low an opinion of women as the author of 1 Timothy might well have argued a double standard of salvation.

In the post-Apostolic age this awkward doctrine became part of the Christian yes to procreation. There is so little in either the Gospels or Epistles which bears directly on the question of parenthood that this poor creature had to bear a good deal of the New Testament part of the load. The fact is that the main figures of the New Testament and their audience were so absorbed with the imminent drama of the Day of the Lord — the supernatural transformation of life — that the question of the natural continuation of life did not seem of moment. This was part of the old world breaking up like the ice on a river in springtime. Neither Jesus nor Paul, so far as we know or can judge from their teachings, had a negative attitude toward human parenthood. It was simply that they were concentrating on a different dimension of reality.

Yet in their insights regarding the fundamentals of marriage, in their differing affirmations, and in their warnings on the limits imposed by higher values, Jesus and his great disciple provided permanent guidelines for Christian thought on the family. Some of these were grasped by the early church, some were distorted or ignored, and some have not yet been understood, for we can be confident, as John Robinson put it, that 'the Lord God has more truth and light yet to break forth out of his Holy Word,' in this aspect of life as in others. It is from this perspective, as well as from the need for a base from which to approach subsequent Christian teaching, that this brief summary has been attempted.

Since that teaching has so often hinged on Scriptural references, attention has focused on the specific texts that have been used in the past or that seem relevant. There is, however, some danger as well as merit in such an approach, for 'the written code kills, but the Spirit gives life' (2 Cor. 3:6). It is possible to become so immersed in the details of the Scriptural records that we miss the larger import of the Word spoken through these records. To be on guard against a Christian legalism is one of the responsibilities of Christian freedom. 'For freedom Christ has set us free; stand fast therefore, and do not submit again to a yoke of slavery' (Gal. 5:1).

X

The Early Church and Parenthood

შ When we speak of the Gospels and Epistles we are already in the midst of the early church. Our earliest Christian writings, the letters of Paul, were written after the middle of the first century to the churches of the Mediterranean basin which he had helped to found. Yet he was not the first missionary; there was already a group of followers of the Nazarene in Antioch when he started on his mission, and there apparently they were first called *Christiani*. The Synoptic Gospels were written somewhat later, setting down the sayings and traditions of Jesus for the second generation Christians, lest the memories and oral traditions of the first generation become dim. The Gospel of John, most critics hold, was written toward the end of the first century, and particularly reflects a living faith about Jesus. Yet this is true of all the New Testament records. They were transmitted by the early church and addressed to the early church.

Our concern here is about the other writings of the first three centuries of Christian life and thought, and their bearing on the Christian approach to parenthood. Also, the Eastern Orthodox Church gives particular weight to the early patristic tradition and the succeeding ecumenical councils. For the writings of the early fathers prior to the Council of Nicaea in A.D. 325, major reliance is placed on the *Ante-Nicene Fathers* (A.N.F.), the American reprint of the Edinburgh edition of 1867.[1] In considering the extant records of early Christianity, it is well to remember that part of the grain has gone with much of the chaff in the winnowing of time and circumstance.

As we review briefly the early patristic writings which bear on the question of parenthood, it is important to recall that a persistent slander against the Christian communities was that they engaged in secret sexual orgies. Tacitus, writing after the turn of the century about Nero's persecution of the Christians in A.D. 64, spoke of the abominable rites practiced in secret. Cannibalism and sexual promiscuity were the popular notions derived from the celebration of the Eucharist and the *agapae* or love feasts, the spiritualized 'church suppers' of the primitive church. The myths about the secret rites persisted. Athenagoras in his *Plea for the Christians,* written to the Emperors Aurelius and Commodius about A.D. 177, says that three things are alleged against Christians: atheism, Thyestean feasts, Oedipean intercourse. Oedipus, who had unwittingly married his mother, was a symbol of illicit and indiscriminate sex relations. To see the ante-Nicene writings in proper perspective, it is important to understand the widespread pagan prejudice concerning sexual vice among Christians. The charge, which seems incongruous coming from the world described by Paul in Romans 1:24f., nevertheless influenced patristic comments on the man-woman relationship, no doubt giving them a more ethereal character by way of reaction than the life of the Christian community exemplified.

In the second century, a major internal challenge arose in the form of Gnostic syncretism and dualism, a reinterpretation of the Good News in terms of a sharp dichotomy between the evil world of the flesh and the higher world of the spirit.[2] As we gather from Christian critiques of the Gnostic heresy, this dualism led to a depreciation of marriage, and particularly procreation, as the imprisonment of souls in evil flesh. It also led, it was charged, to a good deal of sexual license among those who through the necessary knowledge were freed from the world of the flesh. How much the beginnings of this heresy challenged Christian thought in the first century is hard to say. No doubt there were, in any case, in the Christian community tendencies to an otherworldliness which meant neglect of duties in the world, and which later gave Gnosticism its opportunity.

Thus in the earliest patristic writings there is an emphasis on the goodness of marriage and the duty of procreation. The *First Epistle of Clement*, written during the latter part of the first century, adjures the faithful that while we are justified by faith, shall we then 'become slothful in well-doing'? The Creator rejoices in his works: He made man and said 'Increase and multiply.' Let us, says Clement, 'without delay accede to His will, and let us work the work of righteousness with our whole strength.' As for the celibates, 'Let him that is pure in the flesh not grow proud of it, and boast, knowing that it was another who bestowed on him the gift of continence.'

Ignatius, a 1st-century bishop of Antioch, was also concerned about procreation, but equally fearful of lust. The celibate are to be subject to Christ in purity, 'not for the reproach of wedlock, but for the better contemplation of the law.' He names a number of Biblical characters believed to have been celibate, and immediately adds that he is not casting blame on the other blessed saints, the patriarchs, prophets, Peter, Paul, and other apostles who were (he thought) married men. 'For they entered into these marriages not for the sake of appetite, but out of regard for the propagation of mankind.' Justin Martyr expresses much the same view: 'But whether we marry, it is only that we may bring up children; or whether we decline marriage, we live continently.' As the Christian community adjusted itself to a longer perspective on the coming of the Day of the Lord, we find a combination of the Pauline preference for celibacy with the older Hebraic emphasis on procreation.

The only references to family limitation which I find in the early documents are to abortion and infanticide, and these are naturally condemned. Christians, says the *Epistle to Diognetus*, 'marry, as do all; they beget children; but they do not destroy their offspring' — literally, 'cast away foetuses.' The 2nd-century *Revelation of Peter* pictures a special section of hell for 'the accursed who conceived and caused abortion.' Justin Martyr inveighs against the wicked exposure of newly-born children in the pagan

world, because of the injury intended, and more particularly, because most of those exposed 'are brought up to prostitution.'

Paul's teaching about marriage as a remedy for concupiscence is
much diluted in these early writings. Irenaeus refers to Paul's
'precepts in consideration of human infirmity' as helping to explain God's indulgences to His people in the Old Testament. And
the Pastor of Hermas advises: 'If you always remember your own
wife, you will never sin.' But the idea that Christian marriage
purges the lusts of the flesh is more typical. Men and women
should form their union with the approval of the bishop, writes
Ignatius, 'that their marriage may be according to the Lord, and
not after their own lust.'

Most of the descriptions of Christian marriage in the early
patristic literature are designed to refute the persistent allegations
regarding sexual vice, and to distinguish true Christian conduct
from the licentiousness of the heretics. Whether Marcion and his
ilk practice promiscuous intercourse, we know not, writes Justin
Martyr, but it is no mystery of ours. He cites the application of a
Christian in Alexandria for permission to be made a eunuch. In
similar vein, Irenaeus describes the 'mystery of conjunction' practiced by the Valentinians who have the temerity to 'run us down
who from the fear of God guard against sinning even in thought
or word.' Aristides in his *Apology* contrasts the debased morals of
the heathen with those of the Christians whose women 'are pure
as virgins, and their daughters are modest; and their men keep
themselves from every unlawful union and from all uncleanness.'
Tatian, who later felt all sex to be so impure that he joined the
ascetic Encratites, says Christian women are superior to 'lewd,
lovesick' Sappho, for 'all our women are chaste, and the maidens
at their distaffs sing of divine things.' With Christians 'temperance
dwells, self-restraint is practiced, monogamy is observed, chastity
is guarded,' writes Theophilus. And Athenagoras asserts that 'the
procreation of children is the measure of our indulgence in appetite.'

No doubt these claims to virtue made in the heat of apologetic
or antiheretical argument need to be discounted somewhat in the
interest of realism. Yet there is supporting testimony from a dis-

tinguished pagan, the Greek physician Galen, who lived in the
second half of the 2nd century. Galen comments on how the
Christians 'through a certain kind of modesty . . . abstain from
sexual pleasure.' He goes on:

> Indeed there are amongst them men and women who have never
> during their whole lives known the carnal act; nay, there are some
> who, in ruling and mastering their impulses and in their zeal for
> virtue, are not a whit behind real philosophers.[3]

If Christian celibates impressed Galen in this way, it is reasonable
to suppose that many Christian couples were also impressive in
giving a comparatively ascetic character to the married state, in
the belief that sexual abstinence reduced the entanglements of the
flesh. Such abstinence may even have played some role in family
limitation, but if so, there is no reflection of it in the early patristic
writings. It would be interesting to know how the early Christian
family compared in size with its pagan counterpart.

In regard to Christian doctrine bearing on parenthood in the
second half of the ante-Nicene period, the names of five men stand
out: Clement of Alexandria and his pupil and successor Origen,
who gave intellectual luster to the Eastern church; and in the
West, Hippolytus, a Greek disciple of Irenaeus who held a
bishopric near Rome, and two strong bishops of Carthage, Tertullian and his successor Cyprian. The century from A.D. 150 to 250,
when these men lived and taught, represented an important
flowering of Christian thought in the early church. While it was
their theological work that primarily commanded attention, our
concern is focused on the ethical teaching of these men. From this
perspective, Clement, the earliest, is probably the most important
because of the attention he devoted to ethics in general and to sex
morality in particular.

Upon his conversion, Clement brought to the service of Christian faith many of the treasures of Greek philosophy in which he
was trained, including its concern for the good life, the life of
moderation. He shared the Greek distrust of passions which disturb the reason and break down a man's control over himself.

'God's greatest gift is self-restraint.' On the other hand, those 'who run down created existence and vilify the body are wrong' — the body and soul are diverse, not opposite. Not mortification of the flesh, but discipline, self-control, is the road to Christian virtue. Clement is a supporter of the temperate life against the extremes of license and asceticism.

Thus, against the heretics who condemn marriage and the creation of a family, and talk about the uncleanness of conjugal relations, Clement in Book III of his *Stromata* argues the case for Christian matrimony. Will such people reject even the apostles? 'Peter and Philip, indeed, had children . . . And Paul does not demur, in a certain Epistle [the reference is to 1 Cor. 9:5], to mention his own wife, whom he did not take about with him, in order to expedite his ministry the better.' We should admire monogamy, that is a single marriage, as honorable. As to second marriages there is Paul's advice, 'if you burn, join in marriage.' The idea that the children of the Kingdom do not marry refers to the state after the resurrection. The reference in Leviticus 15:18 to intercourse constituting a ritual pollution he interprets as a condemnation of polygamy. He cites the teachings of Jesus and Paul in favor of marriage, and the verses in 1 Timothy about childbearing. There is a telling application to the Christian family of the saying of Jesus that 'where two or three are gathered in my name, there am I in the midst of them' (Matt. 18:20).

Clement not only defends marriage and procreation against the Gnostics (a term he refuses to allow them to appropriate) but at another point in the *Stromata* defends marriage against the claims of celibacy within the fold. The soul needs 'varied preparatory exercise,' a wide experience. Also, 'it is not he who merely controls his passions that is called a continent man, but he who has also achieved the mastery over good things.' So the celibate, considerably free from temptation, is 'not really shown to be a man in the choice of a single life.' Rather it is the man, 'disciplined by marriage, procreation of children, and care for the house,' who is able to withstand the related temptations. The benedict may be inferior to the celibate 'as far as his own personal salvation is concerned,

but . . . superior in the conduct of life.' The discipline of marriage, according to Clement, lies in subordinating lust to Christian
continence, through self-control and prayer. Freedom from the
passions rather than self-indulgence is the objective.

In another chapter on marriage Clement summarizes Greek
philosophical thought on the subject, starting with the legal definition — 'for the procreation of legitimate offspring.' Some of the
philosophers take a low view of marriage and become enslaved in
pleasures. But those who approve marriage constantly proclaim
the command, 'Increase and replenish'; indeed, legislators fine the
childless since such conduct makes for a scarcity of men and the
dissolution of states. Marriage is also important for the care it
provides in sickness and old age. The marriage of others may be
'an agreement for indulgence.' But that of philosophers takes advantage of the married state 'for help in the whole life, and for
the best self-restraint.' While this chapter impresses me as more
descriptive than normative in design, it seems generally congruent
with the views of Clement expressed elsewhere.

In a chapter on procreation in *The Instructor*, Clement condemns coitus other than for the procreation of children as doing
an injury to nature. Matrimony, he says, 'is the appetite for the
procreation of children, not the inordinate excretion of semen,
which is both contrary to laws and alien to reason.' And again,
'he violates his marriage adulterously who uses it in a meretricious
way.' In addition to this general condemnation of the nonprocreative use of sex, Clement condemns the use of fatal drugs which
destroy at the same time 'the fetus and all humanity.' In regard
to the crime of infanticide, he says that 'the man who did not
desire to beget children had no right to marry at first.' He defends
the Pythagoreans, who counsel abstinence, because they abstain
after producing a family. Pythagoras, in fact, he says, banned the
eating of beans, because Theophrastus said they induced sterility
in women. Clement defends marriage not as Paul's remedy for
concupiscence, but as a means to parenthood and a challenge to
self-control.

Origen, the pupil and successor of Clement in Alexandria, a more systematic theologian than his teacher, has much less to say on marital questions. His discussion in *De Principiis*, for example, on the will of the soul being intermediate between flesh and spirit — so that if it yields to pleasures of the flesh, men become carnal, while if it unites with the spirit, they become men of the Spirit — suggests his temper as well as the abstract character of his thought. The main emphasis is on Christian purity. In *Contra Celsus*, Origen again defends the Christians against charges of sexual vice, stating that converts, far from gratifying shameless passion, often keep themselves 'in act and in thought in a state of virgin purity.' He contrasts the action of an Athenian hierophant who took hemlock to check his passions with Christians for whom the Word is able to drive out all evil desires. Origen, incidentally, according to one tradition, had had himself emasculated for the same purpose.

In his *Commentary on Matthew*, Origen regards Paul's support for marriage and for reciprocal marital debts (1 Cor. 7:2f.) as legal accommodation or concession to human weakness. He thinks that a man who makes his wife an adulteress by failing to satisfy her desires may be more culpable than one who divorces his wife for crimes. His conclusion, however, is that although marriage is expedient, celibacy is more expedient. As for celibacy being a gift, he argues that any Christian can 'ask and it shall be given you' (Matt. 7:7). The whole emphasis of Origen's comments is on the ascetic, with marriage very much in the shadows.

Hippolytus, the most eminent theologian in 3rd-century Rome, may also have been a pupil of Clement's. His main work for our purpose is the *Refutation of All Heresies*. In his discussion of Marcion's heresy, he charges him with following the doctrines of Empedocles, who forbade sexual intercourse for his disciples. He asks if Marcion thinks he can escape detection as a follower of Empedocles, when he forbids marriage, the procreation of children, and dissolves marriages 'cemented by the Deity.' Likewise, he describes the Encratites, who forbid marriage and devote themselves to habits of asceticism, as Cynics rather than Christians. His most important passage in connection with our topic is a protest against moral laxity in the diocese of Callistus, Bishop of Rome:

> He permitted females, if they were unwedded, and burned with passion at an age at all events unbecoming, or if they were not disposed to overturn their own dignity through a legal marriage, that they might have whomsoever they would choose as a bedfellow, whether a slave or free, and that a woman, though not legally married, might consider such a companion as a husband. Whence women, reputed believers, began to resort to drugs for producing sterility, and to gird themselves round, so to expel what was being conceived on account of their not wishing to have a child either by a slave or by any paltry fellow, for the sake of their family and excessive wealth. Behold, into how great impiety that lawless one has proceeded, by inculcating adultery and murder at the same time.

Roland Bainton, in his book *What Christianity Says about Sex, Love and Marriage,* says that in the Roman diocese at that time 'women of senatorial rank in the congregations outnumbered the men of equal status.' The children of unequal unions would acquire the status of the father, thereby jeopardizing the wife's inheritance. The dilemma presumably was to sanction concubinage 'within the Lord,' or mixed marriages. It should be added in fairness to Callistus, that while Hippolytus charges him with responsibility for the birth control measures attempted, he does not say that the Bishop of Rome actually approved such measures. It seems a bit ironic, however, that a bishop of Rome, especially the one first called *papa,* should be charged with laxity in regard to birth control.

The question remains whether this is the first example of Christian opposition to contraception. The transposition of a word in the Greek text gives a different meaning to the key sentence. The alternative translation, as stated in an A.N.F. footnote, *ad loc.,* reads as follows: 'women began to venture to bandage themselves with ligaments, and to deal with drugs in order to destroy what was conceived.' In other words, abortion was the purpose in either case. This interpretation would fit more harmoniously the subsequent reference to 'murder.' Also, I gather that an effective abortifacient drug would more likely have been known than an effective sterilizing drug, which is the subject of research by modern medicine. Of course, the text does not indicate that the drug was effective.

In his *Medical History of Contraception*, Norman Himes indicates that among the many superstitions and ineffective methods to prevent conception referred to in ancient literature there were some which may have been fairly effective. Aristotle in his *Historia Animalium* wrote of two oils which Dr. Himes indicates might have been of some effect as mechanical contraceptives.[4] Soranos of Ephesus, 'the greatest gynaecologist of antiquity,' who lived about a century before Hippolytus, listed a number of chemical and mechanical contraceptives which, for relative effectiveness and freedom from admixture with ineffective nostrums, marked a high point in contraceptive knowledge until modern times. Dr. Himes doubts, however, that such expert knowledge was widely shared or easily distinguished from notions without a scientific basis. From the variety of prescriptions mentioned for contraception, sterilization, and abortion, it seems clear that many were tried. Yet I do not find an unequivocal reference to contraceptives in early Christian literature before Jerome.

To complete this brief review of the ante-Nicene fathers, we have still to consider the teachings of two theologians of the Western church, Tertullian and Cyprian of Carthage in the first half of the third century. Tertullian, the son of a centurion, evidently inherited his father's martial spirit, to judge from his vigorous polemics. He was at heart a lawyer, arguing each case as strongly as he could, even though the arguments when taken together contain contradictions. In his later years he embraced the ascetic and premillenarian views of the Montanist sect. Yet the impact of his rigorous and legalistic views on the Western church was important. To judge from his open letters to his wife, advising against remarriage after his death, one would surmise his marriage to have been a curious affair. His wife, however, died before he did.

Tertullian in his arguments against Marcion undertakes to defend Christian marriage. The Creator blessed matrimony as 'an honorable estate, for the increase of the human race.' It is not to be refused because 'when enjoyed without moderation, it is fanned into a voluptuous flame.' Paul, unlike Marcion, at least permits marriage and the enjoyment of it. God in His goodness provided a helpmeet for man, saying it was not good that he be alone. In the treatise *To His Wife*, Tertullian moves at a lower level, arguing that fleshly and worldly concupiscence make marriage necessary for ordinary mortals, and that both should be appeased by one marriage. Monogamy is also indicated by the fact that God used only one of Adam's ribs.

The main villain of the piece is lust. 'It is lust, not natural usage, which has brought shame on the intercourse of the sexes,' he says in his *Treatise on the Soul*, making it clear that the 'normal state' is at least primarily related to procreation. Marcion, by banning marriage, destroys the basis for sanctity, for 'all proof of abstinence is lost when excess is impossible — we do not reject marriage, but simply refrain from it.' Paul taught temporary abstinence that we might learn the profitable character of permanent abstinence; while Paul permitted marriage because of insidious temptations, 'how far better is it neither to marry nor to burn.' It is vain to look for consistency in Tertullian's arguments.

This is particularly true in regard to his views on procreation. At one point, he defines marital union as 'the seminary of the human race, and devised for the replenishment of the earth and the furnishing of the world.' Again he suggests that Marcion may be 'afraid of a redundant population.' But he himself argues that the command to continence (1 Cor. 7:29) has 'abolished that "Grow and multiply," ' which was an indulgence granted 'until the world should be replenished.' [5] Now that indulgence has run its course and we live 'at the extreme boundaries of the times.' In view of the impending distresses in this most wicked world, should we encumber ourselves with the 'bitter, bitter pleasure of children'? Should we seek such burdens 'which are avoided even by the majority of Gentiles'?

In his *Exhortation to Chastity*, Tertullian points out that even if a man marries a barren woman he cannot count on her staying barren, and dissolving 'the conception by aid of drugs' is no more lawful than hurting a child already born. If a man needs a companion he should take a spiritual wife, a widow 'sealed with age,' without worry about posterity — for whom there is no tomorrow. In this way a man can be undistracted by cares and constant in martyrdom.

Cyprian, the student and successor of Tertullian, is less grim in his asceticism but he leaves hardly more room for marriage and family life. Most of his praise is reserved for celibacy, 'the flower of the ecclesiastical seed.' In his treatise *On the Dress of Virgins*, Cyprian explains that 'the first decree commanded to increase and multiply; the second enjoined continency.' The first was made when the world was rough and void, but now 'the world is filled and the earth supplied.' There is still freedom of choice but the Lord exhorts to continence. A great reward awaits those who so choose. Moreover, a virgin need fear neither childbirth nor a lording husband. Another treatise on chastity, attributed to Cyprian but deemed unworthy of him by Erasmus and others, carries this argument a step further: 'if the apostle declares the Church to be the spouse of Christ, I beseech you consider what chastity is required, where the Church is given in marriage as a betrothed virgin.'

Part of such exhortation undoubtedly was motivated by the desire to secure more faithful observance of celibate vows, in view of the less rigorous attitude toward sexual sins then being taken in the Western church. One of the bones of contention between Tertullian and Callistus came from the latter's willingness to forgive sins of fornication and adultery to those who had been baptized. This was also a factor in the revolt of protest led by Hippolytus, so that he is sometimes called an 'antipope' though he later was regarded as a saint. To quote Bainton:

> Whereas in A.D. 220 Tertullian could say, 'Shall we forgive adulterers when we do not forgive apostates?' in 250 Cyprian could ask, 'Shall we refuse to forgive apostates since we do forgive adulterers?' This

relaxation on the part of the church is in marked contrast with the behavior of the state, for this is the very period in which adultery was visited with the severest penalty.

An example is found in Cyprian's own writings, in which he approved the excommunication of certain celibates of diverse sex who had been caught bundling and charged with more — which, if proved or persisted in, would require confession and probation before restoration to the church.

The situation and perspective of the early church was so different from that of the medieval and modern church that it is hard for us to make our imaginations sufficiently sensitive to understand the concerns about marriage and family life which stirred the early fathers. When Tertullian and Cyprian, for example, speak of the world being 'filled up,' they are in the first instance uttering not a demographic judgment, but a conclusion derived from the conviction that they were living, as Tertullian put it, at 'the extreme boundary of the times.' The sword of persecution which hung over their heads was a sign of the 'impending distress,' heralding the long-awaited Day of the Lord. I find a small and insubstantial clue to the different outlook of the early fathers in the Biblical texts they cited increasingly, as the stress on the inspiration of the Spirit in the primitive church gave way to greater reliance on the guidance of Scripture. If we look at the incomplete Biblical indices given in the *Ante-Nicene Fathers,* in relation to some of the passages which have played a role in subsequent Christian thought and debate, a rough tabulation shows the following:

> In regard to marriage there are 47 references to the 'one flesh' passages (Gen. 2:24; Eph. 5:31–3; Matt. 19:6; Mk. 10:8–9); 18 to Paul's remedy for concupiscence (1 Cor. 7:2, 9, 36); 3 to Gen. 2:18, on man's need for companionship; and 3 to Heb. 13:4, on keeping marriage honorable.

> There are about the same number of references oriented to celibacy and continued widowhood: 26 to 1 Cor. 7:1, 7–8, 37–8, expressing Paul's preference for the single life; 23 to Matt. 19:12, regarding 'eunuchs for the Kingdom'; 13 to 1 Cor. 7:39–40, advising against remarriage; and 10 to 1 Cor. 7:32–5, on the divided interests and anxieties of marriage.

There are 23 references to Gen. 1:28, the 'increase and multiply' verse; but only 3 citations of 1 Tim. 5:14, 1 Tim. 2:15, and John 16:21, which refer to childbearing. There are 5 references to 1 Cor. 7:3–4 on mutual conjugal rights. On the other hand, there are 20 references to 1 Cor. 7:5–6, regarding abstinence for a season of prayer; and 14 to 1 Cor. 7:29, enjoining the married to live as if they were not. I find no reference to Gen. 38:9, concerning the sin of Onan.

In attempting to summarize the teaching on parenthood in the early patristic writings, one notes a certain ambivalence in attitude, which may be described in terms of the tension between Paul's injunction to continence in a time 'grown very short' and the defense of the essential goodness of procreation against heretical attack. Against Marcion and other Gnostics who held procreation to be the imprisonment of souls in evil flesh, the fathers championed the basic goodness of the procreative process within God's creative purpose. There are also corollary affirmations of actual parenthood, particularly in the earlier writings. Yet the ascetic and eschatological strain is also present and growing, and not merely in Tertullian, although he is the strongest exponent. The special demands for Christian obedience and virtue in face of the impending distress and the requirements for salvation tend to convert the idea of responsible parenthood into responsible nonparenthood. This is reflected in the increasing stress not only on celibacy as the higher way, but also on abstinence and freedom from the distractions of family obligations within marriage.

Sexual abstinence is the one method of family limitation that is clearly approved. The two pagan methods apparently most common, abortion and infanticide (Tertullian speaks of the Gentiles being decimated by abortion), are strongly condemned. There is the implied approval in Clement of Alexandria of the Pythagorean opposition to the bean as an alleged sterilizing agent, and the possible condemnation by Hippolytus of sterilizing drugs. Even when we discount the descriptions of conjugal relations being limited to the requirements of procreation, and take into account the support for Paul's remedy for concupiscence, it seems to me

fair to describe the early patristic attitude as one generally opposed
to the nonprocreative uses of sex.

Part of this attitude, though not all of it, may well have sprung
from the belief common in the ancient world that the semen was
seed in the full sense, rather than a factor in fertilization. This
point has been stressed by Sherwin Bailey, who says that the male
contribution was regarded as having the properties of the fertilized
ovum, and cites a term used by Clement of Alexandria, *met' oligon
anthrōpon*, something almost, or about to become, man.[6] The
point, it seems to me, merits attention.

In his work, *On the Generation of Animals*, Aristotle says that
Anaxagoras and others held that the 'germ . . . comes from the
male while the female only provides the place in which it develops.' Aristotle, however, has a more sophisticated view. He
calls the semen the 'foundation of the embryo,' the 'form and the
efficient cause,' the female providing the 'material for the semen
to work upon.' He also holds, however, that 'semen both has soul,
and is soul potentially.' From the male, in and with the semen,
comes 'the spiritus conveying the principle of soul,' so that 'while
the body is from the female, it is the soul that is from the male.'

In varying degrees the patristic references broadly reflect the
kind of approach to the nature of semen expressed by Anaxagoras.
Clement has been mentioned, and Tertullian in his treatise *On
the Soul* writes of the soul-producing seed accompanying the body-
producing seed: 'in the seed lies the promise and earnest of the
crop.' He distinguishes three stages of the genetic process, however: the sowing, the forming, and the completing. The 'embryo
. . . becomes a human being in the womb from the moment that
its form is completed.' But abortion is punished at an earlier stage
'inasmuch as there exists already the rudiment of a human being'
(*causa hominis*) which has the 'condition of life and death.' He
thinks the soul is born the seventh month, to correspond to the
seven days of creation.

In the *Excerpts of Theodotus*, once appended to the writings of
Clement of Alexandria, there is another theory: that the soul is
introduced into the womb by an angel, where it unites with the

seed in the process of formation. In the barren woman, the angel fails to act. The man, in ancient times, was never responsible. In the *Recognitions of Clement*, not identified but quoted by Origen, there is a clearer reflection of the concept of Anaxagoras: 'the body . . . takes its beginning from the seed of man . . . and conveyed into the womb as into a soil, to which it adheres . . . is formed into the likeness of him who injected the seed.' The author speaks of the 'germ' but also of the 'foetus being placed.'

It would be wrong to press this point too far. There is also in the patristic view the attitude that any undue conjugal relations are works of the flesh. But it is not unimportant to note that a factor in the patristic opposition to the nonprocreative uses of sex was an erroneous view of the nature of the procreative process.

XI

Eastern Orthodoxy and Parenthood

꿍 A more detailed review of patristic teachings in the first three centuries of the Christian era has been attempted than will be possible for subsequent periods of Christian history. A particular reason for this focus of attention, as indicated at the outset of the last chapter, is that the early fathers and martyrs are given especially respectful attention among the Eastern Orthodox churches, and help to shape their continuing tradition. Since so much of this tradition stems from the early centuries of Christian life and thought, it is convenient to present at this point some notes on the Eastern Orthodox approach to parenthood.

No church is more aware of its history than our Orthodox brethren, who represent an unbroken line of Christian life and worship from the little groups of 1st-century *Christiani* in Antioch, Jerusalem, and other centers of the eastern Mediterranean. When Byzantium, renamed Constantinople, became capital of the empire early in the 4th century, its patriarch became recognized as *primus inter pares* in relation to the other patriarchs, a recognition which the Ecumenical Patriarch still holds among the Greek Orthodox churches. From the Eastern church, Orthodoxy moved into the Slavic world to the north, where it remains the predominant religion. Mention should also be made of the Syrian Orthodox Church in South India and elsewhere, and the Coptic Church in North Africa — ancient, kindred, though independent churches. Indeed, a feature of the Orthodox churches is the degree of administrative freedom they enjoy, while linked by common traditions and liturgy.

The schism between the Eastern and Western church, which came to a head in A.D. 1054, had behind it more than the doctrinal issues which provided the occasion for the separation. There are differences in temper and outlook on life and faith which go rather deep. Arthur McGiffert links the roots of this divergence with two of the early fathers: Clement of Alexandria, the philosopher, and Tertullian, the 'lawyer.' The suggestion seems to me particularly apt for our subject, in that Clement appears to have had a particularly strong influence on Orthodox thinking in regard to marriage and family life. McGiffert's point is that 'in the west from Tertullian's day on dogma was a law; in the east it became in course of time . . . a holy symbol.' The mystical element in Eastern Orthodoxy, as compared with the more legalistic approach of Roman Catholicism, is certainly one of the important distinctions.

This has bearing on our concern because there is a much smaller body of detailed and definitive doctrine among the Eastern Orthodox churches than is the case in the Roman Church. The binding teachings for the Orthodox are found in Holy Scripture, which comprises the Septuagint version of the Old Testament and Greek version of the New Testament, and in Sacred Tradition. The latter is defined in this way in the *Year Book* of the Greek Archdiocese of North and South America:

> Sacred Tradition includes (a) the oral teachings of Christ to the apostles and their oral teachings to their disciples before any of the New Testament was written down, and (b) the decrees of the Seven Ecumenical Councils, gatherings at which both the Church of the East and the Church of the West were represented and which served to define and interpret Christian teachings.

The Old and New Testament teachings which bear on the question of parenthood have been reviewed. It is clear, as Orthodox leaders themselves have stated, that the New Testament, while providing the spiritual and moral framework of a doctrine on parenthood, does not specifically state such a doctrine. The patristic references to 'increase and multiply' (Gen. 1:28) have a strong influence on Orthodox thought, but are regarded as less central than the *mysterion* in Ephesians. Nor did the ecumenical councils deal with such a doctrine. The Council of Nicaea in A.D. 325 pronounced against castration, which is linked with the broader question of bodily mutilation and, by interpretation in the Roman Church, was made the basis of condemning permanent or temporary sterilization. There are specific condemnations of abortion or the use of any means willfully to cause a miscarriage: in Canon 21 of the Council of Ancyra, A.D. 358; in Canon 91 of the Quinisext Council of A.D. 691, which supplemented the Fifth and Sixth Ecumenical Councils in Constantinople; and in the Second Canon of St. Basil, who formulated the rule for the monks of the Eastern Orthodox churches. These clear condemnations of abortion, however, do not add up to a doctrine on responsible parenthood.

The early fathers are especially revered by the Orthodox, both as bearers of the oral tradition and as interpreters of Holy Scripture in the light of this tradition. The patristic writings have great influence and help to shape the ethos of Eastern Orthodoxy. Nevertheless, as we have seen, the ante-Nicene fathers did not set forth a clear or consistent position on the question of parenthood. So the point remains — and an important point it is — that significant aspects of the question of parenthood and the related question of family planning are not covered by official doctrine. These matters remain the subject of continuing study, debate, and interpretation. The Sacred Tradition, in this respect at least, is a living tradition, subject to further clarification under the instruction of the Spirit.

To see this process in perspective, it is needful to understand the rudiments of Eastern Orthodox ecclesiastical organization. Although they may not be married after they have been ordained, priests and deacons may be married or unmarried when ordained. Parish priests, constituting the large majority of the clergy, are married. Only celibate priests, however, are candidates for elevation to bishop, so that the higher members of the hierarchy come from the monastic order. The laity also play an important role,

providing scholars and teachers for the church. Under this ecclesiastical set-up, it is understandable that the more rigorous point
of view may be more often heard, even though it is not fully
representative of Orthodox opinion. If the positions advanced are
seen as part of a continuing debate to clarify the Orthodox position, I think we are on the right track.

There is, however, an established starting point in the conviction
that the primary purpose of marriage is the sanctification of the
couple. Sanctification, rather than procreation, is the primary end
of marriage. This view is based on Ephesians 5:22f., which describes the 'two become one' as a great *mysterion*, illuminating the
relationship between Christ and the Church. This passage plays
an important part in the Orthodox marriage service, and provides
a common point of departure for discussion on other issues related
to marriage and parenthood.

To one not immersed in the Eastern tradition, the variety of
views and practical applications seems a bit bewildering. A memorandum from a lawyer in Athens indicates that there is no ban
on the sale of contraceptives in Greece. An independent lay religious journal in Athens, *Orthodox Thought*, printed a full and
fair summary of an article of mine on 'The Population Problem
and Family Planning,' and concluded with this sentence: 'The
time for considering family planning has come.' The Brotherhood
of Zoë, the vigorous lay movement for the renewal of the church
in Greece, I am told, supports periodic continence as a means to
family limitation.

On the other hand, conversations with members of the monastic
clergy indicate a much more rigorous point of view. Procreation is
elevated as a major purpose of marriage, and patristic citations are
adduced in opposition to any nonprocreative use of conjugal relations. In keeping with these citations, complete abstinence alone
is regarded as permissible as a method of family planning. Stress
is placed on the providence of God in regard to the care and
nurture of children.

In an oral exposition of the more rigorous point of view, an
Orthodox friend stated that while the New Testament was written

for other purposes than defining the doctrine of parenthood, there were some relevant indications on this theme. He cited the term *malakoi* in 1 Corinthians 6:9, where Paul lists categories of people unqualified for the Kingdom. In the Western church, *malakoi*, which has the connotation of 'softness,' has traditionally been translated as 'effeminate,' while the RSV uses 'homosexuals' to represent this and another term used by Paul. But my Orthodox friend would give this word a broader signification, as meaning 'those who use sex for nonprocreative purposes.' Such use was also identified with Scriptural references to fornication, as in 1 Corinthians 6:13. The verse on childbearing, 1 Timothy 2:15, was cited as indicating that the destiny of women must be childbearing. Numerous patristic references — such as Origen's teaching that man must not abuse the sexual appetite, and the opposition of Clement of Alexandria to the nonprocreative use of sex — were adduced in support of the rigorous thesis. The continuing influence of the ancient idea that the 'seed' had the qualities of a fertilized ovum could be seen in the selection of certain citations, in that the distinction between contraception and abortion seemed rather blurred.

Some years ago, I am told, there was a meeting of Orthodox confessors in Athens which debated the question of family planning, or, more accurately, the question of marital relations not oriented to procreation — since all schools of Orthodox thought permit complete sexual abstinence when the husband and wife agree. Part of the group thought periodic continence permissible within the framework of Orthodox doctrine. The others took a more austere position, along the lines indicated above. Their argument included the point that the nonprocreative use of sex is unknown in the rest of the animal world, where mating is always linked with procreation.

Two statements may be cited as reflecting the more rigorous interpretation of Orthodox doctrine on parenthood. One is a letter of the hierarchy of the Church of Greece signed in October 1937 by Archbishop Chrysostom and 55 metropolitans.[1] The keynote of the letter is the Christian duty of procreation, rather than detailed consideration of the means of limitation. The bishops spoke of two manifestations of 'the same unnatural evil: that is, the escape from begetting children and nurturing them.' The first manifestation is abortion and the 'more cruel and criminal . . . rejection of the babies after birth, as "foundlings." ' The second manifestation is the avoidance of conception, the refusal to become parents. It is not quite clear under which of these contraception is subsumed. The term 'neo-Malthusianism' is used in connection with the second, and 'the violent douche of the prematurely killed sperm' is linked with abortion in the first.

The letter argued that methods to prevent the procreation of children are injurious to health, and disturb 'matrimonial harmony and family peace.' As for the argument concerning financial inadequacy, the bishops noted that the wealthy are most prone to avoid procreation, and that financial conditions were never so favorable that insufficiency could not be used as an excuse for the 'revolt against childbearing.' Nations have a duty to improve conditions of life and to assist large families. For their part, families have a duty to avoid luxuries and useless things. Most of all, Christians should have 'confidence in God's providence,' as well as recognize that every Christian is called to carry the cross named 'fatherhood and motherhood.' When extremely difficult conditions make it imperative to abstain from childbearing, 'the only legal way is abstinence from sexual intercourse . . . which . . . seems to be severe and impossible only for those Christians who live in flesh and not in spirit.'

The basic error in the revolt against procreation, the letter held, is that contemporary man has put 'as his first aim in life the enjoyment of lusts, while life's aim is the fulfilment of duty. Marriage's aim at first is the procreation of children and then mutual aid and moral completion of the covenanted relationship of husband and wife through the union of soul and heart.' On the negative side, the Church's tradition teaches us that 'escape from childbearing is an illegal act and a deliberate opposition of man against God's will.' That priests should in some ways consent to marital acts through different methods to frustrate conception is a 'grave and criminal' scandal. Doctors should likewise remember their Hipprocratic and Christian oaths. And the faithful should remember that marriage is 'God's appeal to them to become parents,' as well as that 'the loss of salvation is the consequence of deliberate obstruction of procreation.' The letter ended with a further reference to the legality of abstinence, when a real need exists for avoiding procreation, which Christian husbands can convert from a cross into a crown.

The other item is a statement in 1956 by the late Archbishop Michael, of the American Archdiocese. In this he stresses Orthodox agreement with the teaching of Christ and the heavenly Paul (1 Cor. 7:1–6). 'The purpose of matrimony is perfection of the married couple . . . a cooperation with Divine omnipotence.' Contraception, he thinks, is forbidden and condemned. Sexual intercourse only for the satisfaction of carnal desires causes the 'great mystery' to lose its value and reduces marriage to 'respectable immorality.' Family limitation, if desired, ought to be done by means of abstinence.

From various conversations I gather that the implications of the population explosion have not been considered very much by Orthodox leaders in relation to Christian doctrine on procreation, and that there is a felt need for further theological study. On the other hand, there is McGiffert's point about doctrine as a holy symbol. It seems unlikely that the position of the Orthodox can be spelled out in authoritative or detailed fashion in the near future. It is easier, in the Eastern tradition, to modify the practical application of doctrines — at least when the Scriptures and ecumenical councils do not provide a precise answer — than it is to clarify or develop the doctrines themselves. Consequently, a fairly long process of study and counsel on the patristic teachings and the implications of modern biological and demographic knowledge will undoubtedly be required before real clarification is achieved.

This situation poses a problem in procedure for leaders of the ecumenical movement, in which a number of Eastern Orthodox churches are members. For the Protestant churches in this fellowship are rapidly developing the kind of common understanding and conviction about responsible parenthood which has hitherto been lacking. The Protestant consensus which is emerging is one which calls for all reasonable speed to achieve a public witness — 'without tarrying for any.' How this rapidly evolving consensus can be expressed sufficiently through the agencies of the ecumenical movement, while at the same time equitable room is left for the slower procedures of Eastern Orthodoxy, poses the practical problem for ecumenical leadership.

XII

Roman Catholicism and Parenthood

ह‍‍‍‍‍✒ The key figure in the evolution of Roman Catholic doctrine bearing on parenthood is that giant of North African Christianity, Aurelius Augustinus, Bishop of Hippo. Augustine, the third and greatest of the 'four great doctors' of the Latin Church died at the age of 75, while Hippo was under siege by the Vandals (A.D. 430). He was thus, in the West, the last of the church fathers of the ancient world. The fourth of the 'doctors,' Pope Gregory the Great, who lived 150 years later, was a man of the medieval world, and interpreted Augustine as best he could.

The other two teachers of the Latin Church, who preceded Augustine, Ambrose and Jerome, were much more concerned about the question of celibacy than that of marriage and family life. In them the influence of Tertullian and Cyprian seems strong. Ambrose, a lawyer who became a theologian and noted preacher after election as bishop of Milan, was a staunch defender of monasticism and celibacy. Jerome, the able scholar who prepared the Vulgate translation of the Bible, was more extreme in his ascetic views, attacking bitterly the antimonastic ideas of Jovinian and other rebels. About the only good thing he can say of marriage is that it produces virgins. In his treatise, *On the Safeguarding of Virginity*, as Himes has noted, Jerome writes of women who drink a potion before coitus in order to remain sterile, and who go on to practice abortion by poisonous expedients, going to hell as threefold murderesses — 'suicides, as adulteresses to their heavenly bridegroom Christ, and as murderesses of their still unborn child.' The focus here is on attempted abortion, as the contraceptive or sterilizing drugs were apparently ineffective.

In contrast with Ambrose and Jerome, Augustine dealt at length with marriage and parenthood.[1] In his earlier years as an *auditor* of the ascetic Manichees, he had been indoctrinated on the evil of procreation as the work of the devil, and on the necessity for celibacy as a means to enter the 'realm of light' — though his domestic situation at the time disqualified him from joining the *cathari* or pure ones. Later, the Manichean cult, with its view of flesh and procreation as evil, became the Scylla in regard to Augustine's teaching on parenthood. The Charybdis was provided by Pelagius and his followers, who taught that procreation and the sexual appetite required for it were basically good, that the begetting of children did not transmit the sin of Adam to mar their innocence, and that children were necessary in God's providence to fill the vacancies left by death. Augustine did not so much steer his ship between these heretical rocks as batter them both down.

In the first place, Augustine was not much interested in the social or demographic aspect of procreation, despite the attention he pays to the maintenance of social life in the face of disintegrating factors. The population of the earthly city, the *civitas terrena*, is not a proper concern for Christians nor do its requirements provide an argument against celibacy. Let the heathen tend to earthly replenishment — and if they become converted and abandon this task, so much the better: the Kingdom will be that much closer. No, the proper concern for Christians in relation to procreation is in providing candidates for salvation, for election to replace the fallen angels. It is for this purpose that procreation is ordained by God. Augustine cites 'hold fast what you have, so that no one may seize your crown' (Rev. 3:11) in support of the thesis that the number of elect is fixed. The possible need for replacements, however, sanctions procreation.

On the other hand, procreation in the fallen state involves the 'malady' deriving from sin: concupiscence, upsetting the control by the will and the reason. Indeed, the sexual act is the mechanism by which the sin of Adam is transmitted. Consequently, the good involved in procreation is necessarily below the good of celibacy. Through the sacrament of marriage the sin of sexual union, mortal outside of wedlock, becomes venial, pardonable. As Cole points out, Paul's term *sungnomen*, 'concession,' in 1 Corinthians 7:6, was translated into Latin as *veniam*, 'pardon,' and was taken literally by Augustine.[2] It should be added that Augustine did not attach the greater sin of extramarital procreation to the child of such a union. In the *Confessions* he describes the graces of his natural son, Adeotatus (which means 'God-given'), as a sign of God's goodness, since the only thing of Augustine in the boy was his sin.

The sinful element in sexual intercourse is pardonable within the bond of marriage, in Augustine's view, provided it is linked to the good of procreation. He was too much of a realist to limit conjugal relations to the actual requirements of conception in the manner described by Athenagoras, for example. Augustine indicated that he had never known a couple to restrict themselves in this way. In view of the sacrament, however, marital relations not aimed at progeny can be pardoned: 'although procreation is not the motive of intercourse, [because] there is no attempt to prevent such propagation, either by wrong desire or evil appliance — [the sin is venial].' 'Evil appliance' here means contraceptive device, and 'wrong desire' presumably means contraceptive intent. Cole points out that Augustine's ban on measures to prevent conception included periodic continence. In his treatise, *On the Morals of the Manicheans*, Augustine wrote with reference to his former mentors:

> Is it not you who used to counsel us to observe as much as possible the time when a woman, after her purification, is most likely to conceive, and to abstain from cohabitation at that time, lest the soul should be entangled in the flesh? This proves that you approve of having a wife, not for the procreation of children, but for the gratifi-

cation of passion. In marriage, as the marriage law declares, the man and woman come together for the procreation of children . . . Where there is a wife there must be marriage, but there is no marriage where motherhood is not in view: therefore neither is there a wife.

Augustine's condemnation of both contraceptive method and contraceptive intent leaves little room for any kind of family limitation in his doctrine. In fact the sin of Onan, in his view, is not the spilling of seed but the avoidance of parenthood in relation to sexual intercourse:

> Intercourse even with one's legitimate wife is unlawful and wicked where the conception of the offspring is prevented. Onan, the son of Judah, did this and the Lord killed him for it. (*Adulterous Marriages*, II, no. 12)

Yet, despite his statement that 'there is no marriage where motherhood is not in view,' Augustine does allow room for a nonprocreative marriage through complete abstinence, in which companionship replaces offspring in his threefold definition of the blessings of marriage: 'offspring, conjugal faith, and the sacrament.' As Bainton puts it, 'if both parties by mutual consent should dedicate themselves to chastity they would still be validly married.' What Augustine insisted on was a nexus between procreation and intercourse, to relieve the sinful malady of concupiscence.

When one contrasts his profound concept of sin as essentially pride, the putting of self before God, with this rather narrow concept of sexual sin, one wonders what influence his own chequered experience may have had. In the *Confessions*, he compares 'the restraints of the marriage bonds, contracted for the sake of issue, and the compact of lustful love, where children are born against the parents' will.' Did the loss of his only son from the sub-marital union of youth and early manhood haunt the inner man? Did he blame the death of Adeotatus, the 'God-given,' or the lack of siblings, on the passions of this marriage which was less than marriage? While such speculation is no substitute for objective analysis, a better psychological understanding of the man might help us appreciate more the nontheological factors in his stress on procreation. The theological rationale is not wholly self-evident.

Augustine's elaboration and development of attitudes toward procreation found in some of the earlier patristic writings were modified in a number of respects by Thomas Aquinas in his intellectually brilliant synthesis of Augustinian and Aristotelian thought. On the whole, the Bishop of Hippo's stern ideas on parenthood were made less rigorous and more positive. The hierarchy of God's good creation is in the foreground rather than the economy of God's righteous judgment and election. The essentials of the subsequent Roman Catholic position appear in the two *Summa*'s.

Procreation, as with Augustine, remains the primary purpose of marriage. It is now expressed, however, in terms of natural law, which is a form of divine law written into creation: procreation in man and in lesser creatures is what mating was designed for. It is the end which marriage must serve to fulfill its inherent destiny. Marriage has also acquired a social purpose which it lacked in Augustine: marriage is essential to the preservation of the race. This, of course, does not place an obligation on the individual, who is free to choose the higher good of the celibate life for the better contemplation and enjoyment of God. Nor does it wholly apply to the couple which chooses the way of marriage, for they are free to adopt mutual vows of continence. But from the perspective of the human race it is essential.

Aquinas also brings the family into the picture, a subject rather neglected by Augustine.[3] One of Thomas's arguments for monogamy is on the ground that a 'determinate union' is characteristic of those species in which the young need the care of both parents, a condition particularly true of the human species. Also, the second good of marriage, which Augustine called 'conjugal faith,' focusing on marriage as a 'medicine for immorality,' is now a broader concern for mutual support and family harmony. And procreation itself is linked with education by implication: children should be begotten for the worship of God. This emphasis in Aquinas later led to education being yoked with procreation in Roman Catholic definitions of the primary end of marriage.

Thomas gave a more positive value to sexual desire and enjoyment within the marriage bond than did the mature Augustine, though the two men are agreed that the sex act is the mechanism by which original sin is transmitted. Venereal pleasure is a lesser good as compared with 'temperance' and 'continence,' but it is not evil in itself — though it may be the occasion of sin. It is when it exceeds the requirements of reason that it becomes sinful lust. Marriage has a rightful function to serve, however, as a remedy for concupiscence. By combining Paul's advice on mutual conjugal rights with Aristotelian concepts of justice, Thomas revives in a new form the old Roman concept of marriage as a contract: each partner, so to speak, deeds to the other his or her body. Thus marriage serves the end of justice when 'the debt' is rendered in fulfillment of the contract. As Cole says, 'this whole discussion of "the marriage debt" elaborates a small bit of practical advice from the Apostle Paul into a complex array of legalism.' It should be added that Aquinas makes no more room than did Augustine for measures to prevent payment of the debt from leading to procreation. The debt concept is currently expressed in canon law in this manner:

> Can. 1081, #2 — Matrimonial consent is an act of the will by which each party gives and accepts a perpetual and exclusive right over the body, for acts which are of themselves suitable for the generation of children.
>
> (Code of Canon Law, 1917)

In Thomas Aquinas the main outlines of the Roman Catholic doctrine on parenthood are found. He wove together Old Testament and Greco-Roman, as well as patristic, concerns for procreation as the primary end of marriage; laid the groundwork for the subsequent emphasis on the home as a school for training children in the faith; elaborated Paul's advice on conjugal rights into a set of contractual obligations; and left unchanged Augustine's generalized opposition to any form of family limitation save complete abstinence.[4] This last, however, was oriented to the 'higher good' of reason rather than to the spacing of children.

While the Thomistic doctrine of marriage and family life seems rather cold and formal, there are humane elements in it. Marriage is for the common life and mutual aid, as well as for procreation. The 'marriage benefits,' which are in effect attitudes of consideration, reduce the sin of lust to the pardonable category. Marriage is regarded as an opportunity for the highest friendship. The conception of the man-woman relationship in terms of companionship is a subordinate motif, but it is there. The leaven of the 'one flesh' idea of the Scriptures seems rather weak and dormant in the Scholastic outlook, but it is by no means dead.

Perhaps the most important observation to make about the development of Roman Catholic thought on parenthood since its medieval formulation is that the doctrine has in fact developed — slowly, unevenly, cautiously, but significantly. The necessity imposed by ecclesiastical tradition of carrying its history on its back, so to speak, makes the Roman approach fundamentally conservative. Changes are made gradually and unobtrusively. Yet the situation is far from static, and the general movement is in the direction just referred to, modifying the teachings of Thomas as he modified those of Augustine. The course has its ups and downs, as contending tendencies and parties gain or lose in their influence on the papacy, and progress often seems distressingly slow. But that there is life and growth cannot justly be denied. The problem is whether, in the pell-mell pace of contemporary history, the doctrinal evolution can hope to move fast enough.

Since this brief survey, however, is mainly concerned with the contemporary position, a tracing of this evolution will not be attempted. The main focus will be rather on the chief modern exposition of doctrine in this field — the 1930 encyclical of Pius XI on Christian marriage, *Casti Connubii* — with such references to earlier pronouncements as may aid our understanding of it. The Roman Catechism of 1572, which followed the Council of Trent (1543–63), provides a convenient indicator of both continuity and development. Note will also be taken of more recent developments under Pius XII, which help to set the current scene.[5]

To grasp the Roman Catholic view of parenthood we need to see it in relation to the ends of marriage, the rights of marriage, the blessings of marriage, and the reasons for marriage. By end or *finis operis*, Catholic theologians, following the Thomistic version of Aristotle's teleology, mean the purpose or design built into the institution, the goal which marriage was planned to serve. The way the future shape and flowering of the plant are already embodied in the seed of corn suggests the idea. The frequent use of the term 'nature' or 'intrinsic nature' reflects the concept of an inherent purpose with which God has informed marriage, a purpose which can be ascertained by analysis of the institution. By rights are meant the mutual obligations which flow from the marriage contract, and correspond to the natural ends, the 'essential properties.' By goods or blessings are meant the elements of grace which apply to true matrimony. And by reason or purpose, the *finis operantis*, is meant the motives and intention of the married couple, the ends they seek of their own will in wedlock. Let us look briefly at the view of marriage from these four perspectives.

'Since grace perfects nature,' said the Roman Catechism, 'the order of the matter demands that matrimony be treated first as it exists in nature and as it pertains to the function of nature.' Procreation had been regarded as the chief purpose of marriage in the Western church since the days of the early fathers, and Pius XI speaks of the 'principal ends of marriage laid down in the beginning by God in the words "Increase and multiply"' (*Casti Connubii*, para. 8). In the Scholastic period, education, primarily in the sense of religious training, came to the fore and joined procreation in a twofold primary end. The Code of Canon Law of 1917 puts the view pithily: 'The primary end of marriage is the procreation and education of children; its secondary end is mutual aid and the allaying of concupiscence' (Can. 1013, #1). To these subordinate purposes, Pius XI added 'the cultivating of mutual love,' reflecting the greater awareness in modern Catholicism of the genuine element in the romantic ideal.

At first glance the repeated description of procreation and education as forming a single primary end may seem somewhat curious. Why not a more comprehensive term, such as parenthood, which refers to both begetting and rearing, or alternatively, why not a frank admission that there are two primary ends? The explanation, I think, is that the philosophical framework of Thomism requires a single primary end or formal cause 'by which a union of several is accomplished and specified to be what it is.' In short, marriage requires a unitary and distinctive organizing principle to give it real status. On the other hand, the patristic tradition and related Biblical texts deal with procreation, so that the conservative approach argues for a grafting operation, if education is to be included — 'something else must be added,' as Pius XI says.[6] Education is seen as the projection of the initial responsibility: 'those who began the work of nature . . . are indeed forbidden to leave unfinished this work and so expose it to certain ruin.'

While marriage is given twin responsibilities as its primary end, the marital act remains attached to the older *raison d'être:* 'the conjugal act is destined primarily by nature for the begetting of children.' As the eye is designed for seeing, so the marital act is designed for begetting. This is its 'intrinsic nature.' Note that it is not the sex act *per se* which is given this function, but the sex act in marriage. Marriage and marital intercourse are regarded in the first instance as part of the natural order, the order of creation described in Genesis. Since procreation is defined as the main inherent purpose of the conjugal act, it follows that any other legitimate purpose is subordinate in character and, if it does not serve the goal of progeny, must at least be harmonious with it.

From the perspective of marriage rights, procreation is somewhat less in the foreground. The reason may be that the prime source for the concept was Paul's advice on conjugal rights (1 Cor. 7:3f.) which does not refer to procreation. The Canon Law introduces procreation into its definition of matrimonial consent in this way: 'an act of the will by which each party gives and accepts a perpetual and exclusive right over the body, for acts which are of themselves suitable for the generation of children' (Can. 1081, #2). The Sacred Roman Rota, in a decision of January 1944, went a bit further in describing the principle object of the marriage contract to be 'the "right" to the generation of offspring,' and arguing that the right to community of life and mutual assistance were derivative from this primary right. Even in marriages governed by vows of chastity, it was indicated, it is the exercise of the right to generation rather than the right itself which is excluded. Thus, the marriage rights tend to be oriented toward the primacy of progeny.[7]

Again, from the perspective of the blessings of matrimony, procreation definitely has first place. In his encyclical, Pius XI gives particular attention to these blessings, giving them a much more positive connotation than is found, for example, in the Roman Catechism. There Augustine's three goods — offspring, conjugal faith, and the sacrament — were described as lessening the 'disadvantage' in marriage of which Paul spoke, and lending 'probity' to bodily union, justly condemned outside of marriage. Pius XI speaks rather of the 'extraordinary benefits' conferred by God on matrimony, expressing admiration for these elements of grace. There is no diminution, however, in the emphasis on children as the chief blessing. Pius cites the familiar texts on childbearing, though he omits the reference to woman being 'saved by childbearing,' (1 Tim. 2:15) which had been used in the 1572 Catechism.[8] People are needed to fill the earth and even more to worship God. And Catholic parents are to be mindful of the need for children to become members of the Church.

Under the second blessing, conjugal fidelity, Pius discusses monogamy in the divine purpose: a primeval law fully restored in the law of the Gospel, in the teaching of Christ concerning 'one flesh.' In an important section (para. 23f.), the encyclical develops the theme that conjugal faith grows best in the soil of conjugal love. This love should have as its primary purpose the mutual help of husband and wife 'in forming and perfecting themselves in the interior life . . . above all that they may grow in true love towards God and their neighbor.' One is reminded of

the Orthodox stress on sanctification, an impression strengthened
by the highlighting of the passage in Ephesians. The third good
of marriage, the sacrament, is interpreted primarily in terms of the
permanence and indissolubility of the marriage bond, with emphasis on the assistance of grace for fulfilling the duties of marriage — which brings the circle back to procreation.

It is only in regard to the reasons or subjective purposes for
marriage that procreation tends to stand in a subordinate position.
The Roman Catechism put ahead of the desire for children the
community of man and wife, a community of sex and of hope for
mutual aid 'to bear more easily the hardships of life and the in-
firmities of old age' (Part II, ch. 8). The third reason is the use
of marriage 'as a means of avoiding sins of lust.' It is interesting
that the Catechism states that each person should have in mind
one of these reasons to 'contract marriage piously and religiously.'
In *Casti Connubii*, Pius XI uses the priority given to marital community in this section of the Catechism to reinforce the importance of mutual love. The passage merits quotation in full:

> This mutual inward molding of husband and wife, this determined
> effort to perfect each other, can in a very real sense, as the Roman
> Catechism teaches, be said to be the chief reason and purpose of
> matrimony, provided matrimony be looked at not in the restricted
> sense as instituted for the proper conception and education of the
> child, but more widely as the blending of life as a whole and the
> mutual interchange and sharing thereof. (para. 24)

Here, it seems to me, is one of the growing edges of the Roman
Catholic doctrine on marriage and parenthood. If Pius is speaking
of the theology of marriage rather than its psychology, as appears
to be the case, he is asserting that while the begetting and rearing
of children is the first purpose of marriage within the order of
nature and creation, companionship as a means to spiritual perfection may be regarded as its primary end within the order of
grace and redemption. And since the efficacy of the sacrament
'transcends the condition of natural things' (Roman Catechism),
it is possible to speak of this latter dimension of marriage as being
broader in character. If this interpretation is correct, Pius XI

planted a potentially important seed for the future development of Catholic thought in this area. It can hardly have been an oversight that for several years the English and American translations of the encyclical omitted this passage entirely, or that some of these incomplete translations still are circulated, at least in the United States.

Sherwin Bailey holds that the passage was probably 'designed to allow theologians of the Roman obedience a certain latitude of interpretation in the matter of the ends of marriage.' This, he points out, was in any case the effect produced, with Catholic writers like Wirtz, von Streng, and Doms stressing the personal and relational element in marriage as being at least equal in importance to the genetic, and emphasizing the secondary ends too often neglected in Roman thought.[9]

The official response to this ferment was twofold. Pius XII, in an allocution to the high ecclesiastical court, the Sacred Roman Rota, in October 1941, supported a larger appreciation of the secondary end of marriage, but opposed the 'tendency . . . to divorce it from its essential subordination to the primary end.' The Rota, in January 1944, gave a lengthy supporting opinion. Noting that certain authors 'depart from true and certain doctrine' in giving 'mutual help' an independent and primary status, the Rota asserted that '*all* mutual help, which flows from marriage without detriment to the primary end, is contained within the limits of the secondary end.' Three months later, the Holy Office decreed that the opinion of writers who deny the primacy of generation and education or the essentially subordinate character of the secondary ends cannot be admitted. And Pius XII, in his allocution of October 1951 to the Italian Union of Midwives, stated that 'even the depths of spirituality in conjugal love as such have been put by the will of nature and the Creator at the service of our descendents.' It seems reasonable to doubt, however, that this reaction, which concentrates on one dimension of marriage, is the last word in Roman thought on the subject. And paragraph 24 in *Casti Connubii* provides a basis for new beginnings.

To summarize, the Roman Catholic approach to marriage

from three of four perspectives — or three out of five, if it is correct that Pius XI intended to break new theological ground in paragraph 24 — historically has been pro-fertility. Even with regard to the subjective reasons, the *fines operantis*, which may be different from or contrary to the inherent end, the Rota in its 1944 decision underscored a warning by Pius XI that the contracting parties 'should seek in marriage those ends because of which it was instituted by God.' Whatever the superior merit of religious celibacy, fertility appears as the glory and main redeeming feature of the married state. Thus the Holy Office, for example, worried about the increased propaganda for 'conjugal onanism,' urged in a letter on 30 March 1889 that 'the faithful be taught efficiently that heavenly blessings definitely await the parents of numerous offspring.' Or again, in addressing the Congress of the 'Family Front' and of the Associations of Large Families in November 1951, Pius XII expressed gratitude to 'those generous couples who, for love of God and with trust in Him, courageously raise a large family.' Such reflections of the strong pro-fertility tradition have provided a springboard for what I have called the Roman Catholic 'fertility cult,' referred to below.

Strictly speaking, however, it is marital intercourse rather than marriage itself that is bound up with procreation in the Roman doctrine. For the teaching on marriage leaves room for complete abstinence, and the 'vows-of-chastity' marriage is regarded as valid despite the lack of sexual consummation. The Rota in its 1944 decision cited authorities on canon law in behalf of the thesis that spouses can agree to forgo both coitus and generation,[10] although there is difference of opinion as to whether abstinence can be made a prior condition of marriage. It is in the conjugal act that the possibility of generation must never be denied by human agency. As Pius XI summarized the position in *Casti Connubii*:

> Any use whatsoever of matrimony exercised in such a way that the act is deliberately frustrated in its natural power to generate life is an offense against the law of God and of nature, and those who indulge in such are branded with the guilt of a grave sin. (para. 56)

The wrestling of the papal authorities since the Council of Trent with questions of family limitation by means other than complete sexual abstinence forms an interesting story, which can only be outlined here. The starting point is the dictum of the Roman Catechism of 1572:

> Those who prevent birth violate the law of nature . . . Therefore, the sin of those married couples who by medicine either hinder conception or prevent birth, is very grave; for this should be considered an unholy conspiracy of homicides. (II, ch. 8, q. 13)

Presumably, to judge from the medieval folklore collected by Himes in his *Medical History of Contraception*, the 'medicines' referred to were largely ineffective superstitions in which a few possibly effective spermicides and abortifacients were included. The level of contraceptive knowledge was probably lower than in Greco-Roman civilization.

This judgment is reinforced by the fact that the main ensuing actions of the papacy in this area dealt with a crude form of sterilization — castration — and abortion, rather than contraception. Sixtus V in 1587, in his bull *Cum Frequenter*, placed a ban on marriages by eunuchs, which he said were a frequent occurrence. Since 'no true utility' arises from such unions, which rather 'occasion both temptations and incentives to lust,' future marriages were to be prohibited and existing marriages involving cohabitation to be annulled. The age-old condemnation of abortion was made more precise in a decree of the Holy Office in 1679, which condemned the error that abortion is allowable before animation of the fetus, and the error that a fetus lacks a rational soul and consequently abortion is not necessarily homicide.

Indeed, the early 19th-century references deal mainly with *coitus interruptus* or conjugal onanism, as it was called. The Sacred Penitentiary stated in 1816 that a wife could 'render the debt' in such circumstances, if she would be ill-used in case of refusal. Cardinal de Petro, the Chief Penitentiary, added his opinion that the wife of such a husband could even request the debt if she were in danger of incontinence. The reference to 'ill-used' was spelled out by the Sacred Penitentiary in 1823 as meaning the husband's 'threatening her with beatings or death or some other serious cruelties.' There are subsequent references stressing *inter alia* the wife's duty to try to dissuade the husband from the practice.

In the latter part of the 19th century we find condemnations of contraception in the restricted sense, although the roots of course are old — as in Augustine's mention of 'evil appliance.' In April 1853 the Holy Office indicated that a wife may not offer herself even passively to condomistic intercourse since it is 'intrinsically illicit.' In 1916 the Sacred Penitentiary decreed that a wife in such a situation should 'offer that resistance which a virgin offers to an attacker.' The logical basis for the distinction in degrees of resistance asked for from the wife in the two methods of conception control is not quite clear, but the distinction served to underscore the stern opposition of Catholic authorities to any form of contraceptive device.

The latter part of the 19th century also saw the quiet development of acceptance by papal authorities of periodic continence as a licit method of family planning under certain conditions. In March 1853 the Sacred Penitentiary, having been asked by the Bishop of Amiens whether married people among the faithful, who do not use marriage except on the days when they believe conception cannot take place, should be 'disturbed' by confessors if they have legitimate reasons for refraining, replied that they should not be disturbed 'so long as they do nothing to prevent conception.' This same body, in June 1880, agreed that a confessor 'may suggest, but cautiously, the opinion under discussion to those spouses whom he has vainly tried by another method to lead away from the detestable crime of onanism.' The Penitentiary was silent on the query as to 'whether the danger of a reduction in the number of offspring must be provided against.' Since the medical opinion referred to in the query held that the fertile period occurred in the first days of the feminine cycle, the 'danger' presumably was in any case slight.

Pius XI provided a stronger basis for periodic continence as a means for family limitation when he stated in his encyclical: 'nor are those considered as acting against nature who in the married state use their right in the proper manner, although on account of natural reasons either of time or of certain defects, new life cannot be brought forth.' Since this came in the midst of a world depression, it led to very considerable attention in Catholic circles. Pius XII elaborated the position more specifically. In speaking to the Italian Union of Midwives in October 1951 he said, after mentioning the procreative duty imposed on married couples who have intercourse, that nevertheless 'serious reasons, such as those found in the medical, eugenic, economic and social "indications" can exempt for a long time, perhaps even for the whole duration of the marriage, from this positive duty.' A month later, Pius XII gave additional support when he said: 'One may even hope . . . that science will succeed in providing this licit method with a sufficiently secure basis, and the most recent information seems to confirm such a hope.'

Much has been made by Catholic publicists and others of the distinction between the 'natural' birth control method of periodic continence and 'artificial' birth control methods. This seems to me to confuse the differentiation important to Catholic thought. As has been indicated, for science to provide the licit method with a 'sufficiently secure basis,' procedures as artificial as contraceptives may be involved — temperature charts, chemical tests for ovulation, possibly drugs to help regularize the feminine cycle, or drugs to induce ovulation more surely at the expected time. On the other hand, nonartificial methods of conception control such as *copula dimidiata* and *amplexus reservatus* have been refused the sanction of Vatican courts, while *coitus interruptus* is strongly condemned. The differentiating feature from the Roman point of view must surely be that, in the case of periodic intercourse, 'acts which are of themselves suitable for the generation of children,' to use the canon law phrase, are carried out in the 'proper manner' — that is, in the same way that they would be if procreation were sought. It is the fundamentally procreative manner of the act, without direct or overt hindrance to the possibility of conception, whatever the contraceptive intent, that makes this method, as method, licit for Roman Catholics.

The main internal debate since 1951 has centered around the 'serious reasons' which would justify resort to periodic continence. While Pius XII indicated, in October 1951, the approved categories — eugenic, medical, economic, and social — he did not indicate the degree of gravity required. In fact, in November 1951 he referred to the limits as well as the legitimacy of a regulation of offspring, and said the limits were 'in truth quite broad,' which left the issue even more unsettled. The lack of precise official definition has left open the field of combat for two opposing ecclesiastical factions or parties, the pro-fertility group that I have called the 'fertility cult,' and a group concerned about socially responsible parenthood. Neither group, apparently, is very large or highly organized, but their contention has characterized the Roman situation in recent years.

The aggressive if generally ill-informed 'fertility cult' has been the stronger faction to date. It has been strong chiefly in U.S. Catholic circles, finding a kindred spirit among some of the Dutch theologians, I understand, and formerly having allies in England. To judge from the literature, the point of view still has important influence on much of the material on population and parenthood syndicated to the American Catholic press. In general, the tendency in this group is to cast doubt on demographic predictions so far as possible, to generate the hope of economic miracles from such favorable indications as can be selected, to put the blame for particular population pressures on the lack of international solidarity and charity, to avoid at all costs support for family limitation as part of a solution, and to fall back on trust in divine providence when all else fails.[11] If this review were for the purpose of partisan religious polemics, the literature reflecting the 'fertility cult' point of view would serve as a mother lode of valuable material. I refrain from exploiting it, however, since I cannot convince myself that it is more than a passing aberration, consideration of which would be tangential to the main argument.

It is rather characteristic of the 'fertility cult' to concentrate on demographic and economic calculations of a sort rather than to come to grips with the theological and practical implications of the papal pronouncements. The 'serious reasons' are so circumscribed by members of the cult as to provide the barest sanction for family limitation. The economic and social indications particularly tend to disappear. Periodic continence is judged to be licit only for the welfare of the individual family, not for the welfare of a society. Even for the family, periodic continence is distinctly a second best. As Anthony F. Zimmerman writes in 'Overpopulation': 'The family which courageously and even heroically rears a large number of children in an overpopulated area merits special praise for its virtue.' [12]

In contrast with this radical faction, there is a moderate or constructive group, less vocal than the opposing party, though its voice is now heard with more frequency. The 'responsible parenthood' group appears to be less numerous or influential than the 'fertility cult,' but may have considerable potential support in moderate Catholic circles, particularly outside the United States.[13] In general, people in this camp, if such it can be called, favor more serious Catholic study of population problems and trends, more objective consideration of economic and social development, more liberal or realistic interpretation of the 'serious reasons' — for the regulation of fertility — and more vigorous efforts to provide scientific reinforcement for the licit method.

The rather abrupt halt in the development of the official position on periodic continence after the papal allocutions of 1951 strongly suggests a vigorous reaction from the pro-fertility group and their supporters. In fact I would judge that this point of view, if not dominant in Vatican circles, became strong enough to keep further doctrinal development in abeyance during the succeeding years. Two papal statements during the last year of Pius XII's life hint at the possible waxing and waning of contending groups behind the scenes. In January 1958, in a talk before the Italian 'large family' associations, the aging Pope delivered a homily containing a broad condemnation of 'birth control' and decrying fears of overpopulation much in the manner of the pro-fertility advocates. But on 12 September 1958, he gave a brief address much more like the 1951 allocutions. He referred to the rhythm or Ogino-

Knaus method of family limitation, stating that when this is 'utilized for proportionately serious motives . . . it is morally justifiable.' Thus, the homily in January seems to have been a momentary and passing victory for the 'fertility cult.'

Meantime, the evidence that the days of this faction are numbered accumulates rapidly, not only because of the inescapable questions posed by world population pressures but also because of trends among the Catholic laity. Such data as are available indicate declining Catholic birth rates in several of the more established countries, a phenomenon which Catholic students privately admit implies a wider resort to contraception. An increase in periodic continence, though not effective as yet in many cases, may also play a role. Birth rates in Italy, Spain, and Portugal have now fallen below that of the United States. Studies in England and West Germany show a virtual equivalence between Catholic and non-Catholic birth rates. A 1957 census sample of 35,000 families in the United States indicates that the fertility of couples who call themselves Protestant may be slightly higher than the fertility of those who call themselves Catholic. All this speaks of fairly massive lay disobedience, at least in the Western countries, to the traditional teaching on parenthood. Such a situation can hardly be coped with either by standing pat or trying to turn the clock back. Progress toward a more realistic and adequate doctrine of responsible parenthood seems imperative for the Roman branch of Christianity.

Some have thought that 'the pill' may offer a way forward for Catholic policy. An English bishop, for example, has been quoted as saying that he thought the Church would not oppose oral contraceptives. But what he actually said was that the Church would not oppose, in his judgment, if the use of the drugs proved compatible with the law of God. The evidence appears strongly against the Vatican reaching the conclusion that they are compatible with the 'law of God.' Neither drugs to defer ovulation nor drugs to eliminate the fertilized ovum have any real prospect of Catholic sanction for the purposes intended.

The use of drugs to inhibit ovulation comes up against the

Church's opposition to sterilization and mutilation. Persons, said Pius XI in *Casti Connubii*, are 'not free to destroy or mutilate their members, or in any other way render themselves unfit for their natural functions, except when no other provision can be made for the good of the whole body' (para. 71). During the period of Nazi sterilization practices, the Holy Office was asked 'whether the direct sterilization of man or woman, either perpetual or temporary, is licit,' and replied in February 1940 that 'it is forbidden by the law of nature.' The extension in this manner of the ban on mutilation to cover the temporary impairment of function is now applied to oral contraceptives. On 12 September 1958, Pius XII stated that a direct and therefore illicit sterilization is provoked when medicines are used 'to prevent conception by preventing ovulation.'

The alternative type of drug, namely one to eliminate the ovum after fertilization, comes up against the even stronger condemnation of abortion. Gibbons and Burch, in an article on the oral drugs in the April 1958 issue of *The American Ecclesiastical Review*, point out that while theologians differ as to the time of animation of the human embryo, control measures destructive of a fertilized ovum or embryo must in any case be regarded as more gravely wrong than contraceptive measures: 'For there is involved an attack upon life already in process of growth, which if not actually human, is intrinsically destined to become such.' The Church which forbids the direct killing of the innocent unborn child, even to save the mother's life, can hardly be expected to condone any form or variant of feticide. The same negative conclusion is arrived at if the summary of the general position by Pius XII in October 1951 is considered:

> Every attempt on the part of the married couple during the conjugal act or during the development of its natural consequences, to deprive it of its inherent power and to hinder the procreation of a new life is immoral.

No dramatic new developments, then, are to be anticipated in the evolution of the Roman position. A gradual clarification of the 'serious reasons,' a greater stress on responsible parenthood, more vigorous research to make periodic continence a more reliable means of family planning, greater attention to educating the laity in this method — these are reasonable expectations. We need to recall that it took a century to develop the present position in regard to periodic continence, and that it was a far from easy task. So is the case likely to be in the future. Non-Roman Christians should cultivate understanding attitudes as Rome struggles to move forward. We can also hope for greater Roman Catholic understanding as other churches develop their own doctrines of responsible parenthood in obedience to Scripture and conscience.

XIII

Protestantism and Parenthood

ᘐ Moving from Roman Catholic to Protestant doctrine seems a bit like moving from an elaborate formal garden to a wildwood with many trails. The systematic paths lined with ancient box-wood, carefully pruned, are no longer in evidence, although in Calvinism and certain phases of Puritanism there are some elements of a new legalism. In general, however, Evangelical trails move freely and rather unsystematically through the wildwood. It is only in the present century that we find many separate paths converging and moving in a concerted manner toward green pastures over the brow of the hill. The most exciting part of the Protestant story remains to be written. This may also be true of the Roman story, though the way out of the formal garden seems hard to find.

While issues of sex and marriage formed an important area of dissent from Rome in the Reformation, this is much less true in regard to the doctrine of parenthood. In neither Luther nor Calvin is there any doubt about procreation as a major purpose of marriage, though children are regarded somewhat more as the fruit of conjugal relations and the divine gift which blesses the married state than as the essential and primary end. Luther agreed with Augustine that offspring constituted one of the principle goods of matrimony, though he did not necessarily put it first. He did not quarrel with the thesis that marriage was designed for the increase of the race, but he saw children, in man's fallen state, not so much in relation to a built-in law of nature, as in relation to God's over-riding will, which cannot be thwarted by sinful men, and to God's mercy, which despite the sins of lust, blesses the home with progeny and the gladness of motherhood. 'Propagation is not in our will and power . . . Creation is of God alone.' [1] Luther saw the family, despite its troubles which reflect man's sinful condition, as a 'school for character,' as Bainton puts it, where 'the Christian virtues find their readiest exemplification.'

Calvin, taking more strictly than Luther the Old Testament as valid moral law, was closer to the natural law position of Rome. The injunction to 'increase and multiply' was still normative, and except for the very few granted the gift of celibacy, constituted a positive command to marry. One of Calvin's charges against the Roman priesthood was that they were evading their social responsibility, since most were in the ungifted category. The nexus between sex and procreation was important to Calvin as elevating the man-woman relationship in accordance with its original design.

Neither Calvin nor Luther regarded marriage as a sacrament: it is a sign or symbol, a divine ordinance, but not a special occasion of the Holy Spirit instituted by Christ, as in the case of baptism and communion. Calvin pointed out the inconsistency of Rome in holding marriage a sacrament and yet denying it to the priests and nuns. Both men regarded marriage as fundamentally equal to celibacy in status, and a preferable state except for the gifted few. Both saw it as an essential remedy for concupiscence in man's state of sin, an argument underscored by the low state of morals in the old Church at the time. Luther was particularly impressed by the need to keep in safe bounds the drives of sex, and on occasion was prepared to countenance bigamy as a lesser evil than fornication or adultery. Calvin's less earthy approach stressed not only strict monogamy but also proper decorum within marriage. If sexual immoderation is kept within the bonds of marriage, 'in the case of believers marriage is a veil, by which the fault is covered over, so that it no longer appears in the sight of God.' Thus, for both men conjugal relations served an important negative function, as it had for Paul, in providing a remedy for concupiscence. The question of any control of conception in this connection apparently did not arise, since concern about family limitation was not on the horizon.[2]

Cole seems to me correct in saying that 'procreation remained for them, as for Augustine and Aquinas, the only really positive purpose of sex.' For Calvin particularly, however, marriage itself served another purpose, which he regarded as in one sense more fundamental — namely, the purpose of companionship. This companionship is primarily social and spiritual rather than sexual, a sharing of mind and interest and experience. As Cole summarizes the view expressed in Calvin's *Commentary on Genesis*:

> To him, the decisive words in the creation narrative were those of God's, 'it is not good that the man should be alone.' His design in creating the woman was 'that there should be human beings on the earth who might cultivate mutual society between themselves.'

This concept of marital community, Cole points out, elevated the status of woman as a person, as part of a living organism, in a more just way than was true of Calvin's predecessors. He described his dead wife as 'the best companion of my life . . . the faithful helper of my ministry.'

While the sexual dimension of marriage is somewhat obscured in this version of the 'one flesh' idea, other elements are there and help to keep the idea itself alive in the Puritan tradition. John Milton, for example, in his tract on divorce — which was not untinged with self-interest — appealed to Genesis 2:18 as the first command of God. 'In God's intention a meet and happy conversation is the chiefest and noblest end of marriage . . . The chief society thereof is in the soul rather than in the body.'[3] In such thoughts part of the old contemplative ideal seems to have been transferred to the nonsexual side of marriage, while the sexual side remained in the shadows — perhaps because it was regarded as having shameful connotations or because it was thought of so largely in terms of the duty of procreation. The idea of 'one flesh' was preserved but not given the fullness of its Biblical meaning. It would reappear in more significant form in the 20th century.

There were a number of growing points in the Reformers' thoughts on marriage and family life which might have led to new insights on parenthood, if their implications had been thoroughly examined. Marriage was freed from subordination to celibacy and given a new dignity. It was less tied to the chariot wheel of procreation, or at least the chains were longer. And even in regard to the marital act, children were regarded somewhat more as a divine blessing upon it than as its primary end and justification. Yet the implications for parenthood were not examined in any thorough way for nearly four centuries.[4] Even Anabaptists like Thomas Münzer, and pietists like Count Zinzendorf, who took a more ascetic view of conjugal relations than those in the main stream of development, did not question the nexus between 'conjugation' and propagation. For all practical purposes, the ethos of Wittenberg and Geneva and Canterbury was as strongly pro-fertility as that of Rome.

The nontheological reasons for this result, in regard to the Reformers and their successors, appear to have considerable weight. Underpopulation was a problem in northwestern Europe, as the losses of the Black Death and Hundred Years War had not yet been made good. Britain in the middle of the 16th century probably had a half million fewer inhabitants than two centuries earlier when the plague commenced its ravages. France was striving to recover the third to one-half of her population lost to the twin scourges. The lands of the Reformation together may not have counted more than 25 million souls. There were not only abandoned fields to till, but also new job opportunities in the new commercial and manufacturing developments which preceded the Industrial Revolution. It was precisely this part of Europe that led the economic van. When such factors are considered in conjunction with the high infant mortality and the dearth of reliable contraceptive knowledge, the disposition in favor of high fertility is certainly understandable. The ideal of the large family, particularly among the Calvinists, joined ideals of thrift, sobriety, industry, and responsibility in reinforcing the new economic development.

Similar factors have operated through most of the post-Reformation period, at least for the middle class groups occupying the main pews in the churches.[5] The predominant secular motif until the present century has been economic expansion, reinforced by colonial expansion. Medical advances came gradually, so that population increases seldom outstripped the means of livelihood. Pressures which were engendered could be relieved by migration to North America with its expanding economy and western frontier. The situation itself in these sections of the world was largely favorable to fairly high fertility, and helped Protestant churchmen — particularly in view of the later Puritan taboos surrounding sex — to rest content with the traditional attitude. Any other course seemed to indicate a want of confidence in God's providence.

What were the factors that finally altered the long decades of uncritical acceptance and neglect? I am forced to conclude that again they were primarily nontheological in character. The struggle of the 'birth control' movement to establish itself was conducted, as has been indicated, without much benefit of clergy of any description. Indeed, in the 19th century, official Protestant opposition was only less severe than that of Roman Catholicism. Roman friends are correct, for example, when they argue that the anti-contraception laws on the books in Massachusetts and Connecticut were put there originally not by their ecclesiastical forebears but by mine. Yet it is also true that Protestant lay men and women were active in the 'birth control' movement, at least in the Anglo-Saxon countries, and that its propaganda made important headway among the laity, not merely on theoretical but above all on practical grounds. The concern for the family standard of living, for the health of the mother, for the care of the existing children, and particularly for their education — a major Protestant concern — undoubtedly led to a large increase in the practice of contraception in the Protestant community during the past two generations. This could not but impress the clerical leaders, especially since most of them were married men and faced similar problems.

A second important factor was the massive prod of the great depression, which aggravated many of the considerations arguing for family limitation. This phenomenon undercut the idea of automatic economic and social progress as a sign of natural law, special virtue, or divine beneficence. The first statement dealing with family limitation in a positive sense that my colleagues and I have thus far been able to locate, antedates the depression, but the other early statements seem clearly to reflect the concerns aroused by that prolonged economic paralysis in the West. One reason for stressing the nontheological factors in these early statements is that they give the ethical conclusions much more than the theological groundwork. It should also be added that while Protestant pronouncements do not have anything like the binding character that papal statements have for Catholics, they offer us the best clue we have to the thinking of church leadership, and sometimes play an important role in shaping church opinion.

It is interesting that the lead in this matter, insofar as we have information, should have been taken by the body in Protestantism that has most fully retained the Thomistic system in its theological approach — the Anglican Communion. This is doubly interesting in that both the 1908 and 1920 Lambeth Conferences had condemned 'birth control.' One factor here, no doubt, is that the Church of England as an established church has had more experience with legislative issues affecting marriage than most churches. To her credit, through her Moral Welfare Council and other means, she is giving more persistent and systematic attention to problems of marriage and family life than any other section of Christendom save Rome. As early as 1923, the same year that Marie Stopes opened her first 'birth control' clinic in England, there had been a Church of England statement favorable to the principle of contraception. And in 1930 the Anglican bishops of the Lambeth Conference reversed their earlier stand. While agreeing in resolution 13 that procreation is the primary end of marriage, they went on to adopt, by a vote of 193 to 67, resolution 15, which held that 'where there is a clearly felt moral obligation to limit or avoid parenthood' complete abstinence is the 'primary and obvious method,' but that if there is a morally sound reason for avoiding abstinence 'the Conference agrees that other methods may be used, provided that this is done in the light of . . . Christian principles.' While the Warren Commission, which helped to prepare for the 1958 Lambeth Conference, later called this 'grudging' permission, it was important as a pioneer step toward a Protestant doctrine of responsible parenthood.

Perhaps the most substantial of the early statements was that of the Committee on Marriage and Home of the U.S. Federal Council of Churches in March 1931. The Committee agreed that sex relations between husband and wife 'have their source in the thought and purpose of God, first for the creation of human life, but also as a manifestation of divine concern for the happiness of those who have so wholly merged their lives.' The moral problems of birth control arise from these two functions of sex. There is the question of spacing and limiting children, safeguarding the health of mother and child, and protecting the livelihood and stability of the family. The Committee also referred to 'overpopulation,' though it thought this a fairly distant prospect. The other need is to provide for union 'as an expression of mutual affection, without relation to procreation.' The majority of the Committee, believing that abstinence within marriage except for the few is neither satisfactory nor desirable, held 'that the careful and restrained use of contraceptives by married people is valid and moral.' Three members of the Committee held that the church should 'uphold the standard of abstinence as the ideal, recognizing it as a counsel of perfection.' While the Federal Council did not act on this report, its publication evoked a storm of public debate.

Two recurrent concerns in some of the early United States and Canadian denominational statements are the need for a full personal relationship between man and wife and the need for healthy and stable families. The marriage ideal, said the Congregational Christian General Council in 1931, 'cannot be realized without mutuality and freedom . . . We favor the principle of voluntary child bearing, believing that it sacramentalizes physical union and safeguards the well-being of the family and society.' The General Council of the United Church of Canada, prefacing its 1936 statement with a reference to the dangers in population pressures, pointed out that nature itself destines all but a tiny remnant of reproductive cells 'to find no place in the story of human life'; the right to use present-day knowledge to determine the occasions for procreation implies the right of access to such knowledge, and the establishment of Voluntary Parenthood Clinics is supported. The Philadelphia Yearly Meeting of Friends stressed the importance of approved contraceptives for freedom and spontaneity in the sex relation, often injured by fear of pregnancy, and for family welfare and health through the spacing of children. The General Convention of the Protestant Episcopal Church in 1946 related the proper conveyance of medical information to 'a more wholesome family life, wherein parenthood may be undertaken with due respect for the health of mothers and the welfare of their children.' The Evangelical and Reformed General Synod the following year supported 'in the interest of more stable family life . . . the right of married persons to all appropriate medical aid in the wisest planning of their families.' The pattern of support for the majority position in the statement of the Federal Council's Committee is unmistakable.

The second group of statements came from British church bodies dealing with the question of family planning in the special context of concern over signs of decline in the British and European birth rates. This is no doubt related to the somewhat uncertain voice with which they spoke. The Methodist Conference of Great Britain in 1939 stressed the need for 'a fresh acceptance of the responsibility and obligation of parenthood.' It weighed the value of contraceptives for relieving the nervous strain of inhibition and the exhaustion of frequent pregnancies against the possible development of sensual mental habits and impairment of self-control. Conception control should aim at producing 'the healthiest family in the healthiest sort of way.' The 1943 statement of the Department of Social Responsibility of the British Council of Churches made a theme of its departmental title:

> The use of a contraceptive method can only be justified if the marriage bond and married love are thereby truly honored and not debased, if the obligation to parenthood is the better fulfilled and

not evaded, if family life is enriched and not impoverished, and if increase and not diminution of good comes to society.

The following year a special Commission of the Church of Scotland prepared a report on 'Marriage and the Family.' Again the fears of declining birth rates in Western Christendom were a factor. The Commission asserted that 'the size of an individual family is not the exclusive concern of its parents' who are 'morally bound to consider its size in relation to the welfare of the community as a whole.' Despite the judgment that the practice of restricting parenthood was being abused, the Commission thought that both extreme views of contraception — as turning physical union into sin, or as offering a social service of the first order especially among the underprivileged — contained 'its own germ of truth.'

The end of World War II provides a convenient line of division between the initial pronouncements on responsible parenthood and the more significant as well as representative statements of recent years. If our partial information is not misleading, the initial steps to reform the traditional view of parenthood in relation to the other ends of marriage were concentrated in the churches of the Anglo-Saxon world. The practical issues confronting parents, and the light shed by these issues on the meaning of doctrinal principles, form the dominant note. The more recent statements have somewhat broader dimensions. One reason is the greater awareness of the demographic revolution, which gives additional urgency to finding the right answers. Another is the influence of a more serious wrestling with the theology of parenthood and its context. Before turning to the post-war pronouncements, it may be useful to note briefly a few points in this latter connection.

The major Protestant theologians of our time have not, any more than their predecessors, given detailed consideration to the question of parenthood, but some of their insights are illuminating. They bear more on the man-woman relationship than on the man-woman-child relationship: that is, on the nonparenthood side of marriage, which is the other side of the medal in a Christian doctrine of parenthood.

Emil Brunner seems a partial exception in this respect, being somewhat closer to the traditional approach. The child plays an important part in his understanding of marriage. The child is more than an object of union, which in that case could be temporary in character. The child is another subject, another 'thou' in a community of persons designed to endure. The meaning of monogamous marriage lies in the quality of the person-to-person relationship, which makes the libido a servant rather than master. The sinful element in sex relations is expressed in the 'rent,' the separation of sexuality from its service to personality; lust introduces an impersonal element. While marriage should discipline the libido, Brunner holds that nature itself shows that God intended intercourse to serve mutual love as well as procreation. And since these purposes have equivalent status, contraception is by no means contrary to the will of God — though abstinence is permissible if preferred as a means, despite the Biblical counsel against it.

In his Gifford Lectures, Reinhold Niebuhr also defends the dual purpose of sex, since man is both a child of nature and a free spirit transcending it. The Hellenistic side of Christianity tends to see sex as a particular symbol and consequence of sin. But bisexuality is part of the original creation; it is self-love, the deification of the creature, which is the essence of sin. As for the sexual impulse, 'its force reaches up into the highest pinnacles of human spirituality; and the insecurity of man in the heights of his freedom reaches down to the sex impulse as an instrument of compensation and as an avenue of escape.' Sex, in short, is not sinful in itself, but is made a tool 'for both the assertion of the self and the flight from the self.'

Niebuhr accepts procreation as the prime purpose of bisexuality in nature, but challenges the making of this 'natural fact' into a universally valid 'law of reason,' setting bounds for the human personality. Also, the sexual impulse has 'exceeded the necessities of the preservation of the species from the very beginning.' The freedom of the human spirit, which can use sex for sinful license or for a creative relationship to spiritual values, has its claims:

The prohibition of birth control assumes that the sexual function in human life must be limited to its function in nature, that of procreation. But it is the very character of human life that all animal functions are touched by freedom and released into more complex relationships.

In *Die Kirchliche Dogmatik*, Karl Barth has an interesting section on family limitation.[6] He finds a moral and theological consensus on the need for responsible parenthood, but difference as to means. All four of the choices — abstinence, periodic continence, *coitus interruptus*, and contraception — are 'unnatural' in the sense that they involve human manipulation — interference with 'natural' coitus. Each has certain drawbacks as well: complete abstinence can be calamitous; the 'safe period' may not be safe and requires calculation; withdrawal is wretched and psychologically dangerous; and contraception may be aesthetically uncongenial. If interference is rejected on principle, all four methods are ruled out. Unlimited procreation, however, is not in accord with man's true nature, and a price must be paid if family limitation is accepted as the responsible and truly human course. The choice of method in that case should be made in faith and with a free conscience, in a joint and deliberate decision by husband and wife.

From a practical point of view, the significant item in these references is their agreement on the validity of marital union, apart from the purpose of procreation, which gives a sanction for the limitation and spacing of births. Other theologians tend in the same direction. Paul Tillich in *Love, Power, and Justice*, for example, argues in favor of giving the libido a higher status in theological analysis. It is the 'normal drive towards vital self-fulfillment,' though it needs to stand under the ultimate criterion of the *agapē* quality of love. Pleasure for the sake of pleasure is a perversion. 'Unperverted life strives . . . for union with that which is separated from it, though it belongs to it.' Otto Piper of Princeton Theological Seminary, one of the few people who have given substantial attention to this area, uses Biblical exegesis in *The Christian Interpretation of Sex* to establish an independent status for marital 'knowledge' apart from procreation. He argues that the 'one flesh' passage indicates union is not dependent on procreation, since children are not mentioned in this context. Also, the 'increase and multiply' references are not injunctions but rather blessings spoken by God: 'In other words we have here a promise of children and not an obligation to beget them.' A more extreme argument, to emphasize the spiritual dimension of marriage, is advanced by Jacques Ellul of France:

> Marriage is essentially a new state to which God calls man, not for natural needs but for deeper needs, those of participation in Redemption . . . Consequently, procreation is neither the purpose nor essential element of marriage. The children who ensue can add something, but marriage is fully sufficient without children, being given its spiritual purpose as its principal end.

Although the relatively limited work of the general theologians has and will continue to have an influence on contemporary Protestant thought regarding responsible parenthood, the main theological impact, in my judgment, has been coming from the growing, if still all too few, number of specialists who concentrate on marriage and family guidance problems. On the Continent, the considerable concern in this area among Lutherans stems largely from the Inner Mission. There has been a close relationship between study on the parenthood issues and the establishment of family guidance clinics in Norway and Finland, for example. The practical problems of pastoral counseling provide the setting for a consideration of related doctrinal questions in the writing of men like Leslie Weatherhead and James Pike.[7]

The name that merits mention most of all is undoubtedly that of Sherwin Bailey of the Church of England Moral Welfare Council. He has combined a scholarly approach with practical concern to give leadership on a new theology of marriage both in Anglican and wider circles. His *The Mystery of Love and Marriage* [8] and other writings have focused attention on Christian concern in the relational or personal dimension of marriage as a guiding principle in marital union. He himself cites the influence of the relational philosophy developed by the Jewish theologian, Martin Buber, in his *I and Thou*, which first appeared in 1923, and indeed has ventured the opinion that this may have exerted an influence on *Casti Connubii*. The imprint of Dr. Bailey's thought is clear in the preparatory volume for the 1958 Lambeth Conference, *The Family in Contemporary Society* — called the Warren Report from the name of the chairman. The following from his pen, for example, is found in the South Asia appendix to the Warren Report. It illustrates both the scope of his influence and the caliber of his analysis:

> In human beings, *coitus* is more than a device for reproduction — it is a complex experience, the purposes of which may be described as conceptional and relational . . . The Prayer Book states that the 'first cause' for which matrimony was ordained is 'the procreation of children to be brought up in the fear and nurture of the Lord and to the praise of His Holy Name.' There is sound reason for suggesting that the process of procreation which is begun at conception is not terminated at birth, for parenthood involves many years of creative work with the growing child before that degree of personal maturity is attained at which he becomes fully the human being God intended him to be. Interpreted in this wider sense, the procreative purpose of *coitus* is not limited therefore to the promotion of conception. Those relational acts of *coitus* between husband and wife which cement and deepen their love, relieve their physical and psychological sexual tensions, and contribute to their personal fulfilment and integration, have an effect which naturally overflows the bounds of the one flesh, so that such *coitus* is directly beneficial to the whole family. It cannot too strongly be stressed that the well-being of the family depends to a greater extent than has perhaps been recognized hitherto, on the well-being of the one flesh — and to that well-being regular *coitus* makes a profound contribution.

In efforts such as these to rethink the conceptional and relational ends of marriage we find one of the formative influences on recent church statements regarding responsible parenthood. The new external factor has been the quickening awareness of the population explosion, and the problems of rapid social change it poses for the 'younger churches' of Asia, Africa, and Latin America — or indeed in some cases an appreciation of new population problems in Western lands. Above all, the disruptive effect of these pressures on the stability of marriage and family life impels the Christian conscience to give heed.

Both the internal and external factors can be seen in statements issued in 1951. As for the former, a letter sent out by the bishops of the Church of Sweden stated:

> Every marriage where husband and wife — although normal biological grounds are to be found — do not want to have children has a wrong aim. But the child is not the only purpose. The meaning of marriage is above all to be a communion between man and woman. Sexual intercouse between married couples may be an ample sign of this communion although due to special circumstances it might be necessary to avoid pregnancy. If this view is seriously accepted one must admit that contraceptives may be used under certain conditions.

As for the growing concern over population pressures, the Presbyterian Church in Ireland sent to the presbyteries for discussion a report on 'World Population,' urging study of the question of family limitation in view of the fact that 'the question of food for the world's steadily mounting population has begun to occupy, in recent years, the minds of able men, both here and in America.' Similarly, a consultation in the United States on 'The American Churches and Overseas Development Programs,' sponsored by departments of the National Council of Churches, said rather cautiously:

> Because some areas are overpopulated in relation to their immediately exploitable resources, a balance must be struck between growth in population and growth of food and goods. Increased education and industrialization and laws tending toward later marriages may gradually play an increasing part in reducing birth rates. The possibilities of limiting population by voluntary and socially acceptable means, rather than by famine, pestilence, and war, should be fully explored.[9]

In 1952, the General Synod of the Nederlandse Hervormde Kerk approved the report of its Commission on Civil and Religious Marriage which had been appointed in 1947. This statement, in its wrestling with contemporary problems of the family, impresses me as the most significant document to date from the churches of the Calvinist tradition. It set at the time a new standard for a serious Protestant approach to the question of responsible parenthood. The key point is that new knowledge and new conditions place a new responsibility on husband and wife in regard to creating a family, a responsibility which can rightly include a limitation of pregnancies. The report discounts the objection to family planning on 'natural' grounds, since through medical advances the 'natural' limitation of the family is being successfully attacked, and the 'natural' balance broken. Faith in God's providence, moreover, does not release us from responsibility. In view of the importance of the common life of husband and wife, birth control should not mean cessation of marital relations. As for methods:

> . . . we are here in the field of freedom, because circumstances have here their say . . . Once we have taken for granted that we are jointly responsible for the creation of a family and that this responsibility can also include birth control, then the question of ways and means becomes one that married people must settle between themselves and with their physician in the most responsible way. We already said that it is not the means, but the motives that are determinant.

Two years later, the Augustana Evangelical Lutheran Church in America adopted a statement on 'Responsible Parenthood' compiled from statements prepared by the Commission on Social Relations of the American Lutheran Conference. It offered a new norm of excellence for the churches of the Lutheran tradition. This carefully prepared pronouncement emphasized the right of the child to love, care, and nurture, and made this a test for the decision to space births. Two of the key paragraphs are these:

> So long as it causes no harm to those involved, either immediately or over an extended period, none of the methods for controlling the number and spacing of the births of children has any special moral merit or demerit. It is the spirit in which the means is used, rather than whether it is 'natural' or 'artificial,' which defines its 'rightness' or 'wrongness.' 'Whatever ye do, do all to the glory of God' (1 Cor. 10:31) is a principle pertinent to the use of the God-given reproductive power.

An unrestrained production of children without realistic regard to God-given responsibilities involved in bringing children up 'in the discipline and instruction of the Lord' (Eph. 6:4) may be as sinful and as selfish an indulgence of the lusts of the flesh as is the complete avoidance of parenthood. God does not expect a couple to produce offspring at the maximum biological capacity. The power to reproduce is His blessing, not a penalty upon the sexual relationship in marriage.

Up until now all of the statements we have found have been from the churches of the West. Most of the 'younger churches' of the underdeveloped world have been so enmeshed in problems of survival and elementary questions of religious liberty, so understaffed and so unaccustomed to dealing with broader social issues, that the mounting population pressures and related facts of rapid social change have not received systematic or formal consideration.[10] During the past decade, however, the National Christian Council of India, for one, and the related Christian Medical Association of India, have given more serious attention to the question of responsible parenthood. In a pamphlet entitled 'Christian Marriage and Family Planning,' published in 1953 by the Christian Literature Society for the National Council's Christian Home Committee, in addition to considerations relevant to Indian mores, some of the more universal Christian principles are asserted:

The Bible teaches us that the function of marriage is not only to provide a home for the growing family. God created man, male and female, to be companions, and to love one another, as the stories in the early chapters of Genesis show.

The pamphlet proceeds with a consideration of total or partial abstinence and artificial methods of contraception. More recent unpublished statements of the C.M.A.I. wrestle with the growing question of sterilization, posed by more frequent recourse to this means of family limitation, in view of the inadequacies in regard to currently available contraceptives.

To return to the West, it was in 1956 that the General Conference of the Methodist Church in the U.S. wrote into its church discipline this proposition: 'We believe that planned parenthood, practiced in Christian conscience, may fulfill rather than violate the will of God.' Also, the National Council of the Reformed Church of France, having noted the report of its Medical Commission, uttered certain conclusions. According to Scripture, children are a duty and a joy. But physical union is also an expression of communion desired by God, according to the 'one flesh' concept in the Bible. A certain control of births is legitimate in consideration of maternal health, living conditions of the family, and eugenic disorders. 'To safeguard the unity of the couple is not to give complete license to spouses, but on the contrary to call them to a discipline accepted jointly in mutual respect and temperance, as a victory of their love and of their faith.'

In this same year, the United Lutheran Church in the U.S. adopted an excellent brief statement on 'Marriage and Family Life.' The full unity of the 'one flesh' relation in which husband and wife enrich and are a blessing to each other is the essential characteristic of marriage. In children, moreover, the 'one flesh' idea finds embodiment.

> Husband and wife are called to exercise the power of procreation responsibly before God. This implies planning their parenthood in accordance with their ability to provide for their children and carefully nurture them in fullness of Christian faith and life. The health and welfare of the mother-wife should be a major concern in such decisions. Irresponsible conception of children up to the limit of biological capacity and selfish limitation of the number of children are equally detrimental. Choice as to means of conception control should be made upon professional medical advice.

It may have been about the same time that a report of another Lutheran body, the Church of Finland, stated:

> Scientific contraception serves a rightful purpose by helping married couples to regulate the interval of deliveries when circumstances make it necessary, but it becomes a danger if it is so used that the partners of the marriage through selfish and irresponsible refraining from parenthood avoid the most natural matrimonial duties.

The Anglicans, however, having taken the initiative a generation before, were preparing to seize it again, to show what a mature approach to the population-parenthood problem should be. The preparatory group under Canon Warren of the Church Missionary Society put together a more thorough review of the data and issues — demographic, economic, social, and moral — than any conference in Protestantism had previously enjoyed. Supplementary reports from the United States, Canada, and South Asia were appended to the report. In a theological supplement the problem of contraception is analyzed from three different angles, the meeting point being the judgment 'that a conscientious decision to use contraceptives would in certain circumstances be justified.' The Warren Report itself also records a more affirmative attitude toward properly motivated contraception and asserts that 'to produce children without regard to consequences is to use procreative power irresponsibly.'

The remarkable report on 'The Family in Contemporary Society' produced by Section V at Lambeth in 1958 demonstrates the value of careful preparation. Bishop Stephen Bayne, the chairman, did an outstanding job both in the preparatory phase and in the conduct of the section — for the creative consensus arrived at could not have been achieved without creative leadership. The Section V report and the supporting resolutions of the Conference not only constitute a major development in Anglican thought in regard to marriage and family life; they also mark a significant advance for the whole ecumenical movement, for the influence of the Lambeth conclusions will be felt for a long time. I think it is not too much to say that Lambeth 1958 may prove to be a watershed among the non-Roman churches between the comparative neglect of problems of parenthood in the past and a more responsible approach in the future.

The key resolution of the Conference on family planning, and a related paragraph of the Section V report are quoted in the Mansfield Report found in the Appendix. The report puts the new and positive attitude toward responsible parenthood in a broad theological context. In the Biblical revelation the 'relationship of man and woman — of husband and wife — is rooted in

God's creative purpose equally with the procreative function.' The two insights are not subordinated one to the other, or directly related; their relationship is to be found in 'the place of the family in giving responsible security to the children born of the love of husband and wife.' In this declaration of independence from the doctrine of Thomas and the philosophy of Aristotle, the bishops find not one primary end to which all else is subordinate, but three purposes or functions interwoven in human sexuality: the procreation of children, the fulfillment and completion of husband and wife, and the establishment of a stable environment for a mature family life.

The technical possibilities for controlled conception present new problems for conscientious choice. Responsible parenthood today implies 'a watchful guard against selfishness and covetousness, and an equally thoughtful awareness of the world into which our children are to be born.' As for the means of family planning, the Committee, while giving a sanction in principle to mutual continence and contraception, indicated a rejection of *coitus interruptus* and a strong condemnation of induced abortion, save for medical necessity. The question of voluntary sterilization was the subject of considerable discussion. The reasons why many in the underdeveloped countries are turning to it were recognized, and so were the objections — the abdication of responsible freedom, the unknown consequences, the violation of the human body. But the Committee deferred a final judgment, urging that 'the most prayerful and serious consideration' be given before the choice of sterilization be made.

The Committee also devoted a section to the population problem itself, noting data presented in the preparatory volume. The point of view expressed was this: 'As these problems of population have been created, in a measure, by a Christian concern to combat disease and to save life, so they can be met only by a redoubled concern to help those in need.' The Encyclical Letter, which was issued in connection with the Lambeth Report, included this paragraph on the demographic situation:

There are many lands today where population is increasing so fast that the survival of young and old is threatened. We believe that it is the duty of the better developed countries to help such countries to become self-supporting in food supplies and health measures through technical and other aids. In such countries population control has become a necessity. Abortion and infanticide are to be condemned, but methods of control, medically endorsed and morally acceptable, may help the people of these lands so to plan family life that children may be born without a likelihood of starvation. As the expectation of life in many parts of the world increases, the need to care for the aged therefore becomes more insistent.

While the Lambeth Report is in one sense the climax of the present story, it is also the beginning of a new story, the story of more responsible attention by the non-Roman churches to the issues of population and parenthood. In the months since the Conference, two of the congregationally organized churches, which in general have hesitated to 'invade' the area of parental responsibility with principles of guidance, have begun to speak. The International Convention of the Disciples of Christ in October 1958, in referring to world population pressures, mentioned as minimizing factors the expansion of production and distribution, and migration, for meeting temporary problems, but spoke first of 'population control based on education concerning the use of efficient birth control techniques.' The Baptist Union of Denmark in March 1959 held that 'family planning will always be a matter for every married couple to decide for themselves,' but went on to indicate questions to be taken into consideration: health, family economy, national and international policies affecting conditions for the children, and mutual commitment to a God-given task which overrules other interests. Again, the United Presbyterian Church in the U.S.A. at its General Assembly in May 1959, reversed previous condemnations of birth control. It recognized that marriage involves both companionship and parenthood, and that the former does not require the latter to justify it. Approving the principle of voluntary family planning and responsible parenthood, the Assembly affirmed 'that the proper use of medically approved contraceptives may contribute to the spiritual, emotional, and economic welfare of the family.'

Thus the chorus swells among the Protestant churches, even though many bodies have not yet been heard from. A search of the literature of the pentecostal and faith groups might well indicate that their thinking in this area remains closer to the traditional point of view inherited from Rome than to the insights which now prevail in the mainstream of Evangelical Christianity. Some no doubt have scruples against any kind of doctrinal guidance in this area. But as for the Protestant churches co-operating in the ecumenical movement, can any one doubt, in the light of the evidence summarized above, that a fundamental consensus of conviction on responsible parenthood is rapidly evolving? [11] Much remains to be done to develop this consensus, to provide more solid theological undergirding, to give the consensus cohesion and effective common expression. The hard core of common Christian conviction, however, seems clear.

The implications of all this for the agencies of the ecumenical movement need now to be considered. Consideration of these is included in the succeeding chapter.

The Ecumenical Movement and
the Way Forward

  So we come, at the end of this review, to the question of the way forward for the non-Roman churches, and the related question of Western policy. The questions are related because the principal powers of the Western concert share the ethos of Protestantism, and a clear lead from the churches of the Reformation can, in my opinion, help to overcome the present neglect of the demographic problem in Western and United Nations policy more rapidly than any other factor. As indicated at the outset, the sands of time in this matter are running extremely fast. The mounting consequences of the population explosion particularly in Asia press a claim to attention with an insistency which cannot be long denied. In a few months — two or three years at most — the demographic problem will force its way into a prominent position on the international stage, whether public officials be guided by timid or courageous counsels. Yet, in view of the manifold and stubborn obstacles to a successful population policy, it is of great importance that they be guided by courageous counsels. Nothing, in my judgment, is more likely to bring this to pass than clear evidence of a doctrine of responsible parenthood, rooted in conscience and theological conviction, and commonly held by the churches of the Reformation.

Quite apart from this consideration, however, there is the obligation of our Protestant churches to give more relevant guidance on the problems of marriage and family life in the rapidly changing social environment of today. Christian couples have a right to expect sound pastoral counsel on the problems of parenthood, to help them to responsible decisions on the use of God-given procreative powers. In the discussion at the Mansfield Conference, referred to below, it seemed to be generally agreed that more often than not in Protestant circles it is the doctor or social worker rather than the pastor who provides such counsel as the average couple enjoys. There is need for more specific training in this field in the seminaries — for vigorous denominational and interdenominational family life departments, for consultations and co-operation at every level between pastors and doctors, psychologists, and social workers. This indicates part of the way forward; in the long run it is a more fundamental task than that of public witness.

Both pastoral counseling and public witness need the stimulus, corrective, and reinforcement which the ecumenical fellowship can provide at local, national, and world levels. Consequently, we need briefly to examine relevant developments in the ecumenical movement, both to complete the review of the contemporary religious situation and to assess the prospects for concerted study and action in the period ahead.

The annals of ecumenical consideration of the population and parenthood problems are fairly short if not entirely simple. The fact is that this complex of issues did not loom large enough as a common concern to the founding fathers of the World Council of Churches to call for concerted attention. The demographic problem was not referred to when the 'Aims' of the Commission of the Churches on International Affairs were drafted in 1946. Nor was any provision for a department on marriage and family life written into the structure of the Council itself at the Amsterdam or Evanston Assemblies, despite the fact that a number of the member churches had such departments. The issues affecting the basic institution of society were seen primarily as denominational or confessional matters rather than as challenges to concerted work and witness. This situation could not last, since no institution has been more affected by the social crisis than the family, and no international problem has become more portentous for world order than the population explosion. The moral and human values at stake press an inexorable claim to ecumenical consideration. Little by little that claim is being recognized and responses initiated.

One response was the holding in 1950 and 1953 of conferences on the family at the Ecumenical Institute in Bossey, Switzerland. The composition and orientation of both conferences were exclusively Western and predominantly Continental. The background was not the world population explosion and the related upheaval of rapid social change, but the slower erosion of Christian values in marriage and family life through the impact of secularism and changing social patterns. Two other considerations noted in a report on the 1953 conference were the newer psychological insights into the significance of human sexual life, and new theological insights 'which show that the man-woman relationship is a much more profound and basic conception for the whole understanding of the Christian message than rationalism, puritanism and pietism . . . had believed.'

Growing out of the first conference, a special consultation on birth control was held at Bossey in 1952, which surveyed the various methods and urged the need for more positive guidance by the churches, but did not give very clear clues as to what the guidance should contain. Also, the report remained unpublished, and so had doubly limited influence. The 1953 conference on the family was able to focus on fewer issues than the first, and made somewhat greater headway in clarifying issues. The study group on 'Socially Responsible Parenthood and the Question of Family Planning' agreed that 'it is possible for the unitive end of marriage to be fulfilled independently of the procreative end,' but that 'the two aims should not lightly be separated.' In short, the group spoke with an uncertain voice, reflecting the confusion which still characterized Protestant thought so short a time ago. On one point the conference as a whole resolved: the need to include in the organization of the World Council, and if possible in the Evanston Assembly, a place for 'study of the problems of the family and sexual relationships in their theological and sociological settings.'

This did not come to pass as the conference had hoped, for the time was not ripe so far as ecumenical awareness of the issues was concerned. Yet the situation has changed rapidly since the Second Assembly of the World Council met in Evanston in 1954. For one thing, the International Missionary Council, the older associate of the World Council, which had set up in 1950 a modest Home and Family Life program to counsel with leaders of the 'younger churches' on the special problems arising in non-Christian cultures, held an important conference in Manila in November 1954 on 'The Christian Family in Changing East Asia.' The World Council's Department on the Co-operation of Men and Women in Church and Society has found itself increasingly concerned with theological issues bearing on marriage and family problems. The Study on Rapid Social Change under the Department on Church and Society discovered that the demographic question was a principal concern of the co-operating group in Japan, which undertook a serious study of Japan's demographic situation.[1]

From another angle, the joint agency of the World Council and the I.M.C., the Commission of the Churches on International Affairs, has become increasingly concerned about the impact of population pressures on international schemes for promoting economic and social development within a framework of freedom. As representatives of the ecumenical bodies at the intergovernmental level, C.C.I.A. officers have spoken cautiously in relation to governments, pending a clarification of ecumenical thought and policy. Apprehension over this mounting and neglected problem, however, has underlain the repeated stress since 1952 on the need for longer-range evaluation of programs, for realistic priorities, for a world-wide strategy of development. As the C.C.I.A. Executive Committee stated in 1955:

In the interest of more effective assistance, consideration should be given to greater concentration of efforts on the more crucial projects, and particularly in those densely populated countries where a rapid acceleration of economic and social development is imperative.

C.C.I.A. representatives have been less cautious in private and informal conversations in the corridors of the United Nations and in discussions with churchmen. As the staff member giving primary attention to this area, in the spring of 1955, I developed the concern emerging from our C.C.I.A. work and intensified by the implications of the Chinese census of 1953, in a presentation to the U.S. Conference for the World Council of Churches at Buck Hill Falls, Pennsylvania.[2] The following summer I raised the issue again at the Arnoldshain Conference of European and American churchmen on the responsible society and international affairs. The need for more serious ecumenical consideration and study of the population problem, and the related question of family planning, was endorsed by the conference. The C.C.I.A. Executive Committee concurred in this judgment, stressing the 'need to study the theological and ethical issues involved in family planning and to review the data which will assist in the formulation of policy.' The C.C.I.A. recommendation was received by the World Council's Central Committee at Galyatetö, Hungary, in August 1956.

Nothing much happened, however, at the ecumenical level in response to this resolution during the ensuing year and a half, despite the mounting evidence that the situation was becoming more grave. Consequently, I presented a new analysis entitled 'Population and International Development' to the U.S. Conference meeting again at Buck Hill Falls in April 1958.[3] This time the response was more gratifying. The section of the presentation critical of the Roman position was reported in *The New York Times*, and a hasty 'rebuttal' by the publicity officer of the National Catholic Welfare Conference carried word about the issue across the country. More important, the U.S. Conference, on the motion of Bishop Angus Dun, took special action on the matter:

Resolved that the U.S. Conference for the World Council of Churches . . . being convinced that few problems have greater bearing on the welfare of our fellow men and on world peace than the responsible control of population growth, especially in the under-developed areas of the world, commend this report and the whole subject on which it bears to the member churches of this Conference and to the proper agencies of the National Council of Churches and the International Missionary Council with the hope that the Chris-tian conscience and understanding may be promptly mobilized for a courageous and forthright judgment on this issue, which has been so widely evaded because of its controversial character . . .

The U.S. Conference initiative served as a kind of catalyst. Of-ficers of the National Council decided to undertake a study pro-cedure looking toward a formulation of policy. Bishop Bayne circulated some of the background material to his committee of bishops. Leaders of the United Presbyterian Church set in motion actions which resulted in May 1959 in reversal of former positions on 'birth control.' Social action executives of the United Church of Christ set up a drafting committee to prepare a statement. Of-ficers of the Rapid Social Change Study decided to give more attention to the population problem in their work. And the re-sponse was one of the factors which led the general officers of the World Council and I.M.C. to ask Dr. Norman Goodall, secretary of the Joint Committee of the World Council and the I.M.C., to convene an *ad hoc* study group on the population and parenthood issues, with a view to advice on the way forward.

This study group on Responsible Parenthood and the Population Problem met at Mansfield College, Oxford, on 12–15 April 1959, after having studied a number of preparatory papers. The mem-bers represented various disciplines bearing on these issues and, in a general way, the confessional 'families' in the ecumenical move-ment. The 'younger churches' were present in members from the Philippines, India, and Nigeria, and their active participation made one wish that the modest travel budget could have cared for a larger representation. The meeting was one of those heart-warming occasions when a group of diverse people find a largely common mind by the process of group discussion, in which each makes a contribution, none dominates, and the joint product is something new and meaningful to the group as a whole. Save for the procedural recommendations to the officers of the parent bodies, the text of the Mansfield Report is given in the Appendix. The Report has no authority except the possible merit of its insights, as they may commend themselves to the leaders and members of churches in the ecumenical fellowship. Essentially that is the nature of authority in this fellowship.

After an interesting discussion on the point, the group agreed that the proper framework for the main section of the report was the theological concept of covenant rather than the psychological concept of mutual love and respect. Covenant combines the mutual giving of husband and wife with the divine dimension of marriage. Within this covenant companionship and parenthood have equally fundamental status. Together they make for the fullness of marriage, but companionship is independently justified. Increased knowledge about procreation is a liberating gift from God, which creates a new area for responsible decision. Such a decision needs to take into account the social context and witness of the family, as well as intrafamily claims. When the control of conception is right, the group found there was considerable latitude as to means within the limits of health and Christian conscience. Establishment of conditions of livelihood and knowledge in the underdeveloped world which can give greater reality to free and responsible personal decisions is seen as a proper objective of international development assistance. The Mansfield Report outlines a coherent and relevant doctrine of responsible parenthood — which offers a significant lead for the ecumenical movement.

Two major questions are posed for the ecumenical leadership in regard to next steps. One is how to find a formula on the question of responsible parenthood sufficiently flexible to leave room for the different approach of Orthodox leaders without blunting too much the cutting edge of the Protestant consensus. This is a difficult problem, as may be gathered from the chapter on Eastern Orthodoxy. At the time of writing, the way forward here is not clear. The other main issue is whether there is sufficient conviction on this subject among the churches of Asia, Africa, and Latin America, where the problems show their most insistent side, to make a 'courageous and forthright judgment' truly ecumenical in character. Even though concern about the welfare of peoples and churches in the underdeveloped world is a principal motive in such a judgment, if the church leaders of these continents are not themselves convinced, any ecumenical action might be misunderstood.[4]

On this point, there is an encouraging clue to be found in the East Asia Christian Conference which met at Kuala Lumpur, Malaya, in May 1959. Here there was considerable discussion of the population-parenthood issues. A committee report asserted that, although some churches in the area do not want to discuss such questions, the rapid increase of population, high density, and overpopulation in relation to resources confront the churches 'with issues demanding positive statements for the guidance of the church members and leaders.' The committee also said:

> There can be good Christian reasons for limiting the family apart from demographic considerations of controlling population. Considerations of family welfare must be regarded as supreme.

This is evidence that the concern for the objective of responsible parenthood increasingly is shared by churches East and West.

Turning to the broader question of the public witness and its relation to the Roman Catholic position, I believe every sound consideration argues for a *positive* formulation of Evangelical principles rather than a sterile and unworthy criticism of errors in Roman doctrine and policy. The latter is not the monolithic and unchanging structure that non-Romans often imagine. There are moderate as well as radical or reactionary tendencies; there is widespread lay dissent, at least in practice, in regard to the question of contraception; and there are slow, but real, official efforts to adjust policy to contemporary facts and needs. External criticism only tends to silence and impede the constructive elements in the Roman fold, forcing even the dissenters into a common defense of their religious heritage. A negative approach is seldom strong, and here it seems doubly self-defeating.

Moreover and more importantly, we who share the Protestant

heritage need to appreciate more fully the serious way in which the complex of problems bearing on human parenthood is dealt with under the Roman discipline. The Catholic literature on parenthood and population, at least from the perspective of scholarship and volume, makes our Protestant output look rather amateurish.[5] We have no counterpart to the institute for research in human genetics related to the Vatican, the *Instituto di Genetica Medica e Gemellologia 'Gregorio Mendel.'* However intrusive we may regard the approach of the confessional, and however inadequate we may judge the area left to conscientious personal decision, we must recognize the large amount of attention paid to the training of Catholic seminarians in the problems of marriage and family life. A certain amount of humility for past neglects becomes the Evangelical witness in this field.[6]

Humility, however, is not the same as speaking with a faint and uncertain voice. The consensus which is at last emerging among the Protestant churches, freed from the theological errors and historical impedimenta which so badly handicap Rome, offers the most adequate doctrine of responsible parenthood in today's world. It provides the rationale and framework for a more realistic and effective approach to family planning and population policy than has hitherto prevailed. It points to a *via media* between irresponsible policies of inaction, motivated by fear of Catholic reactions, and irresponsible sanction of 'birth control' without moral standards and safeguards. It represents a point of view which the world of nations desperately needs to hear, and it deserves to be expressed in forthright and confident accents.

The time has come, in fact is long overdue, for the Evangelical voice on responsible parenthood to be heard in the halls of government. Jacques Mertens de Wilmars of Belgium, who currently serves as chairman of the U.N. Population Commission, has written in the organ of the International Catholic Migration Commission [7] of the active part taken by Catholic agencies in the deliberations of the U.N. body. He stresses the need for 'close cooperation' between nongovernmental organizations and the

United Nations in this field, referring to the role of NGO's in 'stimulating interest of governments at [the] national level and assisting the United Nations in their tasks in the demographic field.' I quite agree with him that 'much depends upon the initiative of the Non-Governmental Organizations' in regard to Latin America, Asia, and Africa. Indeed, I would go on to say that a great deal depends all along the line upon the agencies which represent the Protestant churches at the national and international level moving from an unworthy, passive role to a dynamic, constructive role.[8]

The initial key to this result and to much else besides, such as the improvement of pastoral work, is further clarification of the Protestant consensus and its communication to pulpit and pew through the educational process. Until the main points in this common view are known and conscientiously held by our clergy and laity, the Evangelical position will continue to suffer disadvantage. The findings of the 1958 Lambeth Conference and the 1959 Mansfield Report offer major contributions to the kind of clarification we need. Yet since the hammering out of a Protestant consensus is the work of many minds and many traditions, I add a few personal notes on the kind of theological analysis that may offer significant common ground.

The first point is that man is more than nature, the point that Reinhold Niebuhr developed so ably in his Gifford Lectures. As Father Russell puts it:

> God did not create man with the intention that he should aim at a purely natural perfection. From the beginning it was His intention that man's needs and capacities should transcend the natural order; he is destined for a supernatural end which he is intrinsically incapable of achieving by his own efforts.

Despite the grave handicaps from the sin in his nature, man is lifted by the gift of reason and conscience above the rest of the animal kingdom, without wholly escaping it. By this gift he is subject primarily to ethical norms (the moral law) rather than to the norms of physical being (the law of nature). Other animals are constrained by nature to limit mating to procreative needs. But man is not so bound. For him the freedom built into his nature lifts the sex act into the realm of ethical decision.

Man's main hope of making the right decisions rests not in his intrinsic powers but in the grace of a merciful God. Grace does not 'perfect' nature, since man's nature is corrupted by sin. Rather, grace transforms nature, enabling man to do what he cannot do by himself, and to achieve beyond his own deserts. Thus the man — or woman — to whom the gift is given is enabled for the sake of the Kingdom to transcend his sexual nature for the life of dedicated celibacy. This is not the perfection of nature, but its transformation. Celibacy, of course, has merit only for those to whom the gift is given, and no intrinsic superiority over the married state — which, when genuine, also involves a divine gift, the gift of union or *henosis*.

A precondition for the right use of sex is provided by the divine institution of marriage, through which by God's grace husband and wife are enabled to become 'one flesh.' This union is expressed both in physical communion and in parenthood, but it transcends both. It is primarily a spiritual reality, as Jesus taught. Parenthood can be an important fulfillment of marriage, though the childless marriage is not less valid for that reason.[9] Procreation is an important but not essential end of marriage, and the marital obligation in regard to parenthood is contingent upon the total purposes of the marriage.[10] The primary purpose of marriage is the perfecting of the 'one flesh' union itself, whether expressed in parenthood, marital companionship, or both. At a deeper level, the primary purpose of marriage, like the rest of life, is to serve and worship God.

If procreation is not the primary purpose of marriage, even less is it the essential purpose of the marital act. The distinction between the conjugal act as a means to procreation and as a means to the furtherance of *henosis* has always been implicit. But the new knowledge of ovulation and of contraception given to man lifts the freedom of the marital act to a new level of ethical decision. Even if the begetting of children were the primary purpose of marriage, it would not follow that each conjugal act must leave open the possibility of conception. The other purposes of marriage have their rights, and the exercise of these rights through contraception would not of itself determine whether the purpose called 'primary' is served or denied. Only the total marriage relationship determines that. The argument here, however, is that procreation is not the primary purpose of marriage. Consequently, the marital act is even less bound to the purpose of procreation. The decision in regard to procreation is a free ethical decision, insofar as the husband and wife are concerned.[11]

There are various ways to make such decisions responsible: the teachings of the church; the advice of the pastor or other counselor; the prayerful consideration of economic, social, or medical 'indications,' including the claims of existing children. For the Evangelical Christian there is no final substitute for the decision of the couple in prayer before God. It is the husband and wife who are charged to be responsible parents. If they decide that procreation should be deferred, then they have a positive moral obligation to try to prevent conception, and the choice of means is a secondary and derivative consideration. Motives rather than methods constitute the primary moral issue. The licit character of any method is based on the presupposition that the contraceptive intent is morally valid in the concrete circumstances.

While both abstinence and periodic continence have their Protestant supporters as preferable methods for preventing conception, I think a characteristic of the consensus now emerging is the rejection of an *a priori* hierarchy of the various contraceptive methods. The variety of marital situations is too great to judge the question of method in the abstract. The Lambeth Conference of 1958 uses the general term: 'in such ways as are mutually acceptable to husband and wife in Christian conscience.' The Mansfield Report finds no inherent moral distinction between periodic continence, contraceptives, and drugs to inhibit or control ovulation, if made effective and safe. What is right or wrong depends upon the needs and gifts of the particular couple, including the degree of effectiveness required for their situation.[12] The methods, as methods, are morally neutral.

For the majority of Protestant couples who need to defer conception, the choice of a right method narrows down to one or another of the forms of contraception. Consequently, the availability of such means becomes a precondition for the exercise of responsible parenthood. If access to contraceptives is denied to Protestants by law or administrative practice, an important element of religious freedom is infringed, as Bishop Pike has argued. The fact that anticontraceptive laws still extant in certain Western countries are apparently laxly enforced does not change the principle. The means required by most Protestant families for responsible parenthood should be legally available. For this right does not infringe the right of others to refrain from using such means.

This review, however, is less concerned with the rights of Western Protestants than with the needs of the critically situated peoples in the lands of the 'younger churches.' Their hopes for development and a more decent material existence, and their hopes for freedom and peace all stand in jeopardy, especially in the densely populated countries of Asia. The evidence justifies the conclusion that, without more vigorous and effective population policies by governments, and widespread acceptance of family limitation by citizens, the factors of danger cannot be reduced. Unless the population explosion itself is checked, all else will fail.

For the countries which understand this peril and seek help on measures to reduce fertility, it will be a tragedy if the more developed countries fail to respond — through accelerated programs of research on suitable contraceptives, through assistance in providing acceptable materials and reducing their cost, through aid in the organization of clinics and public education. A clear witness to Christian concern in this matter can help to avert or to end such a tragedy. Even now there are signs of a belated awakening by governments to the neglected sector of the development problem. To speed that awakening even by a few months would be a major contribution to the struggle for world order.

The critical importance of this awakening should not nourish the illusion that even vigorous assistance in this field will by itself somehow produce a 'solution' for the perils confronting the underdeveloped world. The reduction of population pressures is only one segment of the problem. The technical problems in this segment, moreover, are tough, and the social obstacles more stubborn. As the Mansfield Report points out, in the poverty-stricken societies we can hardly speak of family limitation in terms of responsible parenthood until there is sufficient improvement in conditions of life to undergird free personal decisions. Only a comprehensive, balanced, and dynamic development effort, in which population policy takes its rightful place but does not displace the other necessary elements, has a real chance of success.

Yet it is the best chance, humanly speaking, that we have. Each of us in the churches can help a little that it not be lost, by helping to build an informed and dedicated Christian opinion on the issues posed by the population explosion and the need for responsible parenthood. There is much else to do, but this task has a special claim from its long neglect. To overcome this neglect and replace it with positive conviction, from the parish level to the international level, is a present call to responsible Christian study, action, and prayer.

Responsible Parenthood and the Population Problem

Report of an international study group on 'Responsible Parenthood and the Population Problem,' convened at the instance of officers of the World Council of Churches and the International Missionary Council, which met at Mansfield College, Oxford, April 12–15, 1959.

Included in the study group were the following: Dr. Norman Goodall, London, Chairman; Dr. Thérese Chausse, M.D., Geneva; Dean William G. Cole, Williamstown, Mass.; Dr. Egbert de Vries, The Hague; Canon G. R. Dunstan, London; Miss Freda H. Gwilliam, London; Dr. Irene Ighodaro, M.D., Ibadan, Nigeria; Prof. A. D. Mattson, Rock Island, Illinois; Mrs. Asuncion Perez, Cabanatuan City, Philippines; Dr. Heinz G. Renkewitz, Arnoldshain, Germany; The Rt. Rev. John Sadiq, Bishop of Nagpur, India; The Rev. Ingmar Stoltz, Stockholm; The Very Rev. Archimandrite E. Timiadis, Geneva; Prof. H. Van Oyen, Basel; Dr. Elizabeth J. Welford, M.B., D.R.C.O.G., London; Dr. Richard M. Fagley, New York, Secretary. Consultants included Dr. Harold Anderson, M.D.; Dr. Madeleine Barot; Dr. R. A. Dudley; Mr. Denys L. Munby; Mr. B. Ch. Sjollema.

The fourth section of the report, dealing with procedural recommendations to the officers of the parent bodies, is omitted here.

I. The Contemporary Setting

1. It has become a truism to speak of a world in crisis. The struggle for self-determination, for dignity and freedom of peoples

round the globe, the economic and technological revolution and the emerging of a world-wide industrial society, these are a few of the facts with which we must learn to live.

2. The larger crisis of our time is reflected in families throughout the whole wide earth. Different regions and different nations produce varying problems, but nowhere is the family unaffected. It, too, is in crisis. The emancipation of women and the growing acceptance of partnership between men and women are revolutionizing the previously masculine-dominated social structures which now appear so patently unjust. Under pressures within and without, age-old patterns of family relations are disintegrating on every side. Out of the ruins of the old must be built the new, but built on foundations of respect and dignity and freedom, not of servitude, injustice and conflict.

3. The rapid improvement and extension of much-needed public health programmes in all continents are bringing dramatic reductions in death rates, particularly in areas where high fertility has hitherto been offset by a tragically high mortality. The world confronts a doubling of the present number of people before the end of this century, and is presently experiencing an annual increase of 50 million persons. While the effects of the mounting population pressures are felt throughout the world, the main thrust is occurring in the economically less developed regions of the earth, and indeed may be intensified by the first stages of industrialization. The crisis here stems less from the size of the human increase in relation to potential resources, than from the rapidity of the increase in relation to the present and practicable rate of development of available resources.

4. The social, political, economic and even religious repercussions of this population explosion are vast and grave. Its shock waves buffet countless human families. Nor is there an easy or quick solution to this crisis. Indeed, it seems probable that only a wise combination of vigorous economic and social development aided by substantial technical and financial assistance, the easing of certain pressures by means of migration, the wide development of education, as well as the extension of 'family planning' can hope to offer an acceptable answer.

5. Living in such a world and confronted with such problems the Church bears her continuing witness that God is at work, as

He has been since the dawn of creation. The Church has survived past times of troubles and stands fast in faith toward the future. The concern of Christian faith for the family is not a new one, born out of the travails of the present. From the very beginning the Church has seen itself as the Family of families, and has known that the Christian witness is necessary and effective in the home, in the relationships between husband and wife, between parents and children. Throughout the centuries Christians have sought to relate the eternal truths of the Gospel to the problems and perils of their times. Yet it must be confessed that in the past Christian thought has, especially in the area of the family and its relationships, often clung to tradition without taking into account new knowledge. In the current age, God is calling upon us not to desert the eternal Christian truth, but to apply it to the changing circumstances of the modern world.

6. We recognize the wide dimensions of the challenge, social, political, economic, medical and educational, and we welcome the fact that various agencies, national and international, are devoting their attention to them. Responsible parenthood does not in itself provide a solution to all problems of social and economic development, including the certainty of rapidly increasing world population. The application of science and technical progress in agriculture and industry and the maintenance of peace and international co-operation will have to play a major role. On the other hand, no acceptable solution seems in sight without responsibility taken by individual parents. In this short report, we attempt to offer what seem to us some fundamental Christian principles on which those who are in Christ may base their personal decisions in faith and not in fear. The family embodies the most intimate of all personal relations and has a rightful privacy of its own, but in these days of annihilated distances and common cause the Christian family must open itself to the wider claims of the world and learn to live responsibly in the love of God, the grace of our Lord Jesus Christ and the communion of the Holy Spirit.

II. Contributions Toward an Ecumenical Consensus

7. We have been impressed and encouraged by the evidence of a growing sense of responsibility for the family on the part of

churches and councils in the ecumenical movement. Within the past decade there have been a number of important statements on Christian marriage and parenthood, and additional studies are being undertaken. A compendium of quotations from documents received is appended to this report.*

8. Particular reference should be made to the 1958 Lambeth Conference Report and related resolutions, on 'The Family in Contemporary Society,' and to the preparatory volume under the same title. The ecumenical movement as a whole is indebted to this undertaking for the serious way in which the problems of the family have been approached and for the substantive contribution made to a Christian response.

9. The degree of agreement found in the available statements of various communions is striking, and indeed significant in terms of a prospective consensus within the ecumenical movement. Yet we are also mindful of the partial character of the evidence so far received. Our information is incomplete and the known silence of important Christian bodies may have diverse meanings. We have in mind in this connection the Orthodox Church, the churches and councils in many parts of Asia, Africa and Latin America, churches in Communist countries, as well as some of the churches in the West. The action of the W.C.C. Central Committee at Galyatetö (1956) in recognizing the need for more serious ecumenical consideration and study of the population problem, and the related question of family planning, is still highly relevant.

10. These facts, however, do not minimize the import of the beginnings that have been made. The combined testimony of the churches that have spoken provides a thesis for future ecumenical study and action. It may be well to note briefly a few of the recurrent themes in the statements at hand, which indicate their common tenor.

> There is repeated stress on the spiritual character of true matrimony, expressed in physical union and transcending it. The 'two become one' is part of God's grace, to be accepted as a mystery and lived in faith.

> The family likewise is surrounded by grace. Children are the gift of God, and procreation is sharing in God's creation.

---

* Not included here.

Christian marriage and family life are consequently described in terms of responsibility; the mutuality of husband and wife, the loving care of parents for children, the love and respect of children for parents, the duties of the family in the service of society, the obligations of all to God and His Church. There is repeated emphasis on the applicability of principles of stewardship to procreation within the marriage bond, and on the duty of the Church to inculcate such principles.

True marriage and parenthood are seen at the same time to be part of the realm of Christian freedom. This means freedom from sensuality and selfishness which enslave. It also means considerable latitude of choice, when the motives are right, in regard to mutually acceptable and non-injurious means to avert or defer conception. Marital freedom, indeed, is the pre-condition of marital responsibility.

11. The principles embodied in the available statements provide significant material for further work by the churches, councils and agencies of the ecumenical movement. To aid that process, we advance considerations which, despite possible differences as to detail, and except as noted below,* find general assent among the members of this study group.

III. THE MEANING OF RESPONSIBLE PARENTHOOD

12. Marriage as a divine institution can be described in Biblical terms as a covenanted relationship within which man and woman receive the grace, security and joy promised by God to those who are faithful to it. Marriage is the 'great mystery' which yet illumines for men the covenant or marriage of Yahweh with Israel (Hos. 2:19f.), and of Christ with His Bride, the Church (Eph. 5:23–33; Rev. 21:9, 22:17).

13. The Christian marriage relationship is a covenant, entered

---

* The historic and doctrinal position of the Orthodox Church necessitates, at certain important points, a different approach to this subject from that reflected in the general course of this statement. The Orthodox member of the group, while sharing the concern of the group and contributing fully to its deliberations, drew attention to 'the different teaching and practice of the Orthodox Church, which holds that parents have not the right to prevent the creative process of matrimonial intercourse; also, that God entrusted to them this responsibility for childbearing, with full confidence that His Providence would take care of material and other needs.'

into with sacrifice in the joyful giving of each to the other; it is confirmed by the exchange of vows to which God's promised blessing is attached; it has its own rules or commandments related by God's ordinance to the nature of man and woman and to the relationship between them. Like every other part of human life, it is redeemed by Christ, it is preserved by His forgiveness, it is enriched beyond human measure by the Holy Spirit dwelling in the husband and wife as members of the Body of Christ, the Church.

14. Thus the covenanted relationship of husband and wife within marriage, is, in the purpose of God, one of total commitment, a total giving of self and a total acceptance of the other, resulting in a union, spiritual and physical, described in the Bible as becoming 'one flesh.' The terms of this union are not those of a human contract. In the Biblical narration the ordinance of marriage is integrated with the very creation of man and woman as such; so its terms, as given by God, are proper to the nature of man and woman, and to the nature of their union. Companionship and parenthood are therefore established together as the purposes of marriage from the beginning, with sexual union as the ordained servant of both. Marriage has its fulness where both are attained (Gen. 2:18–25; Matt. 19:4ff.; 13ff.).

15. The social, cultural and economic circumstances surrounding marriage and family life vary widely from region to region and from age to age. The formation of the family, and of companionship within it, varies accordingly; so does the area of life open to personal decision. The gift of dominion to mankind, within the created order of which mankind is part (Gen. 1:28), reinforced by the command to man to love the Lord God with all his mind (Lk. 10:27), calls upon us to extend this area of decision in humble accordance with our knowledge. Knowledge is thus a liberating gift of God, to be used for the glory of God, in accordance with His will for men. Such use of improved medical knowledge has brought a drastic reduction of infant mortality, and this is to be accepted gratefully as coming from God; at the same time it affects deeply the size of the family and the rate of population growth, and has therefore created a new area for responsible decision.

16. Our concern is therefore with the responsible use of knowledge in family life, particularly in relation to the procreation and

nurture of children. A knowledge of the relation of sexual love to the procreative process gives to a couple the power, and therefore the responsibility, to lift the begetting of children out of the realm of biological accident, or 'fate,' into the realm of personal decision — which is also the realm of grace, where man is free to wait upon God and consciously to respond to His will. Carried further, it enables husband and wife to decide, within the Providence of God, whether any one act of intercourse shall be for the enrichment or expression of their personal relationship only, or for the begetting of a child also.

17. That these two purposes of the act are thus separable, within the divine ordinance of the marriage covenant, is evident from the nature of the act itself, which is known to fulfil the first when it is incapable of fulfilling the second, either through sterility, or in times of periodic infertility and after the age of child-bearing in woman. Sexual intercourse within marriage has in itself a goodness given by God, even when there is neither the possibility nor the immediate intention to beget children.

18. Given this responsibility of choice, founded upon knowledge, what considerations are to guide a Christian husband and wife in the exercise of it? They would surely begin with the general ordinance of God for the marriage covenant, integrating the power of parenthood with the expression of sexual love; so parenthood will be normal and right for them, unless there are specific and compelling indications against it, as, for example, a valid threat to the wife's life or health.

19. This obligation — or fulfilment — accepted, the questions may remain, 'How many children?,' 'At what intervals?' Here the considerations involve:

a. *the integrity of the marriage*: every decision should be a joint one of husband and wife, made in faith and prayer and after deliberation in love.

b. *the claims of children as persons in their own right*: they are to be valued, not primarily as economic or social assets or even to assure the comfort of parents in old age or (as is believed in some Asian societies) their beatitude after death; but as persons with a right to parental care in infancy and youth and to a proper equipment from society to serve God fully in it themselves.

c. *the witness of a Christian family in society:* the Christian family, as a cell in the Body of Christ, has a unique vocation and power to exhibit the fruit of the Spirit, often in what are humanly regarded as the most adverse physical conditions — a witness especially needed in a non-Christian or sub-Christian society. To say this is in no way to deny the complementary witness of celibacy, to which the Christian life adds new power and significance in many societies.

d. *the needs of the social order of which the family forms part:* there are factors of special urgency in regions where rapid multiplication of population co-exists with poverty, insufficient supplies of food and other necessities of life, and a low potential for rapid economic development; responsible parenthood has to take account of these.

e. *Church tradition:* when deciding in conscience, Christians would have proper regard to the teaching or tradition, if any, of their own church, and then offer their own decision to God in faith.

20. What considerations should guide parents in the means they employ for the responsible exercise of their procreative power? Responsible parenthood begins with responsible marriage. Biological maturity alone is not the only criterion of readiness for marriage. Life in the Christian community ought to have prepared the young man and woman to raise their sexual relationship above the domination of mere biological impulse, and to have dominion over it. Further, in the life of grace, not only chastity before marriage but also periodic continence within it, when freely accepted by both the spouses, are virtues of positive worth attainable by Christian people.

21. But this is by no means the whole of the answer. The extremely high rates of abortion in many regions, Eastern and Western, with their toll of human suffering and violation of personality, testify to a tragic determination among parents to find some means, however bad, to prevent unwanted births. The Christian conscience cannot approve of abortion, involving as it does the destruction of human life — unless, of course, the termination of a pregnancy is necessary to save the life of the mother.

22. 'Life,' however, does not begin until the sperm has fertilized the ovum and conception has taken place. Knowing this, what means may Christians properly employ to prevent an individual

act of intercourse from resulting in conception? Granted that the attempt may rightfully be made, there appears to be no moral distinction between the means now known and practiced, by the use whether of estimated periods of infertility, or of artificial barriers to the meeting of sperm and ovum — or, indeed, of drugs which would, if made effective and safe, inhibit or control ovulation in a calculable way. It remains that the means employed be acceptable to both husband and wife in Christian conscience, and that, on the best evidence available, they do neither physical nor emotional harm. Here we would quote some words of a Committee of the Lambeth Conference of the Bishops of the Anglican Communion of 1958:

> It must be emphasized once again that family planning ought to be the result of thoughtful and prayerful Christian decision. Where it is, Christian husbands and wives need feel no hesitation in offering their decision humbly to God and following it with a clear conscience. The *means* of family planning are in large measure matters of clinical and aesthetic choice, subject to the requirement that they be admissible to the Christian conscience. Scientific studies can rightly help, and do, in assessing the effects and the usefulness of any particular means; and Christians have every right to use the gifts of science for proper ends.

23. In conclusion we may quote also Resolution 115 of the same Conference, based on the report of this Committee:

> The Conference believes that the responsibility for deciding upon the number and frequency of children has been laid by God upon the consciences of parents everywhere: that this planning, in such ways as are mutually acceptable to husband and wife in Christian conscience, is a right and important factor in Christian family life and should be the result of positive choice before God. Such responsible parenthood, built on obedience to all the duties of marriage, requires a wise stewardship of the resources and abilities of the family as well as a thoughtful consideration of the varying population needs and problems of society and the claims of future generations.

24. It is to be observed that such deliberation, and such estimation of human, spiritual and social values, as has been outlined above, is well nigh impossible in some of the regions where they are most urgently required. Where there is grinding poverty, a high

birth rate, high death rate and high infant mortality, a fatalistic attitude to birth as to death is almost inevitable, and a high valuation of human personality is difficult to attain. Christians in wealthier regions have a duty to ponder, and to act upon, this truth in order to help their fellows in less developed lands towards conditions in which they can enjoy the freedom to make personal decisions of this sort, and to exercise responsible parenthood for themselves. To secure this help, the Christian is led by his faith to consider such matters as the need for capital investment and hence his opportunities as a citizen for political action. The command to love thy neighbour as thyself (Lev. 19:18; Lk. 10:27) is thus relevant at all points: it defines the duty of spouse to spouse; of parents to their children and of children to parents; of families to other families in society; of churches to churches; and of nations to nations.

(Numbers preceded by # refer to books listed in bibliography)

I — POPULATION AND PARENTHOOD

1. 'Parenthood' avoids the unduly restricted biological connotation which 'procreation' has acquired in secular circles, and is less clumsy than the Roman Catholic 'procreation and education.'

2. 'Responsible parenthood,' in fact, is becoming the preferred term throughout Protestantism for limiting the number of progeny. 'Birth control' fails to distinguish between conception control and abortion.

3. Concern over declining birth rates underlay the main Greek Orthodox statement and several British statements, noted in later chapters. The Director of the Institute for Research in Agricultural Economics, Colin Clark, is still worried over possible depopulation in Britain — cf. his article, 'Too Small Families,' *The Sunday Times*, 15 March 1959. Is not the love of children too strong to regard infertility as more than a passing phenomenon?

4. 'Fertility' here follows English and American demographic terminology, standing for actual births rather than fecundity or the ability to reproduce.

5. Cf. #28, p. 74. The ratio in total G.N.P.'s for the two groups is estimated at 8:1 as of 1976; population growth raises the per capita G.N.P. ratio to 15:1.

6. Exceptions are the work of the U.N. Population Branch and the World Population Conference of 1954.

7. Three of these were undertaken under U.N. and related auspices; one was a Swedish bilateral project.

8. The 1958 reversal by the New York City Board of Health of policy regarding contraceptive advice in city hospitals appears to be a new factor on the other side. The recent refusal in the U.K. of the B.B.C. and Postmaster General to ban a broadcast on behalf of the Family Planning Association is another straw in the wind.

9. For example, Ronald F. Freedman, Pascal K. Whelpton, and Arthur A. Campbell conducted in 1955 a survey of a cross section sample of 2,700

white wives in the U.S. aged 18–39 years: less than 5% expressed un-qualified disapproval of family limitation (13% among Roman Catholic wives); 73% of the Protestants expressed unqualified approval, and 33% of the Catholics did likewise. Of the fecund couples, 83% had adopted contraception; the authors think the total may actually exceed 90%, as couples grow older and seek to limit their families. Cf. #11; summary in *Scientific American*, April 1959.

10. For example, 13 American agricultural experts in a Ford Foundation team reported to the Indian government that by 1966 India will have added '80 million mouths to feed . . . to avert famine in 1966, India must triple its present rate of increase in food production,' *Time*, 4 May 1959. It is of course true that hands go with the mouths, yet even an Indian sweeper's child cannot be put to work before the age of seven — and of course ought not to be until he is at least twice as old.

11. For example, 'in the Far Eastern populations large families are generally welcomed for reasons of familial economy, security and prestige.' M. C. Balfour, R. F. Evans, F. W. Notestein, I. B. Taeuber, *Public Health and Demography in the Far East*, Rockefeller Foundation, New York, 1950, p. 9.

II — THE POPULATION EXPLOSION

1. As Bishop Sherrill said with his usual wit, at a meeting of the U.S. Con-ference for the World Council of Churches, when I mentioned that the world's population had grown by 10,000 during their two hour session: 'I knew we should have adjourned earlier.'

2. In 1945, for example, Frank W. Notestein, the Princeton demographer, summed up the hypothetical figures for the year 2000 as 3.3 billion, though he thought they might be conservative (cf. #30). In 1954 Harri-son Brown arrived at a 4.8 billion estimate for 2000 — *The Challenge of Man's Future*, Viking Press, New York, 1954. It should be added that not all demographers regard the Chinese census of 1953 as accurate; but there seems to be a general consensus that earlier estimates were too low.

3. Cf. the U.N. Population Branch, *The Future Population Estimates by Sex and Age*, Report no. 3: The Population of South-East Asia, ST/SOA/Series A/30, United Nations, New York, 1958 (pub. 1959).

4. Cf. #27. I concentrate here on the projections of the U.N. Population Branch, partly because the work is of a high caliber, partly because the question of projections is not germane enough to this analysis to justify a wider and possibly confusing survey of population estimates. Even the U.N. projections only portray the shadow of present trends, if unfore-seen factors do not intervene.

5. Cf. #4 and W. F. Willcox, *Studies in American Demography*, Cornell Press, Ithaca, New York, 1940.

6. Dr. Nicholas Dietz, Jr., an R.C. sociologist, argues that the explosion will become 'self-limiting,' 'when the birth rates are measured against the

increasing number of senior citizens, and as maximum life span is reached.' But a population which doubles or triples in the process, and then has to cope with the problem of feeding the aged as well as the young can hardly be regarded as escaping the explosion. The critical problems concern the decades immediately ahead, for which the panacea of Professor Dietz offers little comfort.

III — CAUSES AND CONSEQUENCES

1. After the initial repercussions to the first edition of the *Essay* in 1798, Malthus did a considerable amount of research on the Continent to bolster his argument. He also repeatedly called attention to the need for more accurate data and this may well have fostered demographic research. A good short compilation from the various editions is T. R. Malthus, *An Essay on the Principle of Population*, Macmillan, New York, 1929.
2. By the second edition he had discovered that in the back areas of America, population was doubling in 15 years, about the present rate of increase in Mauritius. But he continued to use 25 years as a conservative formula.
3. He included under this head 'all unwholesome occupations, severe labor and exposure to the seasons, extreme poverty, bad nursing of children, great towns, excesses of all kinds, the whole train of common diseases and epidemics, wars, pestilence, plague, and famine.'
4. It is a bit odd that advocates of family planning should be labeled 'neo-Malthusians' since Malthus made clear in the appendix to the fifth edition that he disapproved of checks within marriage:

> I should always particularly reprobate any artificial and unnatural modes of checking population, both on account of their immorality and their tendency to remove a necessary stimulus to industry. If it were possible for each married couple to limit by a wish the number of their children, there is certainly reason to fear that the indolence of the human race would be very greatly increased, and that neither the population of individual countries nor of the whole earth would ever reach its natural and proper extent.

5. *Population and Public Health in Non-Self-Governing Territories*, A/AC.35/L.275, United Nations, New York, April 1958.
6. Public sanitary efforts also contribute — e.g. safer water supply, excreta disposal, and environmental improvements such as housing. In this regard, S. P. Jain stated at the World Population Conference of 1954:

> Though much remains to be done in these directions, the progress made so far seems to have resulted in reducing mortality, particularly that due to infectious and parasitic diseases. Maternity and child welfare services are doing their bit to reduce the high infant and maternal mortality . . .

7. The Secretariat report on meeting 30 of the World Population Conference states:

Hitherto, economic backwardness has been the chief factor in the poor health conditions of the underdeveloped countries. In the most recent years, however, the discovery of certain cheap but highly effective products (antibiotics, sulphonamides and, above all, powerful insecticides) enables these countries to reduce mortality independently of economic development.

8. #26, p. 6of. The last point is a considerable understatement. The document goes on to point out that in the post-war years, when death rates were falling, per capita production of foodstuffs decreased, and the decrease was greatest in the underdeveloped countries.

9. *The New York Times Magazine,* 22 September 1957. Davis says that 'in India a whole household can receive a year's protection from malaria at less cost to the Government than an American spends on one haircut.'

10. The report states, with a sense of relief, that 'since yaws and the other treponematoses seldom kill, the control and eventual eradication of this disease does not raise any demographic issue' (p. 9). The direct and indirect effect of the debilitating diseases on prenatal mortality, however, would seem to have demographic implications.

11. Less headway has been made on the nutritional deficiency diseases, such as beriberi and pellagra, than in regard to the infectious and parasitic diseases.

12. The Chinese demographer, Ta Chen, indicated in regard to the 1953 census that the death rate had declined from an estimated 29 per thousand to 21. He added: 'New China is laying greater and greater stress on public health and personal hygiene, on the more effective control of epidemic and endemic diseases, and on the substantial reduction of infants' and children's diseases (such as neo-natal tetanus and measles).' International Statistical Institute, Stockholm, August 1957.

13. Perhaps the most dangerous frustrations come to those who have acquired an education but find no commensurate job opportunities. The Communist successes in Kerala province in India took place in an area with perhaps the highest level of education in the country. The answer, of course, is not fewer schools but schools geared into a more dynamic development strategy.

14. Soviet aid, in the form of special loans, has grown from very modest beginnings in 1954 to commitments totaling about $1 billion as of June 1958, extended principally to the U.A.R., India, Afghanistan, Indonesia, Burma, and Ceylon, according to the U.N. Report, *International Economic Assistance to the Less Developed Countries* 1957–58, E/3255, United Nations, New York, May 1959, p. 2of. The rate of expenditure has so far been slow, estimated at 10 per cent as of June 1958 by the U.N. survey. Even the full amount constitutes a challenge to the Western powers chiefly in an ideological sense.

15. The 1957–58 totals, according to E/3255, are $90 million in grants, $189 million in loans, with repayments amounting to $34 million. Not

included here are Soviet credits, which are not officially reported to the U.N., but E/3255 notes that the net receipts by India in 1957–58 came to some $18 million, and $64 million in 1958–59. *The International Flow of Private Capital* 1956–1958, E/3249, United Nations, New York, 1959 indicates the total of direct foreign private investment in India to be under $1 billion at the end of 1956, mostly from the U.K., and gross inflow for the year to be around $42 million, some two-thirds of this coming from retained earnings.

IV — MIGRATION AND POPULATION

1. Document no. 2, 'Present-Day Migration of Nationals,' prepared by B. Ch. Sjollema for a study on migration for the World Council of Churches, gives the total number of European migrants including refugees as 8.4 million for the 1946–58 period, of whom 44% went to the U.S. and Canada, 27% to Latin America, 18% to Australia and New Zealand, 6% to Africa — not including French migrants to French territories — and 5% to Asia. A figure of 5.6 million is indicated for net emigration.

2. The full impact of the Arab refugee situation and Israeli immigration upon the demographic problem in the Near East has not yet been felt, though political tensions and military expenditures have no doubt intensified the effect of population pressures, while the effect of Israeli absorption of more than 400,000 Near Eastern and North African Jews is uncertain. But the pressures have been blunted thus far by U.N. relief for the Arab refugees and their children, and by governmental and private assistance for Israel.

3. Document no. 2. Neither the one and one half million Koreans living outside Korea, chiefly in Japan and China, nor the millions involved in the costly exchange of populations between India and Pakistan, after partition, while technically subject to inclusion, have significance for our particular purpose.

4. A major concern of the Department of International Justice and Goodwill of the U.S. Federal Council of Churches in its early years was the injustice in this 'Oriental Exclusion Act.' In 1943, the Chinese Exclusion Act of 1888 was repealed and China given an annual quota of 105 immigrants and granted the right of naturalization. India was treated similarly in 1946. Japan was granted a minimum quota of 185 in the McCarren-Walter Act of 1952.

5. The F.A.O. figures for agricultural area include arable land, land under tree crops, plus permanent meadows and pastures. This last makes the resultant figures for countries like Australia and Argentina, in which extensive grazing is the main form of agriculture, appear low. The purpose of the table is to compare the successive figures for each country, not one country with another.

6. *R.E.M.P. Bulletin*, vol. 2, sup. 2, The Hague, May 1954. The addition of South Africa, Southern Rhodesia, and New Zealand would raise the

total to 3.9 million. The distribution of the five country total is as follows: U.S.A., 38%; Canada, 21%; Australia, 20%; Argentina, 15%; Brazil, 6%. Israel, like West Germany, is in a special category, and its inclusion would distort the general migration picture. Dudley Kirk and Earl Huyek similarly put the 'identifiable net outward movement' of Europeans at 3.2 million for 1946–52, or some 450,000 per year. Cf. #15, p. 218.

7. The regular nonquota immigration from Latin America is not large. The large annual influx from Puerto Rico does not count as immigration. Some hold that the largest element in actual immigration into the U.S. is the illegal migration of Mexican 'wetbacks' across the Rio Grande. All three affect the remaining migration possibilities.

8. Carr-Saunders in 1936 thought Japan, because 'births are coming under control,' the one non-European country likely to benefit from emigration — cf. #3, p. 319. The argument has been strengthened both by the unprecedented reduction in fertility since the war, and by the expulsion of the Japanese from territory previously occupied. Yet it does not affect the generalization, since Japan is not in the same category of underdevelopment that applies to the rest of Asia.

9. Carr-Saunders remarks in *The Population Problem* that overpopulation may be 'characterized by the absence of hope and absence of energy, whereas migration indicates a surplus of energy.'

10. From a technical point of view, the movement of hundreds of thousands of Puerto Ricans into the United States and the recent influx of Jamaicans into Great Britain ranks as internal migration, despite the fact that both instances involve movements from a less to a more developed society. On the other hand the fairly massive migration between Canada and the U.S. or the considerable intra-European movement of people, such as the large number of Polish and Italian settlers in France since the war, is technically international migration, though internal in a continental perspective.

V. — Food and Population

1. The idea of some kind of automatic connection between development and lower fertility is common: for example, Msgr. William F. Kelly of Brooklyn, in a report in the N.Y. *Catholic News* of 5 July 1958, was quoted as pointing to industrialization as presaging a possible drop in the birth rate of backward countries: 'It is possible that their population trends may follow the same pattern as the more advanced Western nations . . .'

2. #26, p. 75. Frank Lorimer points out how little is known about variations in genetic capacities or the influence of environmental conditions: 'The only positive assertions that can be made with assurance are that there are important variations in fecundity among people living in different conditions, but that in general variations among human

populations in natality are more powerfully influenced by social and psychological factors.' #18, p. 22.

3. The F.A.O. 1957 *Yearbook of Food and Agricultural Statistics*, Pt. I, p. 234, indicates a range in daily consumption of animal protein from 71 grams for New Zealand to eight for Pakistan and six for India.

4. The following percentages are given by Josué de Castro: pigs — 20%; milk — 15%; eggs — 7%; beef — 4%. *The Geography of Hunger*, Little, Brown, Boston, 1952, p. 145f.

5. Cf. Ancel Keys in #10, p. 28f. It should be noted, however, that diet is an important determinant of body size, so that present estimates of caloric requirements do not reflect the full needs of many countries.

6. Despite the slowing down of agricultural expansion in recent years as a result of surpluses, the index for total food production in North America increased during this period by 41 points as compared with 33 for the underdeveloped world, and the per capita increase was 12 points. 'The paradoxical situation has arisen that in the more developed countries, where supplies are already abundant or overabundant, technical progress has made possible a further rapid expansion of output if markets for larger supplies could be found.' *The State of Food and Agriculture*, F.A.O., Rome, 1958, p. 1.

7. A highly optimistic view of resources and scientific ingenuity was presented by Kirtley Mather of M.I.T. in *Enough and to Spare*, Harper, New York, 1944. It may be noted that 15 years later the publisher, John Cowles, said, in a commencement address at M.I.T., that the rate of population growth must be checked or the 'world simply won't have the natural resources to maintain its population at anything like the standard of living to which people aspire.'

8. L. Dudley Stamp, an expert on tropical land use, says: 'By and large, if cleared, the equatorial forests would produce vast areas of poor or indifferent soil, liable to become still further impoverished, and further liable to marked soil erosion. The old myth that equatorial soils are of great fertility dies hard' (#32, p. 61). The debilitating effect of the rain forest climate and insect pests upon human energy must also be reckoned.

9. In Paraguay, for example, less than 5 per cent of the cultivable land, suitable for many sub-tropical products, is presently used.

10. *Science*, 23 May 1947. C. B. Kellogg also speaks of a billion new acres in the tropical regions — *Food, Soil and People*, Food and People Series no. 6, UNESCO, New York, 1950, p. 20f.

11. J. J. Christensen stresses the need for research on tree crops useful for human and animal nutrition in #14, p. 103. Such research seems particularly needed if the Amazon basin and Central Africa are to be developed.

12. *Man and Hunger*, Information Pamphlet, F.A.O., Rome, 1957, p. 22f. The Japanese rice yield per acre is about four times that of India, the main factor being the use of inorganic fertilizers in Japan, according to the F.A.O. submission to the Atomic Energy Conference of 1955.

13. F. A. Pearson and F. A. Harper, *The World's Hunger*, Cornell Press, Ithaca, New York, 1945, p. 28. It is indicated that India irrigates nearly one-fourth of its cultivated land, and China about one-half. During the Chinese First Five Year Plan, it is stated that 'the area under irrigation rose by 60 per cent to 37.3 million hectares.' *The State of Food and Agriculture*, p. 18. This would seem to make the earlier estimate too high.

14. The Japanese use some 300,000 small size tractors in their intensive agriculture, but Japan is not an underdeveloped country. Expensive tractors, which rust for want of servicing, are hardly conducive to real agricultural improvement in most of the underdeveloped world.

15. *Second World Food Survey*, F.A.O., Rome, 1952, p. 30. James F. Bonner of Cal Tech, in a study on 'The World's Food: Need and Potential,' asserts that insects, fungi, rabbits, rats, etc. consume one-third of the food grown in the world today. *The New York Times*, 21 May 1956.

16. The estimated annual catch has since risen to 25–30 million tons, which still provides less than 1 per cent of the human diet. *Man and Hunger*, p. 29.

17. Bostwick H. Ketchum writes: 'It was estimated by George L. Clarke several years ago that it takes about 10,000 lbs. of the microscopic plant life (phytoplankton) in the ocean to produce one lb. of fish harvested on George's Bank off the New England coast.' *Oceanics*, vol. VI, no. 2, 1959.

18. To the agricultural economist, Colin Clark, a favorite authority of certain 'anti-Malthusians,' is attributed the view that the world 'is capable of supporting 28 billion people . . . if methods now used by Dutch farmers in their small country are applied to all of the world's good temperate agricultural land' — Anthony Zimmerman in *What's New*, no. 211, Abbott Laboratories, North Chicago, Spring 1959. A higher estimate might be arrived at by using Japanese farmers as the norm. But it may be that Colin Clark is misquoted. Another Catholic priest, E. Colleton in Kenya, says Clark estimates 'that if the cultivable land of the earth were farmed at Dutch standards it would support 10 to 15 billion people in a fair degree of comfort.' The trick seems to be to provide the Dutch climate.

19. Some of the supplies were sold for local currencies, which helped to finance other assistance projects; some, valued at $80 million, were distributed by religious and other welfare agencies, such as the Share Our Surplus program. Far from injuring the farmer, such distribution helps to ease the 'menace' posed by bulging granaries.

20. The West Indian economist, W. Arthur Lewis, now deputy to Paul Hoffman in the U.N. Special Fund, has stated that whereas annual net investment in the U.S.A. is at least 10% of national income, and more like 15% in the Soviet Union or Japan, 'in the underdeveloped countries domestic capital formation is more of the order of 5%' — *Financing the Economic Development of Underdeveloped Countries*, United Nations Association, London, c. 1956, p. 5.

21. *International Economic Assistance to the Less Developed Countries* 1957–58, p. 73. The new loans came to $1,229 million, not including expenditures of Soviet loans outside the Communist bloc, which were estimated at about $100 million; repayments of loans came to $308 million. About 30 per cent of the net loans came through the International Bank.

22. Ibid. This includes technical assistance and other forms of direct aid. It should be noted that at least one-fourth of the total in governmental grants and loans went to three areas: the Republic of Korea, Vietnam, and Algeria. Nongovernmental technical services, in which those provided by Protestant and Roman Catholic missions constitute the largest elements, might raise the total assistance by another $100 million.

23. For example, Adlai Stevenson, in the 7 February 1959 issue of *The Saturday Review*, wrote of the Atlantic Community, with 16% of the world's population, consuming 70% of the world's wealth.

24. Their mineral resources are of little value except for trading until they can industrialize — for which trade is essential. The rapid utilization of minerals by modern industry, intensified by waste, poses a world problem, to which both developed and underdeveloped countries need to give attention. It cannot be assumed that chemistry will provide all the substitutes.

25. The C.C.I.A. Executive Committee in 1956 put as the first of five points commended to the attention of church people:

> Serious attempts should be made to strengthen and broaden, in the less industrialized countries, the basis of their participation in international trade, as a means to accelerate their development; and, in this connection, to seek international consideration of interim measures calculated to lessen the impact of market fluctuations in limited-product countries, which have grave economic and human consequences in these countries.

VI — POPULATION POLICY AND FAMILY LIMITATION

1. Cf. Alfred Sauvy in the French quarterly, *Population*, January–March 1952. The effect of wartime dislocations and enormous casualties complicates a judgment here. The Soviet census data made public in May 1959, showing a total under 209 million, indicate a war toll of some 15 million or more persons.

2. #9. In regard to pro-natalist policies, cf. D. V. Glass, *The Struggle for Population*, Clarendon, Oxford, 1936.

3. A French colleague tells me that these family allowances have helped to increase population pressures in North Africa, by making procreation appeal to many fathers as a means to livelihood.

4. One reason for the high rate of abortion, apart from the smaller cultural opposition than in Western lands, is said to be the fact that many

defective contraceptives were put on the market and overadvertized, leading to many unwanted pregnancies. Evidently, the authorities are trying to improve this situation.

5. Father de Lestapis uses the figure of 600,000 for the number of French abortions which would be somewhat smaller than the number of live births (#8, p. 54). The illegal character of the business leads to a considerable variation in estimates. A Swiss doctor friend, expert in these matters, estimated that as many as 40 thousand women die each year in France as a result of abortions.

6. Among the Chinese it was commonly held, I understand, that a child did not acquire a soul until after infancy, a belief presumably designed to ease the pangs of conscience and parental love over infanticide.

7. In his article previously cited, Father Russell suggests as a 'theoretical' solution for the population problem a vast increase in celibacy, which would permit those who do marry to have large families without being socially irresponsible.

8. The method is sometimes called the Ogino-Knaus method, from work done on it by a Japanese and an Austrian doctor.

9. While unsuccessful in a technical sense, Dr. Stone's valiant efforts awakened much more attention in India to the family limitation issue than would otherwise have been the case.

10. This attempt to summarize medical advice on the technical situation, necessary for an understanding of the total population problem, is strictly for this purpose; those desiring practical counsel should seek professional advice.

11. I am particularly indebted to Dr. Warren O. Nelson and Dr. Sheldon J. Segal, director and assistant director of medical research for the Population Council, for trying to clarify the main points in this complex field.

12. While the drug was thought to inhibit ovulation, the application schedule suggests, I am told, that its antifertility effect may be due to inhibiting implantation of the fertilized ovum.

13. 'Survey of Studies Relating to Vulnerable Points in the Reproductive Process' (1956) by Warren O. Nelson, appended to #21, pp. 206ff. Meier has a good deal of additional material on the oral contraceptives. A more recent paper by Dr. Nelson is 'Present Status of Research in the Biological Control of Fertility' in *Thirty Years of Research on Human Fertility*, Milbank Memorial Fund, New York, 1958, p. 93ff.

14. They also can be used to suppress spermatogenesis but suppress the male libido in the process.

15. MER-25 should not be confused with the antimetabolites, which can destroy the implanted ovum, but also can injure without destroying.

16. A sociological study of family planning efforts in Puerto Rico is found in #16.

17. Events which weaken traditional community controls on reproductive behavior, stress individual importance and dignity, enhance the prestige of women and enlarge the scope of their activities, and stimulate widely new aspirations for education and advancement, were cited as factors

of declining birth rates by Balfour, Evans, Notestein, and Taeuber, op. cit. p. 11.

18. In Africa, aside from Egypt and possibly other parts of North Africa, there is still not too much concern over population pressures; the health of mother and child is more clearly seen. In Latin America, the governments themselves are inhibited by the dominant pro-fertility culture.

19. The government of Sweden is an exception; it is conducting a family planning assistance project. If the recommendations of the Draper Committee in the U.S., mentioned in Ch. I, are put into effect, the situation will begin to change.

VII — PARENTHOOD AND WORLD RELIGIONS

1. The various rites connected particularly with food and vegetation were compiled impressively by Sir James Frazer in *The Golden Bough*, Macmillan, New York and London, 1936.

2. The current fertility cult associated with Shiva, the 'left hand' *shaktism* of the *Tantras*, 'is obviously a survival and a recrudescence of a phase of original Indian religion.' J. C. Archer, *The Faiths Men Live By*, Nelson, New York, 1934, p. 203.

3. In the tale of the Ogress Kālī attributed to 'the Master,' for example, the mother whose daughter-in-law is barren exclaims, 'A sonless family falls into ruin, the line of its succession lost; let me seek out another maiden.' *The Heart of Buddhism*, ed. by K. J. Saunders, Association, Calcutta, 1915.

4. 'Prior to 1921 the growth of population and cultivation were nearly in balance. Population increase was fitful and slow, and increase in cultivation managed to keep pace with it. After 1921, however, population growth has been rapid and uninterrupted, while increase in cultivation, even where it has occurred, has been small and proportionately much less than the increase in population' — *Census of India*, 1951, vol. I, part IB, p. 1, cited in #35, p. 49.

5. *The Heart of Buddhism*, p. 43. This works both ways: another verse describes how a wife is a 'liberated bride,' freed from mortar, butter churn, and 'crooked hunchback lord,' and now 'freedom from birth and death's assured' (ibid.). There is considerable sexual equality in Buddhism.

6. Thomas Burch, however, states that, in regard to Japan, 'neither Shinto nor Buddhism, the two largest creeds in Japan, categorically oppose abortion.' Thomas K. Burch, 'Induced Abortion in Japan,' *Eugenics Quarterly*, vol. 2, no. 3, September 1955.

7. 'It has probably always been true that by far the largest part of Moslem men have had but one wife at a time.' George Foot Moore, *History of Religions*, Scribner's, New York, 1932, II, p. 492.

8. Cf. L. T. Hobhouse, *Morals in Evolution*, Holt, New York, 1915, p. 200f. for additional examples.

9. In one place the Koran appears to regard monogamy as a means to family

limitation. If a man fears he may not be fair, he is to take one wife
— not counting slaves — 'that is more likely to secure that ye be not
over-burdened with children' (4:3). This phrase is an alternate reading
for 'that ye be not partial.' *The Qur'ān*, trans. by Richard Bell, Clark,
Edinburgh, 1939.

10. #17, p. 136. Himes also says, 'In Islam the fetus is not considered
a human being until it has reached a distinctly human form; hence
abortion is not forbidden.' The references to abortion I have seen have
all been strongly condemnatory, except in regard to therapeutic necessity.

11. Cf. #8, p. 42f. Father de Lestapis also cites an opinion by the Grand
Mufti of Egypt in January 1937, concerning a kind of oral tradition
supporting '*azl*: it had been used by the ancient Arabs, had not been
banned by the Koran, and had been discussed by other interpreters;
consequently, it was 'not absolutely illicit' by the precepts of Islam
(p. 45).

12. Confucius said, 'There are three things which are unfilial, but the
most unfilial of these is to have no sons.'

13. My notes are based on a U.N. Secretariat survey (ST/SOA/29) published
in March 1956 but valid for 1951; a 1954 paper by Hope T. Eldridge for
the International Union for the Scientific Study of Population, summarized
in the bulletin of the International Planned Parenthood Federation
for May 1955; and a private memorandum from Athens regarding Greek
legislation.

VIII — The Old Testament, Judaism, and Parenthood

1. Biblical references, except where noted, are from the Revised Standard
Version, by permission.

2. The importance of male succession in Hebrew thought is stressed by
David Mace: 'The need of the Hebrew for a son is the key to the whole
structure of his family life, at least in the early days of the Old
Testament' (#19, p. 201). Millar Burrows, I understand, stresses somewhat more broadly the importance attached to continuance of the
husband's family.

3. On contemporary Jewish views, cf. also Marc H. Tanenbaum's article
'Religion' in *The American Jewish Yearbook*, American Jewish Committee, New York, 1959 edition.

IX — The New Testament and Parenthood

1. Luke's version requires one to 'hate' kin and self for discipleship
(Lk. 14:26–7); J. Alexander Findlay in *The Abingdon Bible Commentary*,
however, writes that the word translated as 'hate' goes back 'to an
Aramaic word which means "love less." '

2. Whether 'one of the noblest of New Testament writings,' as E. F. Scott

rightly calls it, was written by Paul or by a brilliant disciple at a
later date may make quite a difference in contemporary understanding of
Paul's view of marriage; but it is well to remember the influence of
Ephesians on the Christian doctrine of marriage down the many centuries
in which the authenticity of Pauline authorship was unquestioned. And
it remains to be proved that Ephesians does not in fact represent Paul
in every sense. Francis Beane has a useful summary on the question in
his introduction to the Epistle in *The Interpreter's Bible*, vol. 10,
p. 597ff.

3. For example, cf. W. A. Lock, A *Critical and Exegetical Commentary on
the Pastoral Epistles* (International Critical Commentary).

X — The Early Church

1. *Ante-Nicene Fathers*, reprint of the Edinburgh Edition, Scribner's, New
York, 1925. References cited are from vols. I to V, VIII and IX, by
permission of the publisher.

2. For example, cf. Arthur C. McGiffert, A *History of Christian Thought*,
Scribner's, New York, 1932, I, p. 45ff.

3. Translation given in Edwyn R. Bevan, *Christianity*, Holt, New York,
1932, p. 53.

4. Pessaries are also mentioned in Aristotle's *On the Generation of Animals*,
Book II, ch. 4.

5. In his *Treatise on the Soul* Tertullian has some interesting references to
a 'population explosion' at the turn of the 3rd century, cited (and
quite possibly exaggerated) against the Pythagorean idea that the living
come from the dead:

> What most frequently meets our view . . . is our teeming population:
> our numbers are burdensome to the world, which can hardly supply
> us from its natural elements; our wants grow more and more keen,
> and our complaints more bitter in all mouths, whilst nature fails in
> affording us her usual sustenance. In very deed, pestilence, and famine,
> and wars, and earthquakes have to be regarded as a remedy for
> nations, as the means of pruning the luxuriance of the human race
> . . . (ch. 30).

6. Cf. D. Sherwin Bailey, *Sexual Relation in Christian Thought*, #1,
p. 241ff.

XI — Eastern Orthodoxy and Parenthood

1. The text in Greek is appended to *The Problem of Child Birth*, second
edition, Brotherhood of Zoë, Athens, 1947. The phrases used in my
summary are from an unofficial translation.

XII — ROMAN CATHOLICISM AND PARENTHOOD

1. Cf. *Nicene and Post-Nicene Fathers*, Series I, Christian Literature Society, New York, 1888, vols. I to VII, for a number of Augustine's more important writings.

2. #6, p. 60. Cole's chapter on Augustine is instructive at a number of points.

3. Concern for children, however, was not absent in Augustine's thought. In his shorter *Commentary on Genesis*, IX, ch. 7, he wrote that 'children should be begotten of love, tenderly cared for and educated in a religious atmosphere.'

4. This is not to say that Aquinas opposed periodic continence; apparently it did not enter his ken; it might have appealed to his rationalistic approach if it had.

5. I am indebted to William J. Gibbons, S.J., and Thomas K. Burch for the English text of several official Catholic statements which they have compiled for a forthcoming compendium of documents of the Holy See. Quotations from *Casti Connubii* are from *On Christian Marriage*, Paulist Press, New York, 1941.

6. The combination, however, goes back a long ways, indeed as far as Augustine. The Council of Florence in 1439 spoke of 'the procreation and education of children into the worship of God' as the first good of marriage. The contents of the concept of education, however, have grown with time and changing civilization. Education has come to include nurture, physical well-being, and upbringing in general.

7. It should be added that the Rota distinguishes between the right to the marital act and the right to children; it is not asserted that the right to children is unlimited.

8. Another favorite text, from which the Pope abstained, is from the Old Testament Apochrypha, the book of Tobit, or Tobias in Roman circles, which tells how Tobit took Sarah as wife 'not from earthly lust, but only for the sake of posterity' (Tob. 8:4).

9. Herbert Doms, *Vom Sinn und Zweck der Ehe* (Breslau, 1935) was translated under the title *The Meaning of Marriage*, trans. by George Sayer, Sheed and Ward, London, 1939. The argument uses the opening provided by the encyclical to distinguish the meaning of marriage from the traditional concept of procreative purpose. E. C. Messenger, in #22, stresses the point that one motive here was to secure more attention for the secondary ends of marriage, neglected in some Catholic manuals (vol. II, p. 168). Both Doms' book and *Die Zweckfrage der Ehe in neuer Beleuchtung* by Bernardine Krempel (Zurich and Cologne, 1941) were ordered to be withdrawn.

10. E.g. 'spouses are not obliged to coitus except insofar as the other party seeks it . . . nor are spouses positively obligated to the generation of offspring, so long as they neither positively impede generation nor

kill the offspring.' Wernz-Vidal, *Ius Canonicum*, V, no. 521, cited by the Rota.

11. A comment by Father Gibbons seems relevant; he said that too many Catholic apologists have permitted their opponents 'to squeeze them into a position where they find themselves agreeing that the main issue is not the salvation of human souls but the continuance of human comfort.' Interview in *The Sign*, Union City, New Jersey, February 1957.

12. Anthony F. Zimmerman, '*Overpopulation*,' Catholic University of America Press, Washington, D.C., 1957, p. 103. This work was called 'monumental' by the Director of the Family Life Bureau of the National Catholic Welfare Conference in the U.S.

13. Representatives of this general point of view would include such people as G. H. L. Zeegers of the Netherlands; the Catholic social research centers at the Hague and elsewhere; William J. Gibbons, S.J., the Fordham demographer; Thomas K. Burch of Princeton; and Stanislas de Lestapis, S.J., of the social study center in Paris.

XIII — PROTESTANTISM AND PARENTHOOD

1. Cf. #2, p. 79. Bainton also quotes a nice excerpt from *Tabletalk*, #4786, showing Luther's warm love of family, p. 82f.

2. Calvin stressed the malignancy of Onan in refusing his brother the title of father. He also said: 'since each man is born for the preservation of the whole race, if anyone dies without children, there seems to be here some defect of nature.' John Calvin, *Commentary on Genesis*, trans. by John King, Calvin Trans. Soc., Edinburgh, 1850, II, p. 281.

3. Cited in #2, p. 100. Bainton says the Puritan ideal for the man-woman relationship was summed up in the phrase, 'a tender respectiveness,' p. 96.

4. There were some individual efforts, like that of Schleiermacher, but they had little impact on the Protestant ethos.

5. Christian concern, particularly in Nonconformist circles, was expressed over the dreadful living and working conditions in the early stages of the Industrial Revolution in England; but this was expressed in reference to improvement of conditions, not family limitation.

6. Vol. III, pp. 300–311. There is a good summary in #35, p. 147f.

7. Cf. #37 and James A. Pike, *Mixed Marriages*, Harper, New York, 1953. Dr. Weatherhead sanctions contraception for maternal health and the economic necessities facing the modern family. Dean, now Bishop, Pike stresses that avoidance of procreation in certain circumstances may be as strong a moral obligation as procreation in other situations.

8. #1. A new work, *Sexual Relation in Christian Thought*, should also be noted. Mention should also be made of two other able men who have been related to the Council: Canon G. R. Dunstan and his predecessor, the late Canon Warner. Cf. Hugh C. Warner, 'Theological Issues of Contraception,' *Theology*, London, January 1954.

9. In a preparatory committee for this consultation, which I helped to or-

ganize, there was a more vigorous discussion of fertility controls than is reflected in this quotation. The hope that new technical developments in regard to suitable contraceptives would change the situation was a factor in the decision of the preparatory committee not to stress this issue at the time.

10. The condition here described is changing fairly rapidly. The World Council's Study of Rapid Social Change during the past three years has served as a useful stimulus. The co-operating group of churchmen in Japan, for example, undertook a serious study of Japan's demographic situation.

11. The consensus, indeed, may be wider. Alfred Rehwinkel points out that the semiofficial position of the Missouri Synod of the Lutheran Church in the past has been 'that birth control is a violation of God's creation order' but notes that 'some serious doubts as to the validity and adequacy of this position' have arisen in recent years; 60% of those replying to a church questionnaire 'favored a judicious practice of birth control.' Professor Rehwinkel himself argues for such a position. *Planned Parenthood*, Concordia, St. Louis, 1959, p. 43f.

XIV — THE ECUMENICAL MOVEMENT AND THE WAY FORWARD

1. More recently, another co-operating group, the Social Committee of the Swedish Ecumenical Council, has conducted a study project on 'The Problem of Population and Family Planning.'

2. The substance of the argument is in an article entitled 'Too Many People? World Population and Resources,' *Social Action*, New York, May 1955.

3. Printed in *Advance*, 23 May 1958. 'Rebuttals' ranged as far as Kenya where a Roman priest devoted four broadcasts against a garbled version of the argument.

4. There are, of course, other problems: as the uncertain attitude of church officials in Communist countries, and also in some of the churches of the West, which have thus far been silent.

5. I have in mind the serious authors such as Messenger, Hürth, Fuchs, de Lestapis, and Vialatoux, not the exponents of the 'fertility cult' who write some of the family guidance pamphlets circulating in the U.S.

6. Humility is also called for in relation to the pioneer work done by many secular persons and groups; our Lord's saying that 'the sons of this world are wiser in their own generation than the sons of light' (Lk. 16:8) has relevance at a number of points. Movements like Planned Parenthood, the monument to the devoted crusade of Margaret Sanger and others, should not be ignored by the churches. If some of the secular bodies have weaknesses from a Christian perspective, whose fault is it?

7. *Migration News*, no. 2, I.C.M.C., Geneva, March–April 1959. The author refers to the article by Sir Solly Zuckerman, previously cited, as confirming the thesis that there are no 'miracle remedies' for the control of human fertility; but he neglects to point out that the obstacles to such control

call for larger and more determined efforts to cope with these obstacles.

8. An exception no doubt has to be recognized for Protestant minorities in predominantly Catholic countries, until secular and anticlerical forces, and the population pressures themselves, bring about a change in the legal situation.

9. Of course, adoption offers a potential means of fulfillment for the involuntarily childless marriage.

10. Catholic doctrine supports this point in its recognition of the validity of the 'vows-of-chastity' marriage. Pius XII made it clear that only couples using the marital act have the duty of propagation — Allocution of 29 October 1951. The Protestant consensus makes this duty contingent not upon the use of the marital act, but the total purposes of the marriage.

11. Procreation, even with modern contraceptive knowledge, retains its mysterious other dimension, whereby the child is the creature of God. No contraceptive method is 100% effective, and no procreative act is sure. The 'fertility cult' apologists who argue against 'birth control' on the grounds that the 15th child proved to be a genius attribute too much to the human element in procreation. Does the Almighty require unlimited procreation to raise up great men?

12. Periodic continence, for example, is admirable for some couples but, as three demographers with divergent religious backgrounds point out, it is 'appropriate only to the needs of healthy, well-educated and emotionally stable persons.' Frank Lorimer, Jean Bourgeois-Pichat, and Dudley Kirk, 'An Inquiry Concerning Some Ethical Principles Relating to Human Reproduction,' Social Compass, vol. IV, no. 5–6, The Hague, 1957. For those whom this method suits, and for faithful Roman Catholics, one can only echo the hope of Pius XII 'that science will succeed in providing this licit method with a sufficiently secure basis.'

1. Bailey, D. Sherwin, *The Mystery of Love and Marriage*, Harper & Brothers, New York, 1953; cf. also *Sexual Relation in Christian Thought*, ibid. 1959.
2. Bainton, Roland H., *What Christianity Says About Sex, Love and Marriage*, Association Press, New York, 1957.
3. Carr-Saunders, A. M., *The Population Problem*, Clarendon Press, Oxford, 1922.
4. Ibid. *World Population: Past Growth and Present Trends*, Oxford University Press, London, 1936.
5. Chandrasekhar, S., *Population and Planned Parenthood in India*, Allen and Unwin, London, 1955.
6. Cole, William G., *Sex in Christianity and Psychoanalysis*, Oxford University Press, New York, 1955.
7. Cook, Robert C., *Human Fertility: The Modern Dilemma*, William Sloane Associates, New York, 1951.
8. de Lestapis (S.J.), Stanislas, *La Limitation des Naissances*, SPES, Paris, 1959.
9. Eldridge, Hope T., *Population Policies: A Survey of Recent Developments*, International Union for the Scientific Study of Population, Washington, D.C., 1954.
10. Francis, Roy G., ed., *The Population Ahead*, University of Minnesota Press, Minneapolis, 1958.
11. Freedman, Ronald F., Whelpton, Pascal K., and Campbell, Arthur A., *Family Planning, Sterility, and Population Growth*, McGraw-Hill, New York, 1959.
12. Fuchs (S.J.), Josef, *Die Sexualethik des Heiligen Thomas von Aquin*, Bachem, Cologne, 1949.
13. Goldstein, Sidney, *The Meaning of Marriage and Foundations of the Family*, Bloch Publishing Co., New York, 1942.
14. Hatt, Paul K., ed., *World Population and Future Resources*, American Book Co., New York, 1952.
15. Hertzler, J. O., *The Crisis in World Population*, University of Nebraska Press, Lincoln, 1956.
16. Hill, R., Stycos, J. M., and Back, K. W., *The Family and Population Control*, University of North Carolina Press, Chapel Hill, 1959.

17. Himes, Norman E., *Medical History of Contraception*, William Wood, Baltimore, 1936.
18. Lorimer, Frank, et al., *Culture and Human Fertility*, UNESCO, Paris, 1954.
19. Mace, David R., *Hebrew Marriage*, Philosophical Library, New York, 1953.
20. Malthus, Thomas R., *An Essay on Population*, 2 vols., Everyman's Library, E. P. Dutton & Co., New York, 1958.
21. Meier, Richard L., *Modern Science and the Human Fertility Problem*, John Wiley & Sons, New York, 1959.
22. Messenger, E. C., *Two in One Flesh*, 3 vols., Newman Press, Westminster, Md., 1948 (1 vol. edition, 1955).
23. Osborn, Fairfield, *The Limits of the Earth*, Little, Brown & Co., Boston, 1953.
24. Osborn, Frederick, *Population: An International Dilemma*, Population Council, New York, 1958.
25. Piper, Otto A., *The Christian Interpretation of Sex*, Charles Scribner's Sons, New York, 1941.
26. Population Division, U.N. Department of Social Affairs, *The Determinants and Consequences of Population Trends*, United Nations, New York, 1953.
27. Ibid. *The Future Growth of World Population*, United Nations, New York, 1958.
28. Rockefeller Brothers Fund, *Foreign Economic Policy for the Twentieth Century*, Doubleday & Co., New York, 1958.
29. Sax, Karl, *Standing Room Only?*, Beacon Press, Boston, 1955.
30. Schultz, Theodore W., ed., *Food for the World*, University of Chicago Press, Chicago, 1945.
31. Shoulson, A. B., ed., *Marriage and Family Life*, Twayne Publishers, New York, 1959.
32. Stamp, L. Dudley, *Land for Tomorrow: The Underdeveloped World*, University of Indiana Press, Bloomington, 1952.
33. Sulloway, Alvah W., *Birth Control and Catholic Doctrine*, Beacon Press, Boston, 1959.
34. Thompson, W. S., *Population and Peace in the Pacific*, University of Chicago Press, Chicago, 1946; the argument is enlarged and brought up to date in *Population and Progress in the Far East*, University of Chicago Press, 1959.
35. Vialatoux, J., *Le Peuplement Humain*, 2 vols., Les Editions Ouvrières, Paris, 1957 and 1959.
36. Warren, M. A. C., et al., *The Family in Contemporary Society*, S.P.C.K., London, 1958.
37. Weatherhead, Leslie, *The Mastery of Sex through Psychology and Religion*, The Macmillan Co., New York, 1932.